The Environment and the Human Condition

*An interdisciplinary series edited by faculty at the University of Illinois*

Wildlife and People

# Wildlife and People

*The Human Dimensions of Wildlife Ecology*

Gary G. Gray

University of Illinois Press
Urbana and Chicago

Manufactured in the United States of America
C 5 4 3 2 1

*This book is printed on acid-free paper.*

Library of Congress Cataloging-in-Publication Data

Gray, Gary G. (Gary Gene), 1940–
Wildlife and people : the human dimensions of wildlife ecology / Gary G. Gray.
p. cm.— (The Environment and the human condition)
Includes bibliographical references (p. ) and index.
ISBN 0-252-01947-4 (acid-free paper)
1. Wildlife conservation—Social aspects. 2. Wildlife conservation—Economic aspects. 3. Human-animal relationships. I. Title. II. Series.
QL82.G73 1993
333.95—dc20 92-32828
CIP

*To Jasper*
*A very special fox squirrel*

# Contents

# Preface

Wildlife ecology encompasses interactions between and among wildlife populations, habitats, and people (Giles 1971). The most productive approach is therefore likely to be one that treats wild animal population biology, the ecology and management of wildlife habitats, and human aspects of wildlife ecology as coequal components.

Historically, most wildlife problems originated as biological problems that eventually became people problems (Teague 1979). Despite the prevalence of such occurrences, studies related to human dimensions of wildlife lagged behind research on wildlife populations and habitats. Not until the mid-1960s were publications related to human dimensions readily available (Manfredo 1989).

In 1973, a "human dimensions" session at the North American Wildlife and Natural Resources Conference attracted so much interest that a separate workshop was scheduled to accommodate the overflow presentations. A collection of eighteen papers presented either at the technical session or workshop was published under the title *Human Dimensions in Wildlife Programs* (Hendee and Schoenfeld 1973). Since the early seventies there has been a steady stream of publications dealing with human dimensions topics; the 1980s saw an additional surge of interest (Manfredo 1989). This interest in human dimensions of wildlife addresses a concern of the 1973 Committee on North American Wildlife Policy, which reported that "our most neglected and crucial research needs are those concerning human social behavior" (Allen et al. 1973). Two later publications, *Wildlife and America* (Brokaw 1978) and *Valuing Wildlife* (Decker and Goff 1987), both products of important conferences, complete the major book-length contributions to the "human dimensions" literature.

My intent in this book is to provide an introduction to the major subject areas that comprise the human dimensions of wildlife ecology.

A work of this kind is largely a synthesis of the insights, experiences, and research findings of others. The book has its own style and perspective, but it is based on the effort of many scientists and humanists. To them we are all indebted.

I have organized the chapters into fairly brief sections with descriptive headings. This should benefit general readers by alerting them to central concepts and assist those with a wildlife background in finding desired passages. In addition, short essays—identified by the *Perspective* designation—appear at the ends of several chapters. Their purpose is to augment or complement a topic without interrupting the chapter narrative or to suggest an alternative viewpoint in a format that minimizes distraction.

This has been a "lone wolf" project, but I appreciate the contributions of many persons through the years. I particularly acknowledge many conscientious teachers in the Wichita public schools during my youth, Joseph S. Larson of the University of Massachusetts, and C. David Simpson, formerly at Texas Tech.

I extend special thanks to my undergraduate wildlife adviser, Frederick Greeley, now retired from the University of Massachusetts, who read much of an earlier version of the manuscript and made many useful suggestions; to Dave Renwald, whose friendship dates back to our days as "older undergraduates" at the University of Massachusetts for his evocative illustrations; to Richard E. Warner, Durward L. Allen, and several anonymous reviewers for their helpful comments; to the staff of Founders Memorial Library at Northern Illinois University for assistance; to Karen Hewitt, at the University of Illinois Press, for shepherding this project; to my family for their encouragement; and to a few special friends.

Finally, I acknowledge my late father, Cecil T. Gray. Now more than ever I appreciate his love, patience, loyalty, and integrity. He would have been proud to see this book in print. The example of his persistence contributed much to its completion.

# Aboriginal Human–Wildlife Relationships 1

Recent studies of human evolution suggest that the earliest members of the family Hominidae date from about 3 million years ago. Fossil hominids found by Donald Johanson in the Hadar-Afar region of Ethiopia and remains discovered by Mary Leakey at Laetolil in Tanzania have been assigned to one species, *Australopithecus afarensis,* named for the Ethiopian locality that yielded the largest number of specimens. The most complete adult skeleton recovered was also from Afar, the now-famous "Lucy" (Simons 1989).

By the early Pleistocene epoch, 2 million years ago, there were three or four different hominids. Two of these were also australopithecines: *Australopithecus africanus,* a small, slender creature, and *Australopithecus robustus,* squat and massively built with a crested skull. Another, *Homo habilis,* noted for its tool-making ability, is the probable ancestor of the later human species *Homo erectus* and *Homo sapiens* (Fagan 1989).

One million years ago only the *Homo* lineage remained. Java and Peking hominids, each originally given their own Latinized name, have been reassigned to the single genus of humans, *Homo.* However, they are distinct enough from modern humans (*Homo sapiens*) to warrant placement together in a separate species, *Homo erectus* (Fagan 1989).

We might expect that the recent fossil record would yield a clear picture of the emergence of modern humans, but it does not. Anthropologists have yet to discover a transition from the more primitive *Homo erectus* to *Homo sapiens.* Furthermore, *Homo sapiens* includes two entirely different anatomical types—the powerfully built Neanderthals and slim-bodied Cro-Magnons (Fagan 1989).

It has been suggested that some *Homo erectus* groups wandered out of Africa about 1 million years ago, spreading into Southeast Asia and throughout Eurasia. Regional populations in Europe and Western Asia gradually evolved into what we now refer to as Neanderthals (Simons

1989). Recent research suggests that *Homo erectus* groups remaining in Africa gave rise to early modern humans, the Cro-Magnons. Some of the Cro-Magnon groups then migrated to Eurasia where they outbred, outcompeted, or exterminated the Neanderthal populations they encountered (Stringer and Andrews 1988).

Molecular biology is now producing clues to the origins of *Homo sapiens.* A study of mitochondrial DNA (mtDNA), genetic material contained in organelles that store and release chemical energy in cells, showed an extraordinarily high degree of similarity in samples from Europe, Asia, New Guinea, and Australia, as well as one set of African samples. Since mtDNA is transmitted only from mother to daughter, and is not diluted by paternal DNA, it provides a link with ancestral populations. This has led to the "Eve hypothesis"—that the common mother of all present humanity lived in Africa some two hundred thousand years ago (Cann, Stoneking, and Wilson 1987).

Eve was undoubtedly black, one among thousands of similar females. Some bore only sons or daughters who died before giving birth. During thousands of generations, untold lines were lost when daughters produced no female offspring. Eventually, all of the mtDNA lineages were extinguished—except Eve's. Whether this theory survives remains to be seen. What makes it so appealing is the idea we are all related through a common mother—that there really is a "human family."

Three characteristics of early hominids had important ecological and adaptive consequences (Fagan 1989). First, early hominids were large mammals, so they had to range over a large area to obtain sufficient food. This mobility enabled them to utilize a broad range of food items and to make use of seasonal, unpredictable, and patchily distributed food resources.

Second, they were terrestrial primates, exhibiting the upright posture and bipedal gait that are characteristic human features. Life for a primate "coming down from the trees" posed several problems—locomotion in a terrestrial environment with an arboreally adapted body; finding secure shelter in an open habitat inhabited by predators; and competition for high-quality plant food that, though abundant in forests, is widely dispersed in open landscapes.

Third, hominids confronted life in savanna ecosystems where the distribution of water was restricted geographically and seasonally, and there was competition for such water as was available. Furthermore, most savanna plants are grasses, which are generally unsuitable as a food for primates but support a great variety of hooved herbivores.

These ecological challenges promoted such adaptations as a body structure suited to a mobile way of life in a two-dimensional environment, a high degree of behavioral plasticity to cope with a patchy resource base and to experiment with a variety of plant foods, and the introduction of meat into the diet as a way of coping with seasonal plant scarcity (Fagan 1989). In mammals, these characteristics are associated with a trend toward increasing brain size (Eisenberg 1981).

Various approaches to the archeological record of 2 million years ago have demonstrated the problems inherent in trying to use contemporary primitive hunting societies as a basis for conjectures about early hominid behavior. For one thing, they represent two entirely different species (Fagan 1989). It is possible, however, to make some plausible presumptions about the life-style of *Homo habilis.*

Although our knowledge is far from complete, it is probable that *Homo habilis* represents the early scavenger-hunter-gatherer stage of human sociocultural evolution. There is evidence from Olduvai Gorge that meat- and marrow-rich bones were taken to cache sites for processing using simple stone tools (Potts 1984). And there is agreement that these early humans were at least part-time scavengers (Bunn and Kroll 1986). However, studies of carnivorous animals have shown that no large mammal can live solely by scavenging (Potts 1984), so hunting and scavenging emerge as complementary ways of obtaining meat. As for plant foraging, *Homo habilis* limb bones reveal an anatomy far more arboreal than previously assumed for a terrestrial bipedal primate. Thus this hominid must also have been an adept tree climber who relied on fruits and other plant foods, perhaps having a diet similar to that of modern apes (Fagan 1989).

The African savanna was a vacant ecological niche for early humans who made their living by combining scavenging, hunting, and foraging. Excavated sites suggest that *Homo habilis* lived in bands of about twenty-five individuals with a social organization resembling present-day chimpanzees (*Pan troglodytes*) and baboons (*Papio*). A larger brain implies *Homo habilis* infants were born with smaller heads at an earlier stage of mental maturity. This dictated group social needs and daily habits (Fagan 1989).

Subhuman primates live in a world created in their brains by the integration of sensory inputs. More sophisticated inner worlds are a product of greater complexity of sensory inputs as well as higher levels of neural processing. The inner world of *Homo habilis* was more demanding than that of *Australopithecus.* That complexity was a consequence of human social interactions, due largely to the adoption of a broader diet and food-sharing within social groups. In this way, *Homo habilis* embarked upon the first steps of the human journey (Fagan 1989).

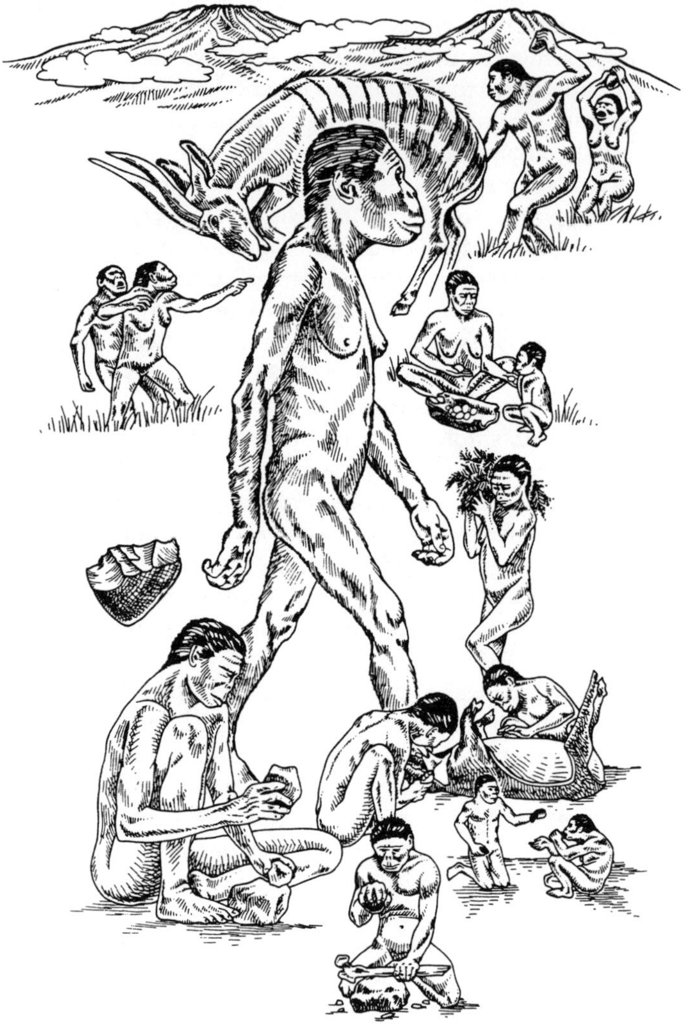

Figure 1.1. A speculative reconstruction of the world of the earliest "true" human, *Homo habilis.* (Reprinted by permission from *Promethean Fire: Reflections on the Origin of Mind* by Charles J. Lumsden and Edward O. Wilson, Cambridge, Mass.: Harvard University Press, Copyright © 1983 by the President and Fellows of Harvard College. Illustration Copyright © 1983 by Whitney Powell.)

*Homo erectus* is thought to have first evolved in tropical Africa about 1.6 million years ago and probably represented an early version of the advanced hunter-gatherer stage of human sociocultural evolution. In functional morphology, *Homo erectus* was fully bipedal and had limbs more distinctively human than those of *Homo habilis. Homo erectus* hunted and foraged for food and may have developed social mechanisms to promote collaboration in food acquisition. The typical tool kit produced by *Homo erectus*'s technology included hand axes, a variety of flake tools, and choppers.

Although earlier hominids probably learned to live with natural fires and were not afraid of them, it is likely that *Homo erectus* was the first hominid to use fire (Fagan 1989). Fire may have been used to flush and drive animals and to promote the growth of lush vegetation that attracts large herbivores. It is possible that attracting large grazing animals to an area was a transition phase between stalking or chasing them and domesticating some of the same animals. In any case, hominids had begun to control and manipulate their environment on a very localized scale.

Several advanced hunter-gatherer societies—including the Kalahari Bushmen Pygmies and Australian aborigines—still exist today. Some of these societies are relatively well off: members may spend only two or three days a week procuring food, devote much of their time to leisure activities, and often live to an advanced age without the benefit of modern medicine (Campbell 1983; Hadingham 1979). Furthermore, their diets are more varied, and in some cases more nutritious, than those of most people in present-day societies. The Bushman diet, for example, includes over twenty species of vegetables and seventeen different species of animal meat.

Looking at both the early scavenger-hunter-gatherers and the advanced hunter-gatherers, it is obvious that their societies were ecologically oriented. Early humans, as well as present-day aboriginal societies, survived by gathering plants, scavenging, hunting animals, and by avoiding predation themselves. Much of their cultural knowledge was and is ecological—how to find potable water and how to locate edible plants and animals.

## THE DAWN OF HUMAN CONSCIOUSNESS

Sir Herbert Read (1965) contended that visual images preceded ideas in the development of human consciousness. The projection of an image into a plastic form, such as a drawing or painting, Read called an icon. Since images, and their resulting expression in icons, occurred prior to

Figure 1.2. A conjectural view of the world of *Homo erectus*, the species of human intermediate between *Homo habilis* and modern humans. (Reprinted by permission from *Promethean Fire: Reflections on the Origin of Mind* by Charles J. Lumsden and Edward O. Wilson, Cambridge, Mass.: Harvard University Press, Copyright © 1983 by the President and Fellows of Harvard College. Illustration Copyright © 1983 by Whitney Powell.)

the beginning of consciousness, they also came before the development of the human aptitudes and skills that depend upon consciousness.

The significance of this theory for our consideration of aboriginal human–wildlife relationships is that most of the oldest surviving drawings and paintings are representations of wild animals. These include the stunning cave "paintings" of large animals, especially bison, wild oxen, and horses, at Altamira in northern Spain and Lascáux in France. Other sites that are less famous also feature impressive wildlife icons—the red and black frieze of early humans hunting several types of horned and antlered mammals at Cueva Vieja in Spain, a kudu from the Nswatugi cave at Whitewaters in southern Zimbabwe, and petroglyphs of desert bighorn sheep (Grant 1980) and other animals at many sites throughout the western United States.

Extrapolating from what is known of primitive religious practices and social customs, Gertrude Rachel Levy (1948) suggested that the first specifically human consciousness was not yet logical nor aware of cause-and-effect relationships. It was, however, aware of synchronicity—able to make a mental association between similar events that are separated by time and location. This primitive mental connection could only be represented in a concrete way by a sign (an image that can be stored in the memory and is therefore separated from the perception).

According to Read's theory, art "has been the piecemeal recognition and patient fixation of what is significant in human experience" (1955: 18). The major concerns of prehistoric humans must have been to secure enough food and to avoid being prey for other animals. Life-or-death struggles with large or fierce animals during countless millennia when human survival depended upon the success of such encounters led to the portrayal of these animals in icons. The dependence of prehistoric humans on wildlife, and their intense scrutiny of animals, gave these hunter-artists an almost instinctive understanding of each animal's essential form. Form follows function, of course, and these wildlife icons vividly express the functions that have allowed various kinds of animals to survive: the flight of birds, the swiftness of deer and antelopes, and the force massed in the heads and hooves of wild oxen and bison.

Herbert Read (1965) also believed that an intense human concern over the availability of food during the drastic, repeated climatic changes of the Pleistocene led to magic—an attempt to evade causality and to influence events secretly, from a distance. Wildlife icons and signs were integral parts of magic rites.

Leo Frobenius related an experience that suggests the kind of cir-

Figure 1.3. A view of the world of early modern humans, *Homo sapiens,* with its more complex culture and greater array of artifacts. (Reprinted by permission from *Promethean Fire: Reflections on the Origin of Mind* by Charles J. Lumsden and Edward O. Wilson, Cambridge, Mass.: Harvard University Press, Copyright © 1983 by the President and Fellows of Harvard College. Illustration Copyright © 1983 by Whitney Powell.)

cumstances under which many of the later prehistoric wildlife drawings may have been done (Frobenius and Fox 1937). During a 1905 African expedition, he met a hunting tribe of Pygmies that had been driven from the plateau and had taken refuge in the jungle of the Congo. Three men and a woman from this tribe were recruited to guide the expedition and soon developed a friendly relationship with Frobenius and other members of the group. One day, when the food supplies were depleted, Frobenius asked one of them to shoot an antelope. He and his comrades seemed astounded, and he then replied that it could not be done that day because no preparations had been made. After much discussion among themselves, the Pygmies conveyed their intention to make preparations at sunrise the next morning. They then went off, as though searching for an appropriate site, and eventually agreed on a high place on a nearby hill. Frobenius described the subsequent events:

> As I was eager to learn what their preparations consisted of, I left camp before dawn and crept through the bush to the open place which they had sought out the night before. The pygmies appeared in the twilight, the woman with them. The men crouched on the ground, plucked a small square free of weeds and smoothed it over with their hands. One of them drew something in the cleared space with his forefinger, while his companions murmured some kind of formula or incantation. Then a waiting silence. The sun rose on the horizon. One of the men, an arrow on his bowstring, took his place beside the square. A few minutes later the rays of the sun fell on the drawing at his feet. In that same second the woman stretched out her arms to the sun, shouting words I did not understand, the man shot his arrow and the woman cried out again. Then the three men bounded off through the bush while the woman stood for a few minutes and then went slowly towards our camp. As she disappeared I came forward and, looking down at the smoothed square of sand, saw the drawing of an antelope four hands long. From the antelope's neck protruded the pygmy's arrow. (Frobenius and Fox 1937:22–23)

Two related books by Charles Lumsden and Edward O. Wilson (1981, 1983) consider the origin of mind from the perspective of evolutionary biology. Their thesis is that a unique coevolution of genetic change and cultural history created the mind and then propelled the growth of the brain (the mind's "machine"), and with it human intellect, at a rate unprecedented for any organ in the history of life.

Genes and culture are inseparably linked so that changes in one inevitably produce changes in the other, endlessly repeating this basic sequence: (1) genetic information encoded in DNA specifies the developmental process by which a brain sufficiently complex to produce a mind is assembled; (2) the mind grows within the environment of its ambient culture; (3) the culture is created anew with each generation from an aggregate of the choices and innovations of society's members; (4) there is a range of variability in the developmental processes through which mind is created, so that some persons are better adapted to survive (and thus more likely to reproduce) than others; and (5) the genes prescribing developmental processes that produce more successful minds tend to spread through the population, and the increasing frequency of such genes is evidence for evolution. "In sum, culture is created and shaped by biological processes while the biological processes are simultaneously altered in response to cultural change" (1983:118). Since culture "is a particular history embedded in the memories and archives of those who transmit it . . . , the way in which memory is implanted and organized is crucial to the creation of culture" (77). From the standpoint of brain physiology, the formation of culture appears to be based on what some psychologists call node-link structures in long-term memory.

Two forms of long-term memory—episodic memory (that recalls specific events to the conscious mind through a time sequence, much like running a clip from a videotape) and semantic memory (which creates meaning by connecting related concepts [fire → hot, burn, dangerous, etc.], and evoking emotional links to feelings)—function in a complementary manner. The concepts and feelings are nodes, or reference points, in long-term memory. Nodes are usually linked to other nodes, so that one memory recalls certain other memories to consciousness. Node-link structures originate in experience, but later can be selectively reassembled in a conceptual sequence to remember episodes or construct narratives expressed through stories or picture sequences (1983).

Events involving various experiences with different kinds of wildlife, and the associated feelings, comprised nodes that must have been almost primal. Node-link structures involving human-wildlife interactions certainly represented the most intense experiences and the most compelling conceptualizations of early humans.

The key to the coupling of genetic and cultural evolution is thought to lie "in the ontogenetic development of mental activity and behavior and particularly the form of epigenetic rules, which can be treated as 'molecular units' that assemble the mind midway along the developmental path between genes and culture" (1981:ix). Thus, in the circuit from the DNA blueprint through the steps of epigenesis to culture and

Figure 1.4. The formation of culture from node-link structures in long-term memory. Here, !Kung hunters associate different kinds of animals and events with traits and names, represented as circles connected by straight lines, and emotional feelings, symbolized by wavy lines. The node-link structures originate with experience, but can be reassembled as a time sequence to recall episodes and to tell stories. (Reprinted by permission from *Promethean Fire: Reflections on the Origin of Mind* by Charles J. Lumsden and Edward O. Wilson, Cambridge, Mass.: Harvard University Press, Copyright © 1983 by the President and Fellows of Harvard College. Illustration Copyright © 1983 by Whitney Powell.)

back to the stored genetic information, the development of the individual mind emerges as the essential element linking genes and culture.

Whether as icons in Herbert Read's theory or node-link structures in long-term memory according to Lumsden and Wilson's scheme, wild animals were a focal point in the experience of all primitive peoples. It seems likely that the intensity of human-wildlife interactions promoted a cognitive awareness that culminated in the emergence of mind. As we proceed to consider the subject areas that comprise the human dimensions of wildlife ecology, we might do well to ponder the possibility that the greatest contribution of wildlife to humanity may very well be nothing less than human consciousness itself.

## HUMAN DEPENDENCE ON WILDLIFE

Glaciers advanced and retreated several times over northern portions of the North American continent during the Pleistocene epoch. The Southern High Plains was never glaciated, but the climate in this region was characterized by cooler summers, milder winters, and more precipitation when the glaciers moved further south (Barry 1983). During interglacial periods the climate was warm and subtropical. A number of archeological sites in the area—particularly along the "breaks" of the Caprock escarpment that forms the eastern boundary of the Southern High Plains and in Palo Duro Canyon of the Texas Panhandle—have yielded fossils of representative animals.

The types of wildlife that would have been available to the Paleo-Indian hunters of this area during the late Pleistocene, from twelve thousand to seven thousand years ago, have been summarized by Schultz (1978). Most notable among the game animals were the mammoth (*Mammuthus*) and bison (*Bison*), although pronghorns (*Antilocapra*), deer (*Odocoileus*), and water birds were certainly present. Fossil remains of other species have been recovered in this area that date from the late Miocene and early Pliocene epochs of the Tertiary Period, from 10 million to 4 million years ago, and some of these species were still present during the Pleistocene. These animals include various kinds of horses (*Equus*), camels (*Camelus*), mastodons (*Mammut*), peccaries (*Platygonus*), pronghorns (*Antilocapra* and *Stockoceros*), ground sloths (*Megalonyx* and *Glossotherium*), armadillo-like glyptodons (*Glyptotherium*), primitive coyotes (*Canis*), saber-tooth cats (*Ischyrosmilus*) and other carnivores, large land tortoises (*Geochelone*), and a number of rabbits and rodents.

The end of the Pleistocene brought an abrupt climatic change. An extended drought settled over the Southern High Plains that lasted from about seven thousand to four thousand years ago. Remains of bison and other large mammals from the area during this three-thousand-year period are very scarce (Hughes 1978). This suggests that the larger game animals could not subsist in the region during the long drought of the Altithermal climatic period. Distinctive artifacts of the early Meso-Indian culture of this region are also largely absent from the Southern High Plains during this time. Apparently the peoples that depended upon this big-game resource virtually abandoned the area as the large animals died off and dispersed. This is just one example of the extent to which aboriginal humans were dependent upon wildlife.

Much farther north, the wild reindeer/caribou (*Rangifer tarandus*) has been important to peoples inhabiting the tundra and northern coniferous forest regions of North America, Europe, and Asia for many thousands of years. Human dependence on this species in circumboreal regions began during the Pleistocene (Banfield 1961:170; Kurtén 1968:170) and continues to the present. Thus the wild reindeer/caribou has been a major human resource over an extraordinarily large geographic area for literally tens of thousands of years. For this reason, Ernest S. Burch, Jr., suggested that this "may well be the species of single greatest importance in the entire anthropological literature on hunting" (1972). Considering the significance of wild reindeer/caribou to primitive humans in tundra and taiga regions throughout the world, it may be useful to review some of the consequences of this dependence on a wildlife species. Burch (1972) examined a number of common assumptions about human populations that hunt this ungulate, based on recent studies of caribou and Eskimos. He has used that evidence to reconstruct what human life is like when *Rangifer tarandus* is a primary resource.

Burch noted that wild reindeer/caribou are very easy to kill. Under aboriginal conditions, the species was successfully hunted with bow and arrow, spear, snare, and—in some areas—with pitfalls. The ease with which they can be killed is mainly due to four behavioral characteristics of the species: they are gregarious (that is, they normally occur in groups), so hunters have a higher probability of making at least one kill for every sighting; they tend to travel in certain directions rather than wandering about randomly, so hunters may be able to predict their route; they are not dangerous, so hunters do not ordinarily have to be concerned about their own safety; and they are not wary animals, so hunters rarely have difficulty approaching them.

Wild reindeer/caribou move in large herds of several thousand animals, but aggregations of one hundred thousand or more are rare events rather than common occurrences. Furthermore, large numbers are not likely in the same herd every year nor in the same locality two years in succession. This means that no area or region would be able to support a dense human population because *Rangifer* herd sizes are likely to vary considerably from one year to the next. Also, wild reindeer/caribou do not necessarily follow the same migration routes each year, and the variability in routes increases as the period of time under consideration increases. Just how different the migration routes will be from year to year is the critical problem for primitive hunters that depend upon this animal.

Hunters of wild reindeer/caribou do not follow their prey during the course of their annual migrations. Instead, hunters have to wait until the herd appears and attempt to make a major kill that will supply them for some time. Thus the only human groups that can afford to be dependent on this species for most of their year-round needs are those living directly between the animals' summer and winter ranges.

Human population density has consistently been inversely related to the dependence on wild reindeer/caribou. That is, areas that supported higher densities of humans must have had a diversified resource base, probably including fish or marine mammals. *Rangifer,* as a single critical resource, would not support a dense human population.

The recurrent themes that emerge from these descriptions emphasize the uncertainty of life when humans are largely dependent upon wildlife. Not merely the quality of life, but existence itself is contingent on such factors as weather conditions, the size of animal herds or flocks, the movement routes of these groups, and the abundance of alternate prey. Under these circumstances, it is little wonder that primitive peoples resorted to myths to explain the unknown, organized their lives around rituals, beseeched various deities for protection, and employed magic in an attempt to exert some control over nature. Considering our present understanding of natural processes, contemporary technological humans, crying out to the heavens for help and guidance, display remarkably little more sophistication than their aboriginal ancestors.

Primitive peoples utilized different types of available wildlife—for variety in diet, for the different kinds of materials each species can supply, and for subsistence in the absence of more favored fare. We should not, however, suppose that they regarded all wildlife as being equally valuable. For example, nomadic peoples of the African Sahara have long depended on Barbary sheep (*Ammotragus lervia*) for meat, hide, hair, sinews, bone, and horns. Nicolaisen (1963:157) remarked that the Ahaggar Tuareg consider Barbary sheep to be of greater value to their economy than any other game animal. In general, we might suppose that the larger ungulates would have similarly been considered prime resources by aboriginal humans because of the larger amounts of meat and greater assortment of useful materials they provide.

Despite the importance of large game animals, it is noteworthy that even small creatures have had a distinctive role in the culture and economy of hunter-gatherer societies. In the course of collecting information on black-footed ferrets (*Mustela nigripes*), Tim Clark (1975) found that ferret and prairie dog (*Cynomys*) skeletal remains have been discovered at several Pleistocene sites occupied by Paleo-Indians in the western United States. More recently, there are records of ferret hides being used by Blackfeet and Cheyenne tribes as pendants on chief's headdresses, of stuffed decorated ferret skins being used in Crow Tobacco Society ceremonies, of stuffed ferret skins being incorporated into sacred Crow medicine bundles, and of a juvenile marmot (*Marmota*) skin used as a medicine pouch by Sioux (Clark 1975). In addition, the elaborate use of porcupine (*Erethizon dorsatum*) quills and bird feathers is well known. It is apparent that aboriginal humans' dependence on wildlife extended well beyond an elemental reliance on animals for food and materials; the essential characteristics of many species were represented in the ceremonial and spiritual activities of these peoples.

## EARLY HUMAN IMPACTS ON WILDLIFE

Hunting techniques used by Paleo-Indians on the Southern High Plains have been reconstructed from the sites selected by primitive hunters, the arrangements of bones at the kill sites, and the positions of projectile points in the animal carcasses. Wendorf and Hester (1962) distinguished two basic hunting patterns. The first method was used at the majority of all the sites they surveyed. The hunters' campsite was located so that animals could be observed as they came to drink at a stream or pond. Once seen, the animals were stalked and killed as they watered. Both mammoth (*Mammuthus*) and bison (*Bison*) were hunted in this way, and from one to thirty animals were killed at a time.

The second method was the stampede, first seen in the Parallel Flaked archeological horizon, and therefore probably not used before nine thousand years ago. Large herds, usually of bison, were driven into an arroyo, stream channel, or over a cliff. Many were trampled to death, crushed, or drowned. James Hester (1967) remarked that, though the uppermost animals were butchered, the remainder were left untouched. If so, this is an early example of the extreme waste of wildlife.

There is also evidence that hundreds of Pleistocene asses (*Equus*)

Figure 1.5. The construction of a Plains Indian war shirt, circa 1850, illustrates the dependence of Native Americans on wildlife for materials used in clothing. The hide from a mule deer was the basis for the shirt, with hair from a bison's tail decorating the chest area. Weasel or ermine tails and feathers from immature golden eagles adorned the shoulders. (Illustration by J. David Renwald, Wildlife Biologist, U.S. Forest Service, © 1992. Used with the permission of the artist.)

were stampeded over cliffs into steep ravines in the Bakhchisarai area of the Crimea in the Soviet Union (Vereshchagin 1967). Herds of other ungulates were ambushed in narrow canyons of this region and killed by hunters using stones, clubs, and spears.

Many of our ideas about the role of hunting in hominid origins and in the subsequent evolution of the human species have come under increasing scrutiny in the past few years. Taphonomic studies—research on the processes that influence (and alter) an assemblage of bones between the time an animal dies and the time its bones are incorporated into the fossil record—have shown that the presence of animal bones and primitive human tools at a common site does not decisively prove that humans were the successful hunters (Behrensmeyer 1987). Humans may have scavenged the remains of animals that died of natural causes or were killed by other predators. Indeed, animal bones may become associated with stone tools in a variety of other ways—for example, redeposition of tools and bones together as "lag" deposits in a stream channel or the use of protected locations at different times by both tool-using humans and bone-carrying canids (Speth 1989).

Even so, many examples attest to the success of early humans in killing big-game animals. These hunters undoubtedly wiped out entire herds of animals on many occasions. Some scientists also contend that overhunting by prehistoric humans was responsible for the extinction of a number of species of large animals at the end of the Ice Age. Over a century ago Alfred Russel Wallace wrote: "We live in a zoologically impoverished world, from which all the hugest, and fiercest, and strangest forms have recently disappeared . . . yet it is surely a marvelous fact, and one that has hardly been sufficiently dwelt upon, this sudden dying out of so many large Mammalia, not in one place only but over half the land surface of the globe" (1876:150).

The major features of this faunal impoverishment can be summarized from circumstances reconstructed by Paul Martin (1967). Toward the end of the Pleistocene a sudden wave of extinction eliminated many species of large vertebrates. Except for small oceanic islands, where smaller animals disappeared, the fauna lost primarily consisted of big-game mammalian and avian herbivores whose adult body weight exceeded fifty kilograms, and the carnivores, scavengers, and commensals that were ecologically dependent upon them. This involved over two hundred genera worldwide.

Two principal explanations have been proposed to account for such a sudden and widespread loss of species (Martin and Wright 1967; Lewin 1983). One, the environmentalist view, asserts that climatic and environmental changes were responsible for the extinction of so many terrestrial vertebrates at the end of the Pleistocene. This theory is supported by the coincidence, particularly in North America, of these extinctions with the end of the most recent glaciation. Explanations based on climatic change and resulting habitat transformations point to perturbations in food availability, pressures on mating patterns and reproductive physiology, and the fragmentation (as well as geographic displacement) of plant communities. Such problems would be compounded for large animals that make greater demands on an ecosystem for space, food, and cover. This could produce the differential extinction pattern indicated by the fossil record: the megafauna perished while smaller animals survived.

One weakness of the climatic-and-resulting-environmental-change hypothesis is the apparent lack of any correlation between extinction events and the glacial advances and retreats, with associated climatic changes, that occurred earlier in the Pleistocene. Other deficiencies include its failure to predict the greater severity of extinctions in both North and South America than in Eurasia or Australia, and the absence of simultaneous extinctions in Africa and tropical Asia (Owen-Smith 1987).

The second explanation, frequently referred to as Pleistocene overkill, is that prehistoric hunters were responsible for the mass extinctions. The argument for this interpretation claims that the timing of extinctions on various continents "follows the chronology of prehistoric man's spread and his development as a big-game hunter" (Martin 1967:75). The level of large mammal decimation implied by this hypothesis may seem to be unrealistic for human hunters. There is ethnological evidence, however, that indicates the normal constraints on hunting are "released" where game is superabundant. Furthermore, simulation scenarios, based on an advancing "front" of prehistoric hunters, show that this explanation is feasible (Mosiman and Martin 1975). Even if early humans did not kill all of a large herbivore species, Janzen (1983) suggested that experienced adult carnivores would have persisted long enough to "thoroughly extinguish" the few that remained. In any case, it is relevant to note that a "prey-mortality rate little more than double the normal would plunge a species precipitously toward extinction" (Lewin 1983).

Critics of the overkill hypothesis ask how, if Clovis humans were able to exterminate so many species, were other species that are equally vulnerable—such as the bison, musk ox, and moose—able to survive. Furthermore, "this fails to explain the simultaneous extinctions of a

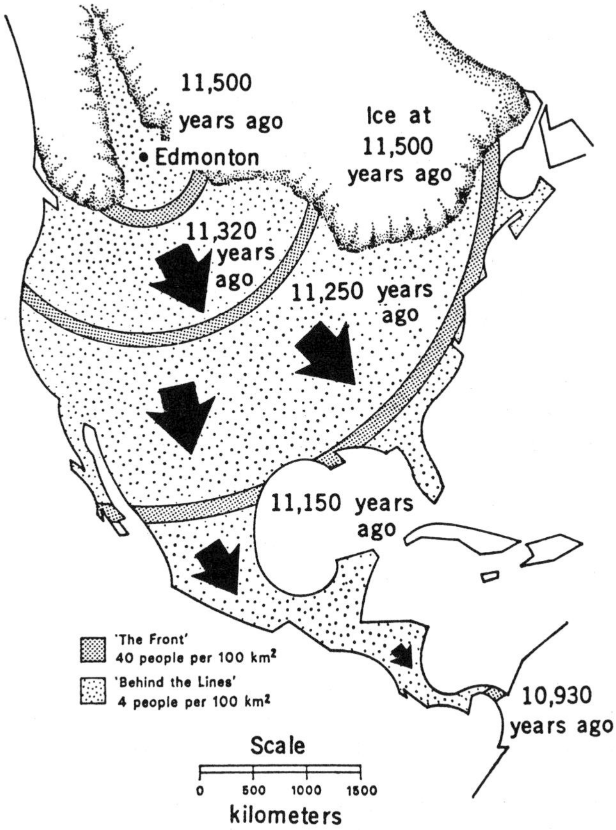


Figure 1.6. Pleistocene overkill by Paleo-Indians is one explanation proposed to account for the mass extinction of large mammals in North America 10,000 to 11,000 years ago. According to this hypothesis, a small band of humans arrived in southern Canada about 11,500 years ago. From there, these big-game hunters and their descendants spread throughout the ice-free portion of the continent along an arc-shaped "front" of human occupation. They killed off much of the megafauna as they advanced, moving relentlessly as the big-game animals were depleted. People remaining in the less densely populated region behind this advancing front lived on smaller game and those large plant-eating mammals that remained. Carnivores that had been the herbivores' natural predators were then probably driven by hunger to seek out the last of their remaining prey. (Reprinted by permission from "The Discovery of America" by Paul S. Martin, *Science* 179(1973): 972. © 1973 by the American Association for the Advancement of Science.)

number of mammalian and avian species not obviously vulnerable to human overkill" (Owen-Smith 1987).

A third hypothesis cites tremendous variations in mean temperature at the end of the Pleistocene as the major cause of extinctions (Fagan 1989:217). More extreme seasonal contrasts in temperature would, according to this idea, have been harder on young animals born in small litters, after extended gestation periods, and at fixed times of year. These traits tend to characterize larger mammals—precisely the kinds of animals that became extinct.

One may wonder why disputes over the megafaunal loss at the close of the Pleistocene always seem to be either/or arguments—either changes in climate, or Pleistocene overkill, or extreme seasonal contrasts. Why not some combination of all three? On reflection, it seems perfectly plausible that the loss of the Pleistocene megafauna might have resulted from dramatic climate-related changes, further accentuated by extreme seasonal temperature contrasts, with unrelenting human predation constituting the final fateful factor.

An explanation that Norman Owen-Smith (1987) called the "keystone herbivore hypothesis" does indeed incorporate a combination of the other ideas, but with an important difference. His proposal is based on the ecology of existing African species of megaherbivores, that is, animals exceeding one thousand kilograms. He summarized it as follows:

> Due to their invulnerability to non-human predation on adults, these species attain saturation densities at which they may radically transform vegetation structure and composition. African elephant can change closed woodland or thicket into open grassy savanna, and create open gaps colonized by rapidly-regenerating trees in forests. Grazing white rhinoceros and hippopotamus transform tall grasslands into lawns of more nutritious short grasses. The elimination of megaherbivores elsewhere in the world by human hunters at the end of the Pleistocene would have promoted reverse changes in vegetation. The conversion of the open parklike woodlands and mosaic grasslands typical of much of North America during the Pleistocene to the more uniform forests and prairie grasslands we find today could be a consequence. Such habitat changes would have been detrimental to the distribution and abundance of smaller herbivores dependent upon the nutrient-rich and spatially diverse vegetation created by megaherbivore impact. At the same time these species would have become more vulnerable to human predation. The elimination of megaherbivore influence is the major factor differentiating habitat changes at the end of the terminal Pleistocene glaciation from those occurring at previous glacial-interglacial transitions. (Owen-Smith 1987)

The controversy over the primary cause of the Pleistocene megafaunal extinctions is not likely to be resolved soon. However, we can be relatively certain that the impact of early humans on wildlife, at least on a local and perhaps even a regional scale, was considerable. This impact was accomplished directly by means of hunting and indirectly through habitat alteration, particularly the use of fire.

## ORIGINS OF AGRICULTURE AND EFFECTS ON WILDLIFE

The beginning of food production—the domestication of plants and animals—was a momentous occurrence in human prehistory. Ten thousand years ago almost all human societies lived by hunting and gathering; by two thousand years ago hunter-gatherers were a distinct minority (Fagan 1989). New economic strategies resulted in an increased, and more stable, food supply, but at the cost of greater energy expenditure. Studies of prehistoric diets also imply a decline in the quality, and perhaps even the length, of human life with the advent of agriculture. There are several theories about the origins of food production; one suggests that human population pressure was an important factor and that people may have turned to agriculture only when there were no other alternatives (Cohen 1977).

The transition from gathering to cultivation of root crops may have been almost unconscious, for many tubers are easy to grow (Fagan 1989). The African yam, for example, can be artificially germinated simply by cutting off the top and burying it. Hunter-gatherer bands familiar with such plants may have cultivated them to supplement food supplies in times of shortage. After tens of thousands of years of digging up wild edible roots with wooden sticks, it would have been a simple matter to have used a digging stick for planting.

Early animal domestication may also have been a natural step. Several types of animals amenable to taming—including canids, goats (*Capra*), sheep (*Ovis*), and wild oxen (*Bos*)—were widely distributed throughout the Old World during the Upper Pleistocene (Fagan 1989). In the case of the dog (*Canis*), the process probably began at least twelve thousand years ago. It is not difficult to imagine how an alliance between humans and canids might have originated. At the end of the Pleistocene Ice Age, people and canids were competing for the same food (Clutton-Brock 1989). A particularly placid or submissive canid pup scavenging around a human camp might survive to adulthood accepting the human group as its pack.

The incentive for domesticating sheep, goats, and wild cattle is also clear: if game animals are not available when meat is required, it is advantageous to have a meat source under one's control. Furthermore, storing meat as livestock is better than trying to preserve dead flesh by drying or smoking it (Clutton-Brock 1989).

Another factor in domesticating game animals may have been the difficulty of simultaneously cultivating crops and being a large animal hunter. The dilemma is that wild herbivores cannot be allowed to eat plants being cultivated for food, but driving them away tends to increase their flight distance, making them more difficult to hunt. Only hooved species with the capacity to become controllable and live in close association with people could be tolerated (Zeuner 1963).

Considering the apparent conflict between cultivating plants and hunting large animals, one of the unexpected findings from the excavation of Tell Abu Hureyra, on the banks of the Euphrates River in northern Syria, is particularly interesting (Legge and Rowley-Conwy 1987). This site was first settled by a group of hunter-gatherers in the Mesolithic period about eleven thousand years ago, but with only a single break it was occupied well into the succeeding Neolithic period. Thus it provides a view of the emergence of agriculture.

For perhaps one thousand years after the beginning of plant domestication at Abu Hureyra, hunting continued to play a critical role in the community's subsistence (Legge and Rowley-Conwy 1987). During that millennium, the major source of animal protein was mass killing of the Persian gazelle (*Gazella subgutturosa*) as herds moved north in the early summer each year. In fact, the mass killings may have been abandoned only when herds were depleted as the mass-killing strategy was adopted throughout the region.

One lesson from Tell Abu Hureyra is that the beginning of agriculture was not necessarily a single revolutionary event, but rather a stepwise process in which the key elements—a sedentary way of life, plant cultivation, and animal husbandry—occurred over an extended period of time. Another lesson is that, within the context of the Neolithic period, agriculture was not necessarily superior to a hunter-gatherer life-style. The early stages of agriculture apparently paralleled the continuation of hunting and gathering until changing conditions made agriculture a more productive and dependable mode of life.

Not all types of wild animals are suitable for domestication. In a nineteenth-century essay, Francis Galton (1865) wrote that six physiological and behavioral attributes are necessary for the successful domestication of animals. First, animals to be domesticated should be hardy, since young animals must be able to tolerate removal from their mother and life in an environment dominated by people. Second, their social behavior should be based on a dominance hierarchy (rather than defense of a territory), so that humans are viewed as the group leader and animals remain submissive even as adults. Third, they should be herd animals that do not flee, so they are tractable with people and can be confined in pens. Fourth, they should be useful as a source of food and materials. Fifth, they must reproduce readily under confined conditions. And sixth, they should be easy to tend—placid in disposition, versatile in feeding habits, yet gregarious—so that a group can be easily controlled by a herder.

It is interesting that, at a descriptive level of analysis, there appear to be few significant differences between the social behaviors of wild and feral species of sheep and goats (Shackleton and Shank 1984). Furthermore, wild sheep and goats captured at an early age can be readily tamed, whereas domestic sheep and goats that are feral as young animals essentially revert to a wild state. Thus, the first stage in domesticating some of humankind's most useful and tractable animals, the sheep and goats, might have involved no more than capturing young or assuming the care of young whose mothers were killed during hunting excursions.

Although the initial incentive for domestication is likely to have been meat, the usefulness of skins for clothing and shelter and hides for shields and armor would have been quickly recognized. The use of by-products such as milk and eggs on more than a token scale would have required selective breeding, however, since only such quantities of milk and eggs as are necessary for animal reproduction would be produced. The development of sheep with woolly coats likewise involved artificial selection, since this type of hair is not normal in wild sheep. Humans also learned to breed animals for specialized tasks—dogs for hunting, herding, draft, or protection; oxen and horses as draft animals (Clutton-Brock 1989).

The early agricultural practices of Neolithic humans affected wildlife by altering or destroying natural habitats, upsetting ecological relationships, restricting normal movements, and causing disturbances that interfered with mating, nesting, or maternal behavior—or resulted in animals leaving an area entirely (Krantz 1970).

Furthermore, early agriculturalists did not depend on wildlife to the extent that hunter-gatherers had, so the extinction of large wild herbivores would have had less effect on early farmers who depended on their crops and herds. Early agricultural humans, like contemporary technological humans, may have thought they could afford the luxury of exterminating wildlife that competed with their needs for space and domestic animal forage. Humans, then as now, may have felt they could destroy wildlife and the natural environment with impunity, because they were no longer directly dependent upon it.

Much of the Pleistocene megafauna has persisted to the present in Africa. Unfortunately, the rapidly growing human population, and poaching for markets in elephant ivory, rhinoceros horn, and other wildlife parts are destroying an irreplaceable wildlife treasure. Paleolithic peoples, with primitive weapons and simpler cultures, could perhaps afford some waste in harvesting wild animals. For modern humans, there is no excuse (D. L. Allen, personal communication, 1990).

---

## SUGGESTED READING

Fagan, B. M. 1989. *People of the Earth: An Introduction to World Prehistory.* 6th ed. Glenview, Ill.: Scott, Foresman. 622 pages. A narrative of human history from the origins of humankind to the beginnings of literate civilization.

# The History of Wildlife in North America 2

During the Pleistocene Ice Ages, from seventy thousand to ten thousand years ago, immense glaciers in the northern hemisphere trapped so much water that ocean levels were 25 meters to as much as 100 meters lower than the present sea level (Hopkins 1982). This uncovered a land bridge, called Beringia, about 1,600 kilometers wide connecting Siberia and Alaska. Herds of grazing animals from northeastern Asia—including long-horned bison (*Bison*), caribou (*Rangifer*), primitive musk oxen (*Soergelia* and perhaps *Symbos*), and the shaggy mammoths (*Mammuthus*)—gradually moved eastward through lush marsh grass and leafy lowland shrubs onto the land bridge (Borland 1975). They were followed and preyed upon by large carnivores. Behind the herds came another migrant: human hunters were approaching the New World.

Even earlier, the two New World continents were joined by an isthmus between what is now southern Panama and northwestern Colombia. This resulted from a combination of tectonic changes in the earth's crust and decreases in the sea level (related to ice-cap formation) about 3 million years ago during the Pliocene.

Representatives of thirty-eight genera of South American land mammals that wandered into North America included an opossum (*Didelphis*), a porcupine (*Erethizon*), a giant armadillo-like glyptodont (*Glyptotherium*), two armadillos (*Dasypus* and *Kraglievichia*), and three ground sloths (*Glossotherium, Nothrotheriops,* and *Holmesina* = *Pampatherium*) (Marshall 1988). Perhaps the most interesting dispersant, however, was *Titanis,* a phororhacoid ground bird believed to have been over three meters tall. Phororhacoids were flightless, carnivorous birds that exhibited specializations for running, and were the only large terrestrial carnivores on the South American continent when the land bridge appeared. *Titanis* has been noted in fossil faunas dating from about 2.5 to 1.9 million years ago in Florida (Marshall 1988).

The immigrants from Eurasia and South America encountered such native North American animals as the pronghorn (*Antilocapra* and *Stockoceros*), mountain beaver (*Aplodontia*), and coyote (*Canis*). Moreover, North America contributed its own migrants to the world's fauna. Ancestors of the modern horse (*Equus*) and camels (*Camelus*), for example, originated here but had disappeared from North America by the end of the Pleistocene (Anderson and Jones 1967; Kurtén and Anderson 1980). They were survived by their descendants, the horses, zebras, asses (all members of the genus *Equus*), and camels (*Camelus*) of Eurasia and Africa and the llamas (*Lama*) of South America.

## BEFORE EUROPEAN EXPLORATION

In history books, the chronicle of North America usually begins with the early European explorers. But by the time Norse, Italian, and Spanish adventurers reached the continent, a thousand generations of North American aborigines had already lived and died. They were descendants of Asian Mongoloid stock and had developed several advanced cultures and more than two hundred different languages (Claiborne 1973). Their cultural adaptations were responses to the same variety of environmental conditions that fostered the diversity of wild animals they hunted.

There can be little doubt that the earliest North Americans were predominantly hunters. For countless generations their Asiatic ancestors had drifted northward with herds of game animals across the Siberian tundra. Far removed from both Atlantic and Pacific weather patterns, Siberia was arid with harsh, dry winters and short, hot summers. Precipitation was so sparse that the great ice sheets seen in Europe and North America during the last Ice Age never formed there. Instead, herds of mammoths (*Mammuthus*) grazed the treeless plains and river valleys, where bands of hunter-gatherers weathered the long Siberian winters (Fagan 1989).

Archaeologists have identified two distinct Upper Paleolithic cultures in Siberia and northeast Asia. However, it was most likely peoples of the Dyukhtai tradition, found mostly east of the Yenesei Basin and known for their bifacially flaked spear points and wedge-shaped cores (used to make microblade tools), that settled North America (Fagan 1989). During the period eighty thousand to twenty thousand years ago, humans gradually adapted to the steppe-tundra conditions of Eurasia (Müller-Beck 1982). Their movement into Beringia may have resulted from the gradual enlargement of hunting territories across an enormous geographical area in which there were few, if any, ecological boundaries (Morlan and Cinq-Mars 1982).

Conditions on the treeless steppe-tundra of Beringia were not hospitable. During the short summers, swarms of ravenous insects reproduced in the wetlands, making existence miserable for humans and animals alike; in winter, there was no protection from the relentless arctic wind. Only the wealth of wildlife made life here barely tolerable (Claiborne 1973). The Beringian large-mammal assemblage was remarkable for its diversity of giant grazers: the woolly mammoth (*Mammuthus*), wild horses and asses (*Equus*), steppe bison (*Bison*), wild sheep (*Ovis*), moose (*Alces* and *Cervalces*), musk oxen (*Soergelia, Symbos,* and *Ovibos*), caribou (*Rangifer*), wapiti (*Cervus*), and saiga "antelope" (*Saiga*) were all present (Guthrie 1982). The caribou, particularly, was a staple resource that could be counted on to return each spring to traditional calving grounds.

The first settlement of Alaska remains an enigma, although it most likely occurred between twenty-five thousand and fourteen thousand years ago. One possible scenario suggests that small groups of big-game hunters moved into East Beringia (that is, Alaska) from the Beringian subcontinent while the Ice Age mammals were still present (Fagan 1989). As the ice sheets retreated fourteen thousand years ago, some of these groups hunted their way southward, through the valley of the Mackenzie River. This opening between the Cordillera and Laurentian glaciers extended south through Alberta and Saskatchewan (Claiborne 1973).

The climate of North America during the Pleistocene was cool and moist. On the northern plains, lowland areas were forested with conifers; most of the higher ground was open grassland. Further south, mixed woodlands and grasslands were interspersed, grading into tall-grass prairie that extended west to the Rockies. Throughout the central sector of the continent, forests occupied the river valleys and woodlands surrounded the numerous lakes. In the Intermountain West, glacial Lake Bonneville covered Nevada, and areas of the Southwest were tropical or subtropical with luxuriant foliage (Barry 1983; Claiborne 1973).

Compared with the rigors of the Siberian tundra and the perils of the North American arctic, groups of prehistoric hunters arriving in eastern Montana and the Dakotas found a verdant paradise. And the continent was inhabited by a bestiary of the most remarkable animals the imagination could conjure: giant moose (*Alces*) with eight-foot antlers, elephant-sized ground sloths (*Megalonyx*), long-horned bison (*Bison*), beavers (*Castoroides*) the size of bears, gigantic mammoths

(*Mammuthus*) and mastodons (*Mammut*), camels (six genera of Camelidae), a tremendous variety of smaller animals, and masses of waterfowl in season (Claiborne 1973). An awesome collection of carnivores preyed upon these plant eaters: the dire wolf (*Canis*), larger than our timber wolf; the saber-tooth cat (*Smilodon*), with upper canines eight inches long; and a giant panther (*Panthera*) that would dwarf today's lions (Claiborne 1973).

Into this natural menagerie came the Beringian hunters from the north. The Paleo-Indians of the distinctive Clovis culture, who appeared on the Great Plains of North America about 11,500 years ago, were direct descendants of the small bands of hunters from Beringia (West 1983). We are still not certain how much the ruthless efficiency of the Clovis hunters contributed to the loss of the rich Nearctic fauna. Perhaps their's was the first massive impact of a human assault on nature that has not yet ended.

## EARLY SETTLEMENT AND COLONIAL PERIOD

Within five years after Columbus made his voyage, another mercenary Italian explorer, Giovanni Caboto (John Cabot), sailed for North America. Ironically, Cabot's party apparently landed on the northern coast of Newfoundland within a few miles of the site of Leif Erickson's settlement almost five hundred years earlier. Cabot's son, Sebastian, reported that the land "is full of white bears, and stags far greater than ours. It yields plenty of fish, and those very great, as seals, and those which we commonly call salmon; there are soles also above a yard in length: but especially there is an abundance of that kind of fish which the savages call baccalaos [codfish]" (Borland 1975:21).

A French fishing excursion was sent to Newfoundland in 1504 (Kimball and Johnson 1978); by 1506 Portuguese ships were returning with large quantities of salted fish (Morison 1971). Scarcely one hundred years later, exploitation by ships' crews started the great auk's (*Pinguinus impennis*) plummet to extinction. This flightless bird, which had no fear of humans, lived on islands near the codfishing areas and proved to be too convenient a resource for the fishermen.

The Spanish were the most active explorers in North America during the sixteenth century. Spanish conquistadores ranged over the Southeast, through Texas to California, and as far north as Kansas. The myth persists that the first important European presence in America resulted from English settlements. However, none of the Jamestown (1607) or Plymouth (1620) colonists was yet born when Álvar Núnez (Cabeza de Vaca) and Hernando de Soto explored Florida and the Gulf Coast

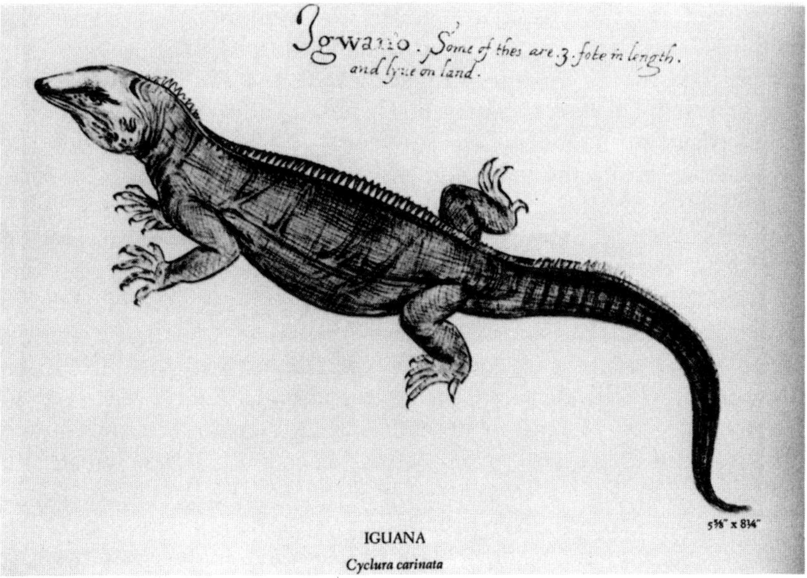
Igwano. Some of thes are 3. fote in length.
IGUANA
Cyclura carinata

Figure 2.1. An "iguana" as rendered by John White, grandfather of Virginia Dare and governor of the ill-fated Roanoke colony in 1587. Thirty-three of his watercolors, reproduced as engravings by Theodore de Bry, were of invertebrates, fishes, reptiles, and birds. These were probably the first paintings of North American wildlife by a European colonist. (Reprinted by permission of the British Library.)

in the 1520s and 1530s, and members of the Coronado expedition gazed into the Grand Canyon in 1540.

Despite the vast territories explored and claimed by the Spanish, their diaries and journals reveal little interest in the wildlife of North America. Coronado had seen "barking squirrels" [prairie dogs, *Cynomys*] and the "great white bears" [plains grizzlies, *Ursus arctos horribilis*] that followed the bison herds, and de Soto surely encountered unusual animals such as the alligator (*Alligator mississippiensis*) in the South, but Núnez's brief description of the American bison (*Bison bison*) is noteworthy mainly because he mentioned the species at all. They looked to him like hunchbacked cows, and he observed that they were about the size of Spanish cattle but with small horns like Moorish cattle, that their hair was long and woolly, and that some were tawny brown and others black (Hallenbeck 1940). The Spaniards were looking for more treasure like that found by Cortez, Pizzaro, and Quesada. Expeditions that discovered only splendid landscapes, the ancient Zuni culture, or teeming wildlife were not successful by their measure.

By contrast, the French recognized the value of North American wildlife almost immediately (Kimball and Johnson 1978). Jacques Cartier reached the St. Lawrence River in 1534 and sailed upriver as far as the present location of Montreal. He noted puffins (*Fratercula arctica*) on an island in the Gulf of St. Lawrence, and a Jesuit priest with the party remarked on the large numbers of geese, ducks, herons, cranes, swans, coots, and other water birds (Borland 1975).

It was not until Samuel de Champlain began to explore the region in 1603, however, that the French really began exploiting the resource. By 1608 Champlain had established a trading post at Quebec and was buying pelts and skins from the Native Americans. Later in the century, Jolliet and Marquette explored the Great Lakes and the Mississippi River in the 1670s; Robert Cavelier, Sieur de La Salle, went clear to the mouth of the Mississippi in 1680; and La Vérendrye ventured onto the Northern Plains sixty years before Lewis and Clark (Kimball and Johnson 1978).

If herds of game animals prompted prehistoric humans to cross the land bridge into Alaska and schools of fish lured Europeans across the North Atlantic to Newfoundland, then it was the beaver (*Castor canadensis*) that first enticed the colonists to explore the interior of the continent (Borland 1975). And if North American exploration was dominated in the sixteenth century by the Spanish and in the seventeenth century by the French, then the eighteenth century largely belonged to the English.

English and Dutch colonists confined themselves to coastal settlements along the eastern seaboard during the early decades of the seventeenth century. Nevertheless, their reports contained numerous references to North American wildlife. In 1624 inspectors sent to the Plymouth Plantation from England reported, "The country is annoyed with foxes and wolves" (Bradford 1952). In 1626, a single ship from the Dutch West India Company's Manhattan trading post contained 7,246 beaver skins, 675 otter skins, and mink, muskrat, and wildcat pelts from the upper Hudson River valley (Borland 1975).

The abundance of wildlife in North America was the subject of wonder by the English colonists. William Wood wrote: "If I should tell you how some have killed a hundred geese in a week, fifty ducks at a shot, forty teals at another, it may be counted impossible though nothing [is] more certain" (Cronon 1983:23). The spring spawning runs of alewives, smelt, and sturgeon elicited even more amazement.

Only one wildlife species, though, could match the alewives for sheer numbers. John Josselyn wrote that the passenger pigeons (*Ectopistes migratorius*), during their semiannual migrations, numbered in the "millions of millions," and Thomas Dudley described a March day in 1631 when "their flew over all the towns in our plantations . . . many flocks of doves, each flock containing many thousands and some so many that they obscured the light" (Cronon 1983:23).

The abundance of some mammals also impressed the English, though their numbers were slight compared with those of alewives and passenger pigeons. Thomas Morton regarded New England deer (*Odocoileus*), including the elk (*Cervus*), as "the most usefull and most beneficiall beast" in the region (Cronon 1983:23–24). During the spring, one could see as many as one hundred of them per mile, and they remained numerous enough year-round to ensure a steady supply of meat. Still, it was thought that deer numbers might be increased if wolves (*Canis*) could be eliminated. William Hammond probably expressed a common sentiment: "Here is good store of deer," he wrote; "were it not for the wolves here would be abound, for the does have most two fawns at once, and some have three, but the wolves destroy them" (Cronon 1983:24). Such thinking prompted the Massachusetts Bay Colony to authorize a bounty on wolves in 1630, and the town of Portsmouth, Rhode Island, to establish in 1646 a closed season on deer hunting from May 1 to November 1 (Kimball and Johnson 1978). By 1720 all the colonies had adopted this prohibition on deer hunting during part of the year.

In the late summer of 1754, the young Scottish physician Alexander Garden journeyed north to escape the oppressive heat of Charleston. His destination was the extraordinary estate of Cadwallader Colden west of Newburgh, New York. During Garden's visit they were joined by John Bartram, a Quaker farmer who had been looking for plants in the nearby Catskill Mountains. This meeting, described by Garden in an enthusiastic letter to Carl von Linné at the University of Uppsala, brought together three of the colonies' finest botanists. They were all amateur naturalists by today's definition, but virtuosos by any standard. The activities of these men helped to usher in the age of great adventurer-naturalists in North America.

Several naturalists were well known for their accounts of flora and fauna during this period. Nearly all were botanists first, but most devoted some attention to the wildlife of colonial America. Mark Catesby roamed through the southern colonies on foot for four years beginning in 1722, with many of his specimens going to the collections of his European patrons. The first volume of his work, *The Natural History of Carolina, Florida, and the Bahama Islands,* established Catesby as the first real American ornithologist (Kastner 1978).

William Bartram, John's son, also spent four years exploring in the Southeast (beginning in 1773), traveling five thousand miles on foot and horseback. His journal, published as *Travels through North and South Carolina, Georgia, East and West Florida,* included illustrations (a sandhill crane [*Grus canadensis*], for example, that he drew before eating it for dinner) and 175,000 words of detailed biological observations mixed with anecdotes, social commentary, and philosophizing in a style of "poetical description laced with homely fact" (Kastner 1978:87).

André Michaux, sent by the French government to search for useful plants, was another of this group. He had "herbalized" with Lamarck in France and collected plants in Persia. Within a short time after his American arrival in 1786 he had gained a reputation for being one of the very few collectors who could find new plants in an area already covered by the Bartrams. His wanderings ranged from the Carolina mountains and Florida swamps to Lake Mistassini in Quebec. Present-day books on botany studded with the attribution "Michx." attest to the breadth of his impact (Kastner 1978).

The period of European settlement and colonization has been called the "Era of Abundance" in the history of American wildlife conservation (Shaw 1985:7), and to a large extent it was. Even in this period, however, there were indications that numbers of some species were greatly diminished. In 1748, South Carolina traders alone shipped 160,000 buckskins to England (Borland 1975). It was in response to this kind of exploitation that closed deer seasons had become necessary. At about the same time the Swedish botanist Peter Kalm—one of Linné's prize pupils who was traveling and collecting in America—was told by a ninety-year-old man that when he was young, a hunter could "shoot eighty ducks in a morning but at present you frequently wait in vain for a single one" (Kastner 1978:37). The excessive and wasteful killing of wildlife would become even more flagrant as the frontier was pushed westward in the nineteenth century.

## THE NINETEENTH CENTURY: WESTWARD EXPANSION AND WILDLIFE EXPLOITATION

Long before the American Revolution a few restless wanderers had headed west and become frontiersmen, hunting and trapping for a living. One of the best known of them, Daniel Boone, led a party of twenty-eight axmen in 1775 that began cutting a trail (later called the Wilderness Road) from Virginia through the Cumberland Gap into Kentucky. Early settlers in the Ohio Country found enormous trees in the forests, gigantic fish in the rivers, and game animals everywhere.

Flocks of one hundred spruce grouse (*Canachites canadensis*) were common (Borland 1975). Naturalists, too, were eager to explore the frontier.

Michaux, apparently never satisfied with past accomplishments, enlisted the support of the American Philosophical Society for his plan to journey overland to the Pacific. Thomas Jefferson, a leading member of the society, drafted a detailed response to the proposal, and the money was raised. In 1793, Michaux's plans were compromised by his association with another Frenchman, who was involved in a scheme to enmesh the United States in France's continuing war with England and Spain on the frontier (Kastner 1978).

While contemplating the trip by Michaux, Jefferson heard from his Virginia neighbor, Meriwether Lewis, then a young army officer serving on the western frontier. Lewis had learned of Michaux's plans and volunteered to accompany him (Kastner 1978). Ten years later—in the spring of 1803—Jefferson was president, Napoleon had sold the entire Louisiana Territory to the United States, and Captain Lewis was commander of the Corps of Discovery (Thwaites 1904). In retrospect, the departure of the Lewis and Clark Expedition from St. Louis the next May was symbolic: it prefigured the westward movement of tens of thousands of persons during the 1800s, all on their own journeys of discovery.

The Lewis and Clark party was en route at a time when wildlife abounded in the West. Estimates put the number of bison (*Bison bison*) on the Great Plains at 50 to 60 million; there may have been 40 million pronghorn (*Antilocapra americana*) (Borland 1975). Several hundred plant and animal specimens were collected by members of the famous expedition, of which about two hundred remained intact. Its scientific data were overlooked, however, because the initial publication of the expedition's journals omitted most of them. Late in the century, naturalists who went through the original accounts were impressed with the true scope and depth of their findings. The "discoveries" of naturalists who followed were very often merely rediscoveries of Lewis and Clark's findings (Kastner 1978). Of all the animals they described, only two now honor their names—Lewis's woodpecker (*Asyndesmus lewis*) and Clark's nutcracker (*Nucifraga columbiana*) (Borland 1975).

There were other expeditions during the first half of the nineteenth century, but none as famous or productive. Colonel Zebulon Pike led an official army reconnaissance of Colorado and New Mexico in 1806 (Jackson 1966), and Major Stephen Long was sent by the army to explore the region between the Missouri River and the Rockies in 1819. Long's group included artist-naturalist Titian Peale and zoologist Thomas Say (Kastner 1978). Other prominent naturalists traveled and recon-

Figure 2.2. Although Audubon's bird paintings are usually considered to be much superior to those of Alexander Wilson, Audubon apparently plagiarized several of his older contemporary's illustrations (Welker 1955). Audubon's Mississippi kite (*left*), for example, is almost a mirror image of Wilson's original (*right*). (*Left:* Reprinted by permission from *The Birds of America,* vol. 1, by John James Audubon [New York: Dover, 1967]. © 1967 by Dover Publications, Inc. *Right:* Reprinted from *American Ornithology; or The Natural History of the Birds of the United States,* Popular Edition, vol. 1, by Alexander Wilson and Charles Lucian Bonaparte [Philadelphia: Porter and Coates].)

noitered on their own. Among the best known were two self-taught artist-ornithologists—a lanky peddler and schoolteacher, Alexander Wilson, from Scotland; and the illegitimate son of a French sea-faring merchant and a French Creole girl, Jean Rabin Fougère Audubon (John James Audubon), born in Santo Domingo (Ford 1951; Kastner 1978).

By midcentury the pace of settlement and exploitation had quickened. Gold was discovered near Sutter's Fort in California in 1848 and in the Colorado mountains ten years later. The trickle of settlers became a torrent. After the Civil War, ranchers went West followed by a flood of homesteaders. All of these new arrivals relied to some extent on wildlife for sustenance, and all dispossessed animals from their traditional haunts.

During the last half of the century free-living bison were all but exterminated, but as early as 1843 Audubon wrote that "even now there is a perceptible difference in the size of the herds, and before many years the Buffalo, like the Great Auk, will have disappeared" (Ford 1951:48). Francis Parkman thoroughly comprehended the bison's role in the economy of the Plains Indians, and he commented: "The buffalo supplies them with the necessaries of life; with habitations, food, clothing, beds, and fuel; strings for their bows, glue, thread, cordage, trailropes for their horses, coverings for their saddles, vessels to hold water, boats to cross streams, and the means of purchasing all that they want from the traders. When the buffalo are extinct, they too must dwindle away" (Matthiessen 1987:147). This conclusion was also apparent to the white settlers and their representatives in Washington. They bitterly opposed measures to limit the killing of bison, and in the end their will was done. Although Congress eventually passed protective legislation, President Grant yielded to political pressure and never signed the bill. The carnage continued unabated.

Changes in European fashion, from beaver-felt hats to high silk hats, practically eliminated the beaver (*Castor canadensis*) skin trade in the late 1830s, but the beaver streams were almost trapped out anyway. Late in the century, the plumed birds were nearly extirpated, also because of the demands of fashion. High style dictated that women powder their faces with swansdown puffs, fan themselves with fancy plumes, and adorn their hats with splendid feathers. This put enormous pressures on species such as the trumpeter swan (*Olor buccinator*), roseate spoonbill (*Ajaia ajaja*), and the egrets, both the reddish (*Dichromanassa rufescens*) and the snowy (*Leucophoyx thula*) (Borland 1975).

The slaughter of American wildlife during the 1800s was so staggering in its dimensions as to be almost inconceivable. If it were somehow possible to catalog all the abuses, it is unlikely that many could bear to peruse the full account. Even a brief sampling of these incidents makes painful reading.

An 1838 New York law forbidding the use of batteries (that is, multiple guns) in the shooting of waterfowl was later repealed because it was ineffectual. Commercial shooters had taken to wearing masks to conceal their faces and vowed to execute any informants who revealed their identities (Matthiessen 1987).

On August 29, 1863, Eskimo curlews (*Numenius borealis*) and golden plovers (*Pluvialis dominica*) appeared in such numbers on Nantucket Island, Massachusetts, as to practically darken the sun. Some seven to eight thousand were shot that day, and the killing stopped only when the island's supply of gun powder and shot was exhausted (Matthiessen 1987).

The largest nesting flock of passenger pigeons ever recorded appeared in the sandy scrub-oak barrens of south-central Wisconsin in 1871. It occupied an area of more than 290 square kilometers (approximately 47 kilometers by 6 kilometers) and was estimated to include 136 million birds. News of this incredible concentration was spread throughout the adjacent states by means of the recently invented telegraph, and literally thousands of market hunters descended. Millions of dead birds were shipped out at a wholesale price of fifteen to twenty-five cents a dozen. Within two months the markets were glutted, the pigeons were scattered, and most of the exploiters had departed. They left behind a rancid wasteland (Matthiessen 1987).

An 1886 bulletin of the American Ornithologists' Union, entitled "Destruction of Our Native Birds," estimated that 5 million birds were killed in America each year for decorations on womens' hats. On two occasions during that year Frank M. Chapman strolled through the streets of New York City, taking note of the headgear worn by women. Out of 700 hats he counted, 542 featured mounted birds. Chapman saw twenty-some species, including owls, grackles, grouse, and a green heron (Matthiessen 1987).

The list of abuses seems almost endless. Considering the vengeance with which virtually all wild animals were killed during this period it is amazing that the outcome was not even more disastrous. Fortunately, there were also signs that a more enlightened attitude toward wildlife was emerging. Ralph Waldo Emerson's essay *Nature,* published in 1836, had introduced the idea of conservation long before there was any such word. The English aristocrat Henry William Herbert, who immigrated to America in 1831, began writing a series of magazine articles in the late 1830s under the pen name Frank Forester. These articles, which were expanded into several books, discussed sporting etiquette, lamented the commercial destruction of wildlife and habitat, and called for sportsmen to band together and protect their interests (Reiger 1986). Still, the extinction of the great auk in 1844 apparently caused little stir (Kimball and Johnson 1978). It was the drastic reduction of bison and passenger pigeons, present in such astronomical numbers only a few years before, that first attracted public attention. George Perkins Marsh's book *Man and Nature,* published in 1864, documented many other natural resource abuses and sounded a clarion call to conservation action.

Most of the conservation efforts during this period were attempts to reduce the numbers of game animals killed. In 1852 Maine was the first state to hire salaried game wardens, and twelve years later New York instituted the first state hunting license (Shaw 1985). State wildlife agencies were organized by California and New Hampshire in 1878 (Matthiessen 1987). Meanwhile, Connecticut and New Jersey took the first steps to protect nongame wildlife. Laws were passed in 1850 protecting songbirds. Unfortunately, famine in the South after the carnage of the Civil War years led to the continued consumption of robins and other large nongame birds (Matthiessen 1987).

The establishment of Yellowstone in 1872 as the world's first national park was a signal step in conservation progress. Actually, the idea for a "nation's park" had been proposed by George Catlin as early as 1833 (Matthiessen 1987). Although the park was not created solely for wildlife, it became the "first federal preserve and as such benefited wildlife by eliminating local hunting and preserving natural habitat" (Shaw 1985:8). However, additional legislation was necessary; the Park Protection Act of 1894 further protected the fledgling reserve, including its wildlife, from continued exploitation (Matthiessen 1987).

There is a common misconception, even among environmental historians, that no real conservation movement existed until the twentieth century. In fact, American sportsmen "who hunted and fished for pleasure rather than commerce or necessity, were the real spearhead of conservation" (Reiger 1986:21). The appearance of three national periodicals in the 1870s gave sportsmen a public forum as well as a means of communication among themselves. *American Sportsmen* (1871) was the first of these publications, followed by *Forest and Stream* (1873), and *Field and Stream* (1874). All of them concentrated on the interrelated subjects of hunting, fishing, natural history, and conservation—and all crusaded against the commercial exploitation of wildlife.

George Bird Grinnell, a prominent naturalist and editor of *Forest and Stream,* championed the moderate and responsible use of wildlife in the pages of that journal. In 1886 he sponsored a pledge, supported by several periodicals oriented toward youth, not to kill birds or wear their feathers. Within three years this spontaneous group numbered over fifty thousand members and was known as the Audubon Society. Such local groups were formally chartered in Massachusetts and Pennsylvania in 1896 and were so widespread that a national association of these groups was organized six years later.

As the century came to a close, there were several additional events of significance to wildlife conservation: establishment of the Division of Economic Ornithology and Mammalogy in 1886, a federal agency that eventually became the Fish and Wildlife Service; organization of the Boone and Crockett Club by Theodore Roosevelt and George Bird Grinnell in 1887; notable individual conservation efforts like the salvation of the snowy egret (*Leucophoyx thula*) by E. A. McIlhenny, whose private refuge in Louisiana was set aside as a preserve in 1892; and the Supreme Court decree (in *Greer vs. Connecticut,* 1895) that wildlife belongs to the states rather than to the federal government or individual landowners (Matthiessen 1987). This Supreme Court decision meant that the citizens of each state own the resident wildlife of that state in common. This principle underlies the subsequent history of wildlife conservation in the United States.

## WILDLIFE IN THE TWENTIETH CENTURY

With a new century came new conservation leadership. After McKinley's assassination in 1901, Theodore Roosevelt became president, and his inauguration "was one of the most auspicious and timely events in the history of American wildlife" (Matthiessen 1987:178). Roosevelt was a Phi Beta Kappa graduate of Harvard (class of 1880) and ranched in North Dakota soon after the slaughter of that state's last great bison herd. Renowned as an outdoorsman and a big-game hunter, he was also an astute amateur biologist and naturalist. That Roosevelt's interest in wildlife encompassed nongame as well as hunted species is apparent from his own words: "I need hardly say how heartily I sympathize with the purposes of the Audubon Society. I would like to see all harmless wild things, but especially all birds, protected in every way" (Cutright 1956:86). This attitude was translated into action with the creation of the first wildlife refuge on Pelican Island, Florida, in 1903; he added thirty-one more in the next six years (Borland 1975).

Progress in wildlife conservation at the state level was still rather halting during the early years of the century. A Wild Game and Birds Protection Act, prohibiting commerce in waterfowl and game mammals, became law in Texas in April 1903. It contained some loopholes, however, including one that set a daily limit of twenty-five ducks per gun. Wealthy hunters who could afford to employ gun bearers frequently made extremely large kills that were nevertheless quite legal (Doughty 1983). At times there was even sanctioned violence. Audubon warden Guy Bradley was murdered by a Florida plume hunter on Oyster Key one summer day in 1905. Worse yet, Bradley's killer was set free by an indulgent jury (Matthiessen 1987). The message sent by this trial panel was obvious: the protection of wildlife was a low priority, and persons choosing this vocation were, like the animals they sought to protect, fair game.

Passage of the Weeks-McLean Act in 1913 gave responsibility for the management of migratory game birds to the federal government. This provided a basis for eventual protection of beleaguered shorebirds and waterfowl. The Federal Tariff Act, which was also approved in 1913, prohibited importation of wild bird plumage into the United States (Matthiessen 1987). International cooperation in dealing with the problems of migratory birds in North America came in 1916 with the Migratory Bird Treaty between the United States and Great Britain (acting on behalf of Canada). The Migratory Bird Treaty Act, passed by Congress in 1918 to implement the 1916 Treaty, instituted a crucial partnership for the conservation and management of game birds that migrate across international boundaries. These actions bolstered the fortunes of many avian species.

About 1910 a rift developed in the fledgling conservation movement, with one viewpoint emphasizing conservation and the other preservation. The conservationists—including Roosevelt, explorer and geologist John Wesley Powell, and forester Gifford Pinchot—espoused the view that public land resources can be used and managed wisely so that they remain available for future generations. Preservationists were led by naturalist and writer John Muir, who promoted the idea that large tracts of public land should be set aside as wilderness and thereby protected from any kind of development. Debates over the relative merits of these two schools of thought, as well as what actually constitutes wise use (rather than abuse and exploitation), continue today.

It is significant that Aldo Leopold, the "father of wildlife management," encompassed both attitudes. He was a pioneer in promoting wilderness preservation and was mostly responsible for establishing the Gila Wilderness Area in New Mexico (the first area in the National Forest System to receive wilderness designation). Furthermore, his philosophical essays, especially *A Sand County Almanac* (published posthumously in 1949), have a definite preservationist tone. Yet his theory of game management, which first appeared in a 1925 article in the *Bulletin of the American Game Protective Association,* was certainly consistent with the tone of scientific conservation. Leopold's ideas were expanded in a series of lectures at the University of Wisconsin in 1929 and refined in his classic text, *Game Management,* published in 1933 (Borland 1975; Meine 1988).

The early application of wildlife management and conservation concentrated on waterfowl. Duck numbers were much reduced on the inland flyways during the twenties, a consequence of wetland drainage with the expansion of cultivated farmland after the World War I. Waterfowl refuges were proposed to protect and restore feeding, resting, nesting, and wintering areas for ducks and geese. Passage of the Upper Mississippi River Wildlife and Fish Refuge Act in 1924 started this

Figure 2.3. Leaders of the two contending schools of conservation thought in the early twentieth-century. Sportsman, naturalist, conservationist, and President Theodore Roosevelt (*left*) is shown here with writer, naturalist, wilderness preservationist and Sierra Club founder John Muir at Yosemite. (Courtesy of the Library of Congress.)

trend, but the Duck Stamp Act, which became law ten years later, was (and still is) the major impetus and source of funds for preservation of wetland habitats on a continental scale.

Several programs launched by Franklin D. Roosevelt, when he became president in 1933, helped restore and preserve natural habitats, as well as providing jobs during the depression years. These included the Civilian Conservation Corps, the Soil Conservation Service, and the Tennessee Valley Authority. Perhaps FDR's most important contribution to wildlife was his appointment of Jay N. "Ding" Darling as chief of the Bureau of Biological Survey in 1934 (Borland 1975). Darling, an active conservationist and Pulitzer Prize-winning political cartoonist, was responsible for instituting the Cooperative Wildlife Research Unit Program at land-grant colleges in 1935 and for the first North American Wildlife Conference convened by President Roosevelt in 1936. Furthermore, he was the force behind the formation of the National Wildlife Federation, also in 1936.

Another landmark action during the the thirties was the passage by Congress of the Federal Aid in Wildlife Restoration Act of 1937, also called the Pittman-Robertson Act. This legislation placed an excise tax on sporting arms and ammunition, with proceeds apportioned among the states for wildlife research and restoration. The sporting arms and ammunition industry had provided financial and political support for state and federal conservation efforts from the early years of the century. Passage of this law was important, however, because it forced states to meet certain standards, ensuring honest and efficient administration of wildlife programs at the risk of losing substantial amounts of federal funding.

War years are wasted years, years when respect for any form of life—wild or human—is diminished (Borland 1975). The years from 1941 through 1945 were no exception. Many of the first wildlife professionals, newly trained in the late thirties, were sent off to battle in the early forties; some never returned. Wildlife refuge lands were neglected as human and fiscal resources were directed to the war effort. Valuable wildlife habitats were conscripted for military bases and artillery ranges.

The forties also ushered in the era of widespread pesticide use. DDT proved effective in killing a wide variety of insect pests, thus controlling such diseases as malaria and typhus during World War II. After the war, DDT and other chlorinated hydrocarbons were used in the United States and throughout the world by public health agencies, farmers, and homeowners. Although some environmental scientists and conservationists called attention to evidence these chemicals were harmful to wildlife, it was not until the publication of Rachel Carson's book

Figure 2.4. An example of the work of Jay N. "Ding" Darling, a Pulitzer Prize-winning political cartoonist, whose special concern was conservation. Darling's influence was so great that President Franklin Roosevelt appointed him as chief of the Bureau of Biological Survey (the agency that later became the U.S. Fish and Wildlife Service) in 1934, a position "Ding" used to launch several pivotal programs in wildlife conservation. (Courtesy of the Jay N. "Ding" Darling Papers, Special Collections Department, University of Iowa Libraries.)

*Silent Spring* in 1962 that the consequences of extensive pesticide use became generally known.

Eisenhower's administration during the fifties had a calamitous impact on conservation. Less than halfway through Ike's first term Bernard DeVoto wrote: "In a year and a half the businessmen in office have reversed the conservation policy by which the United States has been working for more than seventy years to substitute wise use of natural resources in place of reckless destruction for the profit of special corporate interests" (1954). Douglas McKay, who was to characterize conservationists as "punks," had been appointed as secretary of the interior to reward his support of Eisenhower's candidacy. McKay's lack of any natural resource experience may have been exceeded only by his arrogance. He pursued a political vendetta against the Fish and Wildlife Service that eventually caused a number of dedicated wildlife professionals—including Alfred Day, Clarence Cottam, and Durward Allen—to leave the agency. Partisan politics is nearly always anathema to conservation. As "Ding" Darling remarked, "The worst enemies of wildlife are the Republicans and Democrats" (Matthiessen 1987:228).

With the sixties came a reawakening of environmental consciousness. Conflicts between competing uses of public lands led to passage of the Multiple-Use Sustained-Yield Act in 1960. This legislation mandated that the Forest Service and Bureau of Land Management try to balance the demands for various uses—timber, grazing, mineral extraction, watershed, outdoor recreation, and fish and wildlife habitat—on public lands. In 1964 the National Wilderness System was created by an act of Congress. This provided for designating certain undeveloped tracts of federally owned land to be maintained in an undeveloped state. The Endangered Species Preservation Act of 1966 was the first of several federal laws directed to protecting animals "threatened with extinction" and their supporting habitats.

Finally, the decade ended with passage of the National Environmental Policy Act (NEPA) of 1969. NEPA contains some cosmic language and idealistic concepts, but also requires all federal agencies (except the Environmental Protection Agency) to submit an environmental impact statement (EIS) for any project or piece of legislation that would have a significant effect on environmental quality. Citizens and conservation organizations have gradually discovered that the EIS process allows them a powerful oversight role in environmental decision making; likewise, federal agencies have learned that they must be responsive and responsible in their environmental planning and management activities.

It is no exaggeration to refer to the seventies as the environmental decade. Earth Day on April 22, 1970, focused public attention on a broad range of environmental issues, including problems involving wildlife. Although that event was not the beginning of an environmental revolution, as some have suggested, it certainly was a turning point (Borland 1975). Previous conservation movements concentrated on individual problems or resources. This environmental movement was different: it was more comprehensive than the two previous waves of conservation, spurred by the two Roosevelts, earlier in the century; its concern encompassed the entire earth and all of life (Shanks 1984). Several important legislative initiatives affecting wildlife were successfully passed during these years—revised Endangered Species Acts in 1973 and 1978; the National Forest Management Act (1976) that regulated clear-cutting on national forest lands; and the Federal Land Policy and Management Act, or so-called BLM (Bureau of Land Management) Organic Act (also in 1976), that provided substantial direction in the management of 180 million hectares of federal land in the West and Alaska—and an entirely new federal regulatory organization, the Environmental Protection Agency, was created (1970). Other congressional edicts enlarged the National Wilderness System, established new national parks and wildlife refuges, placed a moratorium on the taking and importation of several marine mammals, provided for payments to maintain certain wetlands, increased penalties for shooting eagles, banned the shooting of wildlife from aircraft, and prohibited the dumping of hazardous substances in coastal areas (Borland 1975).

At decade's end the emergence of a "sagebrush rebellion" was a reminder of fundamental disagreements over natural resource conservation and public land policy. The philosophical differences trace back to the very beginnings of the republic, to the struggle between Alexander Hamilton (representing the aristocratic view) and Thomas Jefferson (who advocated a democratic policy) over the use of the public domain lands (Shanks 1984). In its most recent incarnation, the confrontation involved six western states, led by Nevada, which filed court suits claiming state ownership of federal lands (Shay 1980). Some congressional representatives from these states also introduced legislation to accomplish the same end. Apparently the ultimate goal was the transfer of national forest and BLM lands into private ownership, or at least private control. Although the "sagebrush rebellion" got its start with two groups that have exercised dominion over the western public lands for many years, the livestock and mining interests, it was soon joined by the energy corporations. The underlying themes of this movement are part of a pattern that has recurred throughout the nation's history: "worthless" public lands become valuable (as the natural resources on more valuable private holdings are exploited and exhausted); greedy economic interests create controversy and turmoil; and politicians placate the special interest groups (Shanks 1984). This course of events has repeatedly caused the plunder of wildlife and widespread destruction of wildlife habitats and the extinction of species.

Probably the dominant influence on American wildlife in the eighties was the environmental policies of the Reagan administration. Reagan's first secretary of the interior, James Watt, engineered the transfer of more than $1 trillion worth of public resources into private control. The large energy corporations were the primary beneficiaries of Watt's unconscionable largesse. Not since the Teapot Dome scandal of the twenties (when Secretary of the Interior Albert Fall went to jail for leasing naval petroleum reserves in California and Wyoming to Harry Sinclair and his Sinclair Oil Co. for a $200,000 bribe) has a secretary of the interior violated sacred public trust in so flagrant a manner (Shanks 1984).

The magnitude of Watt's virtual gift of natural resources to corporate and private business interests is not yet generally understood by the American public. The full impact of these giveaways on wildlife is even further removed from public comprehension. It will be fifty or one hundred years from now, as the human population burgeons and demands on public lands and their resources are even more intense, before the true consequences of these political deeds will become apparent. Then, once again, the rape of American wildlife will be obvious.

Early impressions of George Bush's presidency with respect to wildlife and natural resource conservation were mixed. The appointment of William Reilly, a career conservationist and capable administrator, to head the Environmental Protection Agency was widely applauded; however, Bush's naming of Manuel Luhan, a former New Mexico member of Congress with a dismal environmental record, as secretary of the interior caused disbelief and consternation among citizen conservationists and natural resource professionals alike. As months have passed into years, the hope that Bush would fulfill his pledge to be "the environmental president" has largely faded. Just as his famous admonition to "read my lips" now means, "Guess I sneaked that tax issue past you dopes," his promise of "no net loss of wetlands" has also been violated. Sadly, the White House position on environmental matters seems to have deteriorated into a "good cop, bad cop" routine, with Bush typically expressing pious support for worthy initiatives while former White House Chief of Staff John Sununu and Budget Director Richard Darman effectively sabotaged them. The hostility of Ronald Reagan's presidency to the environment was a disappointment, but no great surprise. People who perceived George Bush as having a genuine concern about environmental quality, and a gut-level appreciation of how the natural world operates, are sad to see him politicize environmental issues at a time when the American people finally seem ready for effective action.

PERSPECTIVE

## A Conflict of Wildlife Ideals

Wildlife cannot exist apart from the natural environment of which it is an integral component; likewise, the fate of wildlife in the past several hundred, if not the past few thousand, years cannot be separated from a consideration of human history. Several recurrent patterns are evident in the history of American wildlife. One of the most important is the clash of aristocratic and democratic ideals (Shanks 1984).

According to the Roman legal and social tradition, wild animals were "commons": like the air and the oceans, wildlife belonged to everyone and to no one. Once an animal had been killed or captured, however, it became the property of the hunter (Shanks 1984). This practice was introduced into England while that country was still an outpost of the Roman Empire.

The successful Saxon invasion of England in 1066 installed a new philosophy. William the Conqueror confiscated lands and greatly expanded the royal forests. Hunting on crown lands was a privilege accorded only to royalty. Poaching was a deadly serious activity. The French historian Nonnemere commented, "The death of a hare was a hanging matter, the murder of a plover a capital crime" (Shanks 1984:194). Against this background, the exploits of the twelfth-century outlaw Robin Hood became legend. His deeds included poaching the king's deer. Such acts gave encouragement, and even sustenance, to starving commoners during times of famine.

The signing of the Magna Charta in 1215 marked the beginning of a gradual liberalization of English law with respect to wildlife (Shanks 1984). There remained, however, "qualification statutes" that still tended to restrict hunting to persons of prominence or property who were considered by the crown to be trustworthy (Bean 1978). These statutes had two significant social functions: first, they promoted widespread discrimination based on social class; and second, they prevented persons regarded as being unfriendly to the monarchy from legally possessing weapons (Lund 1980).

After the American Revolution, the English notion of sovereign control over wildlife was incorporated into the legal and social framework of the new republic. Since there was no monarch, the question of whether that sovereign authority belonged to the states or resided with the federal government was the source of a long and bitter dispute (Bean 1978). Still, there were never laws or customs favoring one class or group over another in the use of American wildlife. Thus, inherent in our own legal and social traditions are aspects of both aristocratic and democratic control over wildlife and other public natural resources.

There have been abuses of the worst sort by both groups: special interests and corporations (embodying the aristocratic model) have often successfully enhanced their own welfare by exploiting a natural resource until it was exhausted, whereas hordes of individuals collectively comprising the public (and representing the democratic principle in action) have usually not tried to conserve a natural resource that belonged to everyone and therefore to no one. Historically, aristocratic exploitation corresponds to the actions of a selfish despot; democratic abuses represent examples of the "tragedy of the commons" (Hardin 1968).

The upshot of this abuse and exploitation is a tragic record of species pushed to extinction: the great auk, the heath hen, the Labrador duck, the Eskimo curlew, the Carolina parakeet, the passenger pigeon. There is plenty of blame to go around; the American aristocrats and democrats can share the responsibility for countless instances of unbridled greed and shortsighted stupidity that have deprived the nation and the world of a part of its wildlife heritage. The evolutionary biologist Edward O. Wilson has said, "The one process that will take millions of years to correct is the loss of genetic and species diversity by the destruction of natural habitats. This is the folly our descendants are least likely to forgive us" (1983).

## SUGGESTED READING

Borland, H. G. 1975. *The History of Wildlife in America.* Washington, D.C.: National Wildlife Federation. 208 pages. An engaging and lavishly illustrated chronicle of American wildlife from prehistory to the present.

Matthiessen, P. 1987. *Wildlife in America.* New York: Viking. 332 pages. A readable account of wildlife in America that does not shrink from the unpleasant task of recounting the impacts of human exploitation.

Reiger, J. F. 1986. *American Sportsmen and the Origins of Conservation.* Revised ed. Norman: University of Oklahoma Press. 316 pages. An interesting exposition of the contributions of the sportsmen who initiated and supported the conservation movement in nineteenth-century America.

# Consumptive Uses of Wildlife 3

Consumptive uses of wildlife are those that involve the killing of an animal—for a product its body yields or an experience its body signifies. Although wild animals have been taken by humans for hundreds of thousands of years, it is only in recent times that hunting and trapping have become recreational pursuits rather than subsistence activities. Even in twentieth-century America, however, a significant segment of the population has sometimes found it necessary to rely on wildlife for material needs. As recently as the depression years of the thirties, many rural families hunted and trapped for food and to supplement a meager income.

## ATTITUDES TOWARD HUNTING

George Reiger contended that public attitudes toward hunting "are linked to shifting definitions of property and ownership" (1978). Before European colonization of North America, hunting was a prerogative of the ruling classes of Europe and Asia, and it was perceived as being a desirable—even a prestigious—activity. Such class privilege lent an air of exclusivity to hunting and also provided protection to wildlife and other resources: access to the immense forest preserves was restricted to royalty and their game reeves, or wardens, so wood and wildlife could be harvested in a controlled manner without endangering basic stocks.

The deferential attitude of commoners toward game animals began to change within a generation of Columbus's landing. "After all, it was difficult to maintain a proper awe of the great cats, for example, when the lowliest army sentry was expected to kill with his service arbalest [crossbow] any Jaguars or Pumas he found roaming too close to camp. Soldiers serving in Florida and Central America ate parrot breast, bear hearts, and deer tongues—food fit, quite literally, for kings—and the privates and corporals must have wondered on occasion about the protocol that refused them such delicacies in Spain" (Reiger 1978).

With the colonization of North America, public attitudes toward hunting were further altered by the abundance of wildlife at a settler's very doorstep. Hunting quickly passed from an activity that had been prohibited to one that was often necessary for survival. We can speculate on whether the clash of Old World prohibition with New World opportunity made the colonists feel like "legal poachers." Certainly, there was no tradition of restraint in the killing of game animals to fall back upon. In the absence of moral or legal constraints, overexploitation was a natural consequence.

Early in the nineteenth century, hunting began to evolve in two different directions (Reiger 1978). One was exemplified by market hunters who expanded the practice of exploitation and directed it toward making handsome profits by sending fresh game meat to larger cities by way of a growing network of canals and railroads. The other was personified by sport hunters who often ate game meat that was available commercially, but preferred to do the hunting themselves. By the 1830s, reduced numbers of game began to diminish the recreational opportunities for sport hunters. Commercial and sport hunting were on a collision course.

"When sportsman-naturalist Henry William Herbert arrived in New York City from England in 1831, he stepped into an America which was changing so rapidly and so extensively that it is barely imaginable today" (Reiger 1978). Herbert was an aristocrat, a hunter, and an author. Writing under the pseudonym Frank Forester, Herbert promoted a new attitude toward hunting; indeed, his views amounted to the germ of a new ethic. Although he had no formal training in game or forest management—these disciplines did not exist at the time—Herbert understood that both wildlife and sport hunting were endangered by habitat destruction and overshooting. He continually urged fellow sportsmen to outlaw destructive shooting practices, to enforce existing wildlife laws, and to halt spring hunting (Reiger 1978).

The writings of Frank Forester were well known to such prominent nineteenth-century political leaders and sportsmen as Daniel Webster and Robert Barnwell Roosevelt. They in turn inspired the next generation, which included Theodore Roosevelt, George Bird Grinnell, C. Hart Merriam, and Charles Sheldon (Reiger 1978).

There have been several generations of revolutions in transportation, communication, and social attitudes since Henry William Herbert first glimpsed a changing America in 1831. But the trend toward urban-

Figure 3.1. "The Life of a Sportsman," as depicted in one of the Currier and Ives lithographs of nineteenth-century Americana. (Courtesy of the Library of Congress.)

ization has continued unabated. Until 1920, most Americans lived in rural areas (Carey 1986). Now, two-thirds of the population is crowded into less than 2 percent of the landscape (Lipske 1986). Many urban dwellers have little contact with wildlife, but their attitudes influence the fate of wildlife and those who do wish to use the resource.

In New Jersey, the nation's most densely populated state, public attitudes toward hunting have been monitored on a biannual basis since 1972 (Applegate 1984). The number of resident firearm hunters in New Jersey declined from 186,774 in 1971 to 132,065 in 1981. This decline was reflected in data from telephone surveys of the general population: 9.3 percent of residents described themselves as "active hunters" in 1972 compared to only 4.9 percent in 1982.

There was relatively little change in attitudes toward deer hunting in New Jersey during this period. Overall, about 52 percent of residents expressed approval and 40 percent disapproval. However, Applegate (1984) anticipated increasing opposition to hunting over the next decade, and he suggested three contributing factors: first, declining participation in hunting; second, continuing urbanization, so that increasing numbers of residents will live in high-density population areas;

and third, the loss of rural land to development, which reduces available wildlife habitat and so decreases hunting opportunities.

A study conducted in Michigan examined attitudes toward hunting and sought the social and psychological determinants of these attitudes. Members of three wildlife interest groups—Michigan deer hunters, Michigan Audubon Society members, and Michigan supporters of the Fund for Animals, Inc. (an organization that opposes hunting)—responded to a self-administered questionnaire (Shaw 1975). The survey form was designed to measure a variety of variables reflecting respondents' personal backgrounds and attitudes in addition to the dependent variable, which was their attitude toward hunting. All thirteen of Shaw's hypothesized predictors were significantly correlated with attitudes toward hunting, but a combination of three background predictors accounted for 45 percent of the variance in hunting attitudes: urbanization of early background, level of education, and experience with bloodshed. In general, persons opposed to hunting tended to come from urban backgrounds, to have higher education levels, and to have had less exposure to killing and bloodshed of animals when compared with persons who approved of hunting. Shaw concluded that attitudes toward hunting, whether pro or con, were "highly developed and supported by a broad range of related beliefs, attitudes, and background experiences" (1975). Furthermore, opposition to hunting was "based more on legitimate philosophical differences than on ignorance or biological naivete as is often suggested by hunting advocates" (1975).

An Iowa study of attitudes toward hunting indicated that "the formation of anti-hunting attitudes was associated with background variables which in turn were associated with values and beliefs related to hunting" (Wywialowski 1977:26). Background and socioeconomic characteristics associated with an antihunting attitude included being female, having an urban childhood residence, being over sixty or under thirty years of age, having a four-year college degree or more, being a student or having a professional occupation, and having a low family income. Values associated with an antihunting attitude included an opposition to cruelty, violence, guns, and killing. Individuals opposed to hunting did not believe that hunting renewed human ties to the environment, nor that it required skill. In fact, they felt hunting has a detrimental effect on the natural world and that animals have no chance against guns. Responses to the questionnaire revealed that beliefs and values were more strongly associated with a person's attitude toward hunting than were socioeconomic and background variables. Several measures were favored by all groups of respondents as ways of improving sport hunting (see Table 3.1), but a required hunter-safety

Table 3.1. Percentage of survey respondents who believed that a particular management option would improve the present hunting system.

| | Attitude categories | | | |
|---|---|---|---|---|
| Management options | Prohunt ($N$ = 652) | Neutral ($N$ = 160) | Antihunt ($N$ = 226) | Overall ($N$ = 1,038) |
| Require a hunter safety course | 71.8 | 76.3 | 79.2 | 74.1 |
| Require some knowledge of wildlife, determined by test[a] | 48.9 | 50.0 | 63.4 | 52.3 |
| Require a certain degree of accuracy in shooting[a] | 43.4 | 50.0 | 58.1 | 47.6 |
| Require a vision test[a] | 42.6 | 48.8 | 59.6 | 47.3 |
| Eliminate hunting in roadside rights of way[a] | 33.9 | 47.5 | 53.7 | 40.3 |
| Restrict hunter numbers[a] | 22.9 | 25.0 | 45.4 | 28.1 |
| Raise the license fee so only the highly motivated would hunt[a] | 11.2 | 14.4 | 32.3 | 16.3 |
| Liberalize hunting seasons | 9.7 | 7.5 | 6.2 | 8.6 |

Source: Adapted from Wywialowski 1977:25, table 19.

Note: Respondents could check as many options as they felt would improve sport hunting.

[a] Differences among attitude categories were very highly significant, chi-square text, $p < 0.001$.

course was selected by the highest percentage of all groups (Wywialowski 1977:26).

The conflict between persons for and against hunting is especially troubling because it pits two groups, both of which are vitally interested in wildlife and concerned about preserving wildlife habitat, against each other. Their major point of contention is how wildlife should be utilized.

One finding in a study of hunters and nonhunters in Ohio (Peterle and Scott 1977) was also disturbing. It showed that the hunting habits and attitudes of 591 hunters who responded to a 1961–62 questionnaire had changed when they were resurveyed in 1973–74. Unfortunately, their responses to several questions suggestive of their hunting ethics indicated their values had eroded. For example, fewer in 1973–74 thought that they gained satisfaction from hunting if no game was killed; fewer thought that a hunter should always track down a wounded animal; fewer thought that firearms training should be required; and fewer would report game law violators (Peterle and Scott 1977).

George Reiger summarized some of the findings of a study of antihunting sentiment in these words: "The nonhunting public has no problem with the killing of wildlife so long as it is done humanely.

What the nonhunting public does object to is the crippling and nonrecovery of game. Furthermore, it believes the typical hunter is untrained, incompetent, and ignorant of the law" (1978:46). If hunting is to survive public concern over the competence and behavior of hunters, Reiger contended, "hunter education must evolve into intensive mandatory courses in natural history and wildlife management, in bird identification and wilderness medicine, in ethics, courtesy, and tradition" (1978:47). In addition, "all hunters should be tested for firearms familiarity and marksmanship at regular intervals—say, every 5 years—and the hunter's license stamped to qualify him for rifle, shotgun, or trapping" (1978:47)

Clearly, one critical challenge to wildlife professionals is to bring pro- and antihunting groups together. Both groups share a concern for the welfare of wildlife; their common commitment should be to stop the decline and degradation of wildlife habitats. Realistically, however, we must recognize that ultimately the forces behind the fragmentation and reduction of wildlife habitat are economic, operating through land-use decisions. Any effective remedy will require legislating changes in economic incentives and land-use regulations. Another significant challenge, one where wildlife professionals can have a more direct influence, is to institute the reforms in hunter education and licensing that are necessary to restore the confidence of the general public in the competence and behavior of hunters.

Humane concerns of the antihunting public are commendable, but they are often misdirected. Substantial efforts to oppose the killing of individual animals are largely unnecessary. Unless the species is endangered or threatened, taking moderate numbers of animals has no lasting effect on the population. Still, hunters and trappers need to review their practices to ensure that animals are killed humanely, and fishermen should not fillet their catch before first killing it. Wildlife biologists, too, should promote humane treatment of animals. "We are the professionals; therefore, we should be taking the initiative in dealing with the treatment of the wildlife resource" (Schmidt and Bruner 1981).

## ECONOMICS OF HUNTING

The economic returns from hunting are immense, yet they are too often underestimated by the general public. In plain terms, hunting is big business. In 1985, 16.7 million persons in the United States participated in some form of hunting, spent a total of $10.1 billion, and were involved in 334 million recreation days—spending an average of $603 per hunter (U.S. Fish and Wildlife Service 1988). Approximately 18 percent of all men (16 years of age and older) and 2 percent of all women hunted at least once during the year. The expenditures for several types of hunting in the United States are shown in Table 3.2.

As impressive as these numbers seem, we should view them realistically. Compared to the 1985 gross national product (GNP) of $3.957 trillion, the $10.1 billion contributed by hunting represented only about one-quarter of 1 percent. When the contribution of other uses of wild plant and animal resources are factored in, however, the importance of all wildlife resources becomes more apparent. The contributions to the GNP by several sectors of the economy are indicated in Table 3.3.

Resource economists William Martin and Russell Gum (1978) used two different measures to estimate the monetary value of outdoor recreation in Arizona. One, the *total benefit value,* is based on the idea that for each consumer there is a price he or she would be willing to pay rather than do without a certain commodity. That price must be equal to or greater than the price actually paid. The difference between the actual price and the price he or she is willing to pay is a measure of benefits. Estimating the average value of this benefit for each user (or purchaser) of a commodity, and multiplying this average by the number of users, yields the total benefit value. By this measure of economic value, the total benefit value of hunting in Arizona was estimated at $34.5 million in 1970.

The other measure of a commodity's monetary value used in this study was the *maximum collectible revenue value.* This method assumes that one person owns an entire resource and wonders, "What single price could be charged (perhaps as an entry fee to a hunting area) that would maximize the total revenue from users of this resource (such as mule deer) for a particular activity (hunting)?" In this hypothetical case the price chosen would be the *optimal entry fee*—neither too high nor too low—that would generate the most revenue. The maximum collectible revenue value for Arizona hunting in 1970 was $13.9 million.

The usefulness of these monetary value estimates becomes apparent when they are converted to values per unit area of land. This allows a comparison of land values for hunting with those for livestock production. Even using the maximum collectible revenue value model—which produced the smaller estimate of monetary value for hunting—one square kilometer of huntable range in Arizona's Management Region 5 had an average value of $229 for hunting, whereas the average sale value for cattle ranching was only $137 (Martin and Gum 1978). It should be emphasized that these dollar values are estimates. Income derived from livestock sales is concentrated among a relatively small number of producers in a few well-defined industries and can therefore

Table 3.2. Expenditures for the principal types of hunting in the U.S. in 1985.

| Type of hunting | Number of hunters (millions) | Number of days (millions) | Total spent (billions) | Amount spent per hunter | Amount spent per day |
|---|---|---|---|---|---|
| Big game | 12.5 | 131.3 | $ 6.0 | $476 | $45 |
| Small game | 10.8 | 132.3 | 1.8 | 168 | 14 |
| Migratory bird | 5.0 | 41.7 | 1.1 | 216 | 26 |
| Other | 2.8 | 47.1 | 0.4 | 125 | 8 |
| Combined | 16.7 | 334.0 | 10.1 | 603 | 30 |

Source: U.S. Fish and Wildlife Service 1988.

be estimated with reasonable precision. Income from hunting, by contrast, is diffusely spread in fairly small amounts among many individuals and a large array of small businesses, which complicates estimates of economic benefits.

A study of hunting expenditures by deer hunters on selected wildlife management areas (WMAs) in Mississippi was conducted by Whiteside, Guynn, and Jacobson (1981). They employed a *user expenditure approach,* which "assumes that dollars spent for recreation are appropriate measures of recreational benefits." An estimate of the average total expenditure per hunter suggested figures of $128 and $126 to hunt deer on the Choctaw and Tallahala WMAs, respectively, during the 1977–78 season. If these expenditures were representative of amounts spent by all deer hunters using WMAs in Mississippi, the statewide total exceeded $11.3 million for that season. This does not include money spent by deer hunters on private lands, nor does it account for the *multiplier effect*—the ratio of additional business income generated by each dollar of the original expenditure as it passes through the economy. Each dollar spent on hunting has been estimated to generate an additional three to four dollars of business (Hartman 1973).

The *travel cost method,* a widely recognized technique for valuing recreation, was used to estimate the consumer surplus value of firearm deer hunting on eight quarter-townships in northern lower Michigan (Feltus and Langenau 1984). The advantage of the travel cost method is that it uses observed consumer behavior and actual costs. The *consumer surplus* is the amount of money that persons are willing to pay beyond their actual expenditures, and was determined in this case by a regression of the number of visits per site against the travel distance to that site. The consumer surplus value of firearm deer hunting averaged $236.12 per square kilometer per year, and the value associated with a checked deer was $174.66 (both expressed in 1974 dollars).

Table 3.3. Contributions to the Gross National Product of the United States by several sectors of the economy in 1985.

| Economic sector | Billions of dollars |
|---|---|
| Manufacturing[a] | $ 795.800 |
| Wholesale and retail trade[a] | 652.600 |
| Services[a] | 639.400 |
| Finance, insurance, real estate[a] | 626.600 |
| Transportation, public utilities[a] | 374.400 |
| Construction[a] | 182.200 |
| Mining[a] | 122.800 |
| Agriculture (including forestry and fisheries)[a] | 91.500 |
| Farms only[a] | 75.500 |
| Fishing[b] | 28.100 |
| Amusement, recreation[a] | 19.600 |
| Timber production[c] | 19.600 |
| Nonconsumptive wildlife use[b] | 14.300 |
| Hunting[b] | 10.100 |
| Medicine (wild plant derived)[c] | 8.000 |
| Commercial fisheries[c] | 6.800 |
| Wild genetic resources[c] | 0.342 |
| Food and industrial products[c] | 0.229 |
| Gross National Product[a] | 3,957.000 |

Sources: [a] U.S. Bureau of the Census 1986.
[b] U.S. Fish and Wildlife Service 1988.
[c] Prescott-Allen and Prescott-Allen 1986; these numbers are from 1980.

Revenue from firearm deer hunting on six of the eight areas averaged $214.89 per square kilometer per year compared with only $83.18 from timber sales, yet deer hunting represented only about 14 percent of the total recreation (Feltus and Langenau 1984).

Under certain conditions, a system of leases for daily or seasonal fee-hunting on private land can augment the income from agriculture. The profit realized from hunting has, in some cases, been sufficient to keep landowners financially solvent in spite of increasing costs, changing market conditions, and the continual hazards of blizzard and drought. It also provides an incentive for landowners to maintain or improve wildlife habitat and may allow them to reduce stocking rates for domestic livestock (to maintain range condition in dry years and improve it in normal years). Fee-hunting is generally limited to large farms or ranches where wild game is still fairly abundant or where game animals and habitats are actively managed.

In a symposium paper, Tom Christian (1980) discussed the development and operation of his Palo Duro Shooting enterprise, which is primarily oriented to hunting free-ranging aoudads (Barbary sheep, *Ammotragus lervia*) on the Figure 3 Ranch in Palo Duro Canyon of the central Texas Panhandle. In 1979, hunters paid eight hundred dollars for a one-week hunt, including room and board at a rustic lodge in the canyon, guides, and other services. Gross income from hunting amounted to approximately two dollars per acre per year, and total revenue varied from about one-fifth to one-third of ranch income. Christian indicated that hunting has added flexibility to his ranching operation and furnished necessary operating capital in years when market prices for cattle were low.

Another alternative to traditional hunting is the shooting of exotic big game on commercial hunting ranches. Questionnaires returned to Attebury, Kroll, and Legg (1977), in response to a survey of exotic big-game ranches in the United States, suggested that most such commercial operations are located in Texas; however, there are some in at least six other western states and four eastern states. Ten species of exotic game were stocked by five or more ranches, with fallow deer (*Dama dama*) and mouflon sheep (*Ovis musimon*) being the most popular. The average trophy fee per animal ranged from $180 to $1,167, depending on species. These costs, in 1974 dollars, are presented in Table 3.4 for several species. The average area for shooting on these commercial ranches was 1,179 hectares (2,912 acres), which had an average per hectare value of $1,460. Investments in the facilities provided for hunters averaged $40,779 (range $1,000 to $75,000), and the average return on capital (including land) was 1.4 percent (Attebury, Kroll, and Legg 1977).

Although there are various objections to exotic big-game shooting on commercial ranches, it apparently provides some people with an acceptable substitute for the reduced quality and availability of traditional hunting experiences in many locales. Furthermore, exotic game ranches may help to perpetuate game species that are endangered in their endemic regions. There are probably more blackbuck antelope (*Antilope cervicapra*) in Texas, for example, than in their native India (Attebury, Kroll, and Legg 1977).

Fee-hunting on private lands, which is undoubtedly most common in Texas, is an outgrowth of demand for hunting opportunities in places where suitable public land is scarce. Texas declared its independence from Mexico in 1836 and was a republic when it joined the Union nine years later. One condition of statehood was that Texas be allowed to retain sovereignty over all its public land, so only a tiny percentage of the land in the state is not privately held. Wildlife may be owned

Table 3.4. Trophy fee and costs for selected exotic game species on commercial hunting ranches in the United States (1974 dollars).

| Species | Percentage of ranches offering ($N$ = 31) | Average trophy fee | Average invested cost | Average replacement cost |
|---|---|---|---|---|
| Aoudad (Barbary sheep) | 35.5 | $ 632 | $293 | $ 319 |
| Axis deer | 38.7 | 621 | 308 | 362 |
| Blackbuck antelope | 32.2 | 600 | 295 | 362 |
| Corsican sheep | 29.0 | 236 | 55 | 58 |
| Fallow deer | 51.6 | 398 | 212 | 223 |
| Mouflon sheep | 51.6 | 338 | 149 | 159 |
| Sika deer | 38.7 | 408 | 246 | 256 |
| Wapiti (American elk) | 19.4 | 1,167 | 639 | 1,000 |

Source: Attebury et al. 1977.

by the states, but access to wildlife in Texas is controlled by the landowner.

The whole concept of fee-hunting on private land, which is nonchalantly accepted as the norm by Texans, very often provokes violent opposition elsewhere in the United States. There is nevertheless some indication that the practice is spreading. In many parts of the country, ever greater proportions of rural private land are posted to prohibit hunting, and Guynn and Schmidt (1984) found that most closures of private land to hunting in Colorado were related to problems of vandalism and unacceptable hunter behavior. Colorado landowners who charged a fee for deer hunting were the ones most satisfied with their attempts to manage the number and actions of hunters on their lands; they also reported better hunter cooperation. Responses to a survey from 516 landowners (having a minimum of 40 hectares each) indicated that "the major benefit to a landowner of charging fees was to regulate hunter behavior; income was less important" (Guynn and Schmidt 1984:18). Fifty-seven percent of 529 deer hunters who responded to the survey questionnaire were willing to pay a fee to hunt deer on private lands, but nonresidents were more willing than residents to pay for the opportunity.

## ECONOMICS OF WILDLIFE EXPLOITATION: AN INTERNATIONAL OVERVIEW

Deer stalking in the Scottish Highlands yields economic benefits and has the added advantage of being complementary with sheep farming. Landowners' clients are charged about one hundred pounds a day for the privilege of stalking, with fees increasing as much as 50 percent during October. Clients keep only the antlers; the venison is sold by the landowner (Eltringham 1984:101). Antlers are worth twenty to thirty pounds, and exceptionally large sets having many tines (pointed branches) may be valued at several hundred pounds for their trophy value. The total dressed carcass weight of red deer (*Cervus elaphus*) approximates one thousand metric tons each year, and had a value of about £1.5 million in 1977 (Mitchell, Staines, and Welch 1977). Deer stalking is the only profitable use for many properties in the Scottish Highlands, and although earnings are meager, costs are also quite low.

Musk from the Himalayan musk deer (*Moschus* spp.) is worth about fifty thousand dollars per kilogram in Japan (Eltringham 1984:104). From 1974 to 1982 an average of 263 kilograms of musk were imported to Japan, representing the killing of about forty-two thousand of these deer each year (Green et al. 1983). This illegal trade has largely been responsible for the musk deer being endangered over much of its range. The sad irony is that musk can be extracted from live deer as a renewable resource, and "musk farms" have been operating in China for more than twenty years.

The high potential productivity of wild African ungulates has been advanced as a rationale for game cropping; for example, Hirst (1975) estimated an average yearly productivity of 0.97 kilocalories per square meter from a community of seven ungulate species having an average standing crop of 7.46 kilocalories per square meter per year. This was about twelve times the productivity of a comparable standing crop of range cattle. Unfortunately, there are formidable problems associated with harvesting, processing, and marketing wild game meats (Eltringham 1984:105–15); hence, an informed appraisal of African game cropping was generally pessimistic. Two possibilities mentioned did seem to have some promise of success: game ranching rather than the cropping of free-ranging game animals and cropping of zebra (*Equus* spp.) rather than other species (Eltringham 1984:122–23, 126). The meat from zebra is as valuable as any other wild game meat, and the value of a zebra skin (a minimum of fifteen pounds each in 1974) is several times greater than that of virtually any antelope species. A cautionary note: the game cropping programs often cited as economic justification for protecting wildlife have usually been culling operations with a harvest well above the "maximum sustained yield" (Eltringham 1984:121).

For practical purposes, hunters are tourists whose activities benefit the host country by bringing in foreign exchange just as conventional tourists do. Clarke and Mitchell (1968) attempted to assess the economic impact of big-game hunting in Kenya. During 1966, a total of 496 hunting licenses was issued to visitors and 155 more were held by residents. The average safari-related expenditure totaled £2,076 for each hunter. Some money was spent in Tanzania and Uganda, which many safaris entered, and about 22 percent represented travel from the country of origin, but most of the money was spent in Kenya. The revenue to East Africa from hunting in 1966 was £945,600, or about 6.5 percent of the total foreign exchange derived from tourism. Thus the current ban on hunting in Kenya has deprived its economy of sizable earnings.

The demand for ivory extends back at least to the days of the Roman Empire and may have led to the extinction of elephants (*Loxodonta africana*) in North Africa by the early years of the first millennium A.D. Before firearms were available, 23,000 kilograms of ivory were imported into Holland each year between 1608 and 1612 from a single port at the mouth of the Congo (Eltringham 1984:137). Estimates of the ivory trade in the late 1970s were calculated at 680 to 991 metric tons per year (Parker and Martin 1982). These figures were considered to be conservative, however, because they did not take into account smuggling, corruption, bureaucratic incompetence, and quantities destined for countries importing relatively small amounts.

In the 1970s, the price of ivory shot up to fifty-five pounds per kilogram due to the decimation of elephants in Central Africa. Ivory carvers who rely on this commodity are most numerous in China, Hong Kong, and India (Martin 1980; Martin and Martin 1982). An effective ban on trading in ivory and ivory products would certainly hurt many individual traders and carvers, but only in the Central African Republic, where it has amounted to 4 percent of all foreign exchange earnings, and possibly in Tanzania is the ivory trade a significant factor in the country's gross national product (Douglas-Hamilton 1979).

There certainly have been ample opportunities for humans to demonstrate a modicum of restraint—to hunt elephants at levels that would assure a sustained-yield harvest of ivory—yet we have repeatedly failed to do so. Elephants were nearly extirpated from West Africa by 1900 and, within a few years during the late 1970s and early 1980s, two-thirds of Kenya's elephants and fully 90 percent of those in Uganda were killed to satisfy the tusk trade (Eltringham 1984:138). Apparently only a complete ban on ivory trading will assure that some elephants survive.

The trade in rhinoceros products has imperiled these pachyderms to an even greater degree than elephants. Rhino horn is used medicinally in the Far East, where its alleged mystic properties are supposed

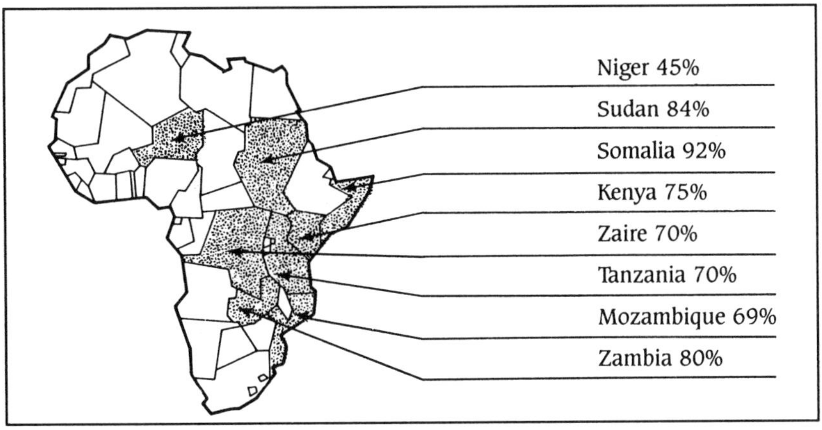


Figure 3.2. Percentage decline of the African elephant in selected countries from 1981 to 1989. Elephant numbers in Africa were reduced by more than half from 1979 to 1989. (Courtesy of the World Wildlife Fund and the Conservation Foundation, Inc., Membership Department circular #WF-E-207.)

to relieve sexual impotence and other maladies, and for ceremonial dagger handles in North Yemen. At one time Yemeni men could not afford rhino horn, but the high wages paid to migrant workers in the Saudi Arabian oil fields have eliminated this barrier. Between 1969 and 1977, 22,645 kilograms of rhino horn, taken from about eight thousand of the animals, were imported by North Yemen. In 1978, one dealer sold rhino horn to carvers for $677 a kilogram; the shavings from the ornamental handles were exported to Hong Kong for an additional $150 per kilogram (Martin and Martin 1982). The slaughter of rhinos throughout Africa, beginning about 1975, has been responsible for losses of up to 80 percent, so their future is very much in doubt.

Asian rhinoceroses—the Javan (*Rhinoceros sondaicus*), Sumatran (*Dicerorhinus sumatrensis*), and Indian (*Rhinoceros unicornis*) species—are mostly protected in reserves. Their horns seem stunted compared with the African (*Ceratotherium simum*) animals, but there is nevertheless some poaching. The reason: 1980 wholesale horn prices ranged from six thousand to eight thousand dollars per kilogram (Eltringham 1984:147).

Rhino horns can be removed on a sustained-yield basis because they continue to grow, like sheep's wool. Immobilizing wild rhinos presents problems, however, and the animals undoubtedly need their horns for defense and social interactions. Other rhino products also have commercial value: the skin of a white rhino has an estimated worth of twenty-one thousand dollars (Eltringham 1984:147). Even the excretia have medicinal uses, and keepers in Indian zoos conduct a lively trade in rhino urine and feces collected from their charges. It is unfortunate that the exorbitant demand for rhino parts is not confined to these products, of which there will be ample amounts as long as there are rhinos.

At present there is a ban on importation of elephant ivory and rhinoceros horn into the United States under provisions of the Convention on International Trade in Endangered Species of Wild Fauna and Flora (CITES). This agreement has produced progress but its enforcement depends upon the vigilance of exporting and importing countries. Unfortunately, there is considerable variation among countries in their ability and motivation to enforce it. Furthermore, only nations that have signed the agreement are bound by it.

The success of CITES in protecting species depends on eliminating markets by securing export and import bans. Elephants and rhinoceroses are killed by poachers who often use assault-type automatic firearms and channel the ivory and horn into international black markets to circumvent such controls. These black markets will continue to operate as long as high price and strong demand dictate. The long-term survival of elephants and rhinos is therefore not assured.

The consumptive exploitation of many other animals, though perhaps not as well known as that of the elephant or rhino, is nevertheless economically important on a regional basis around the world. Gorillas (*Gorilla gorilla*) and chimpanzees (*Pan troglodytes*) costing several thousand dollars each are captured for zoos and medical research centers, but the quantity killed for food dwarfs the number taken alive (Eltringham 1984). The number of monkeys eaten by Peruvian Indians was said to be far greater than the 139,000 exported alive each year (Grimwood 1968).

Songbirds are common table fare in continental Europe. Approximately 150 million migratory birds are killed each year in Italy alone, where the density of shooters is reputed to be the highest in the world ("Hunters in Italy" 1981). The sale of equipment and ammunition for this activity is economically significant, with additional yearly revenue contributed from the trade in netted birds (Eltringham 1984:174). Exotic birds, mostly passerines, are much in demand for the trade in caged birds. The primary sources are tropical countries where the most colorful species are abundant, and estimates of the numbers involved range from 5.5 to 100 million annually (Bruggers 1982). The hill mynah is one of the more highly sought Asian birds because of its ability to mimic sounds. Some 250,000 are reportedly exported each year, bringing prices of £150 each in London.

Numbers of a rare Bolivian bird, the caninde macaw, total only five hundred to one thousand, of which about sixty were exported in 1981; prices are in the range of $15,000 a pair. There is a continuing demand from Arab countries for birds of prey to be used in falconry. The peregrine falcon is a prime object, with smuggled birds bringing prices of £4,000 each (Eltringham 1984:176).

As indicated, animals are often captured live for medical research or the pet trade. Although the animals themselves are not killed—if one ignores the high mortality during capture, holding, and transportation—they are permanently removed from their natural habitats and cease functioning as "wildlife." This use is consumptive in the sense that they are no longer able to contribute reproductively to their breeding populations.

There is no doubt that the economic worth of wildlife is enormous, but Eltringham contended we should not be seduced by money value alone. In his words, "Economics is a dangerous game for the conservationist to play, and the arguments for protecting our wildlife heritage should be based on the same ethical and aesthetic grounds as those advanced for the preservation of ancient buildings and historic monuments" (1984:122).

## ETHICS OF HUNTING

The guiding principle of Albert Schweitzer (1923), a renowned theologian, physician, and humanitarian, was *Ehrfurcht vor dem Leben,* which is usually translated as "reverence for life" but really is much stronger than just reverence—more like a combination of honor and awe for life (Clarke 1958). Schweitzer wrote, "A man is really ethical only when he obeys the constraint laid on him to help all life which he is able to succour, and when he goes out of his way to avoid injuring anything living. He does not ask how far this or that life deserves sympathy as valuable in itself, nor how far it is capable of feeling. To him life as such is sacred. He . . . tears no leaf from its tree, breaks off no flower, and is careful not to crush any insect as he walks" (1928:254).

Schweitzer himself recognized that in attempting to live by this principle one would be in constant conflict with the realities of human existence: "The absolute ethic of reverence for life makes its own agreements with the individual from moment to moment . . . [and] forces him to decide for himself in each case how far he can remain ethical and how far he must submit himself to the necessity of destroying and harming life and thus become guilty." Ironically, Schweitzer (1922) tells us he kept a gun in his Lambarene compound that he used to kill snakes and birds of prey. Even the modern hunter's ethic would have justified his killing only those particular animals that presented an immediate danger (Clarke 1958).

Two writers, Joseph Wood Krutch and Cleveland Amory, have been emphatic and outspoken in their condemnation of consumptive uses of wildlife. A 1974 book by Amory entitled *Man Kind?* is an emotional description of barbarisms perpetrated on animals in the name of hunting. In truth, most hunters would probably be appalled by these accounts. The widely read magazine article by Krutch (1957), "A Damnable Pleasure," condemned killing for sport. His appraisal of hunting was summarized succinctly: "When a man wantonly destroys one of the works of man we call him Vandal. When he wantonly destroys one of the works of God we call him Sportsman."

By the late 1980s, earlier verbal assaults on hunting by Amory and Krutch had escalated to actual aggression by a new generation of protesters as some antihunters abandoned lobbying or marches and adopted a militant stance. In a widely publicized incident in Montana's Gallatin National Forest, several animal-rights activists tried to disrupt a hunt of bison that had wandered outside the boundary of Yellowstone National Park. Dan Jacobs, one of the lottery-picked hunters, agreed that their activity fell short of sport. "I don't even call this a hunt. It's just a shoot," Jacobs said. "But that's what the old buffalo hunts were, too. In those days you sat up on a hill and shot as many as you could kill in a day" (Knox 1990).

As Jacobs raised his rifle, a dozen people burst whooping and hollering from the surrounding forest. He lowered the firearm and watched in amazement as they dashed in among the bison obstructing his shot, then tried to drive the animals back to the safety of the park. They also taunted Jacobs and his two hunting companions: "Does this make you feel like a big, tough man?" Later, after three bison had been killed, a protestor dipped her hand in the blood from one of the shaggy beasts and smeared it on a hunter's face hissing, "The war is on" (Knox 1990).

Militant antihunters manifest a moral certainty like that of anti-abortionists who throw blood on pregnant women entering Planned Parenthood clinics. The quasi-religious fervor of antihunting activists makes it easier for hunters to dismiss their arguments, yet many non-hunting outdoor recreationists are unhappy at having to dodge bullets on hiking trails between Halloween and Thanksgiving (Knox 1990).

"Increasingly," wrote Margaret Knox (1990), "a host of people who don't hunt want answers to a wide range of questions about hunting:

Who should control wildlife policy, and what should their goals be? With wildlife habitats shrinking and more people visiting them, is hunting still appropriate? Is killing animals for sport morally acceptable?"

Though such tough questions put hunters on the spot, even the most pacifistic nonhunters are implicated in current wildlife quandaries. Kevin Lackey of the Rocky Mountain Elk Foundation reminds us, as others have, that vegetarians eat food grown on lands that were once wildlife habitat, and that habitat loss is the biggest threat to wildlife (Knox 1990).

In 1989, Maine housewife Karen Wood was killed in her own backyard by a .30-06 slug in the lung when a hunter mistook her white mittens for a fleeing deer. The *Bangor Daily News* blamed her for not wearing blaze-orange, and a grand jury in that prohunting state refused to indict the hunter. "Such callousness by the hunting community probably creates as many anti-hunting converts as any animal-rights propaganda" (Knox 1990).

Outdoor writer John Husar (1986) wrote that he periodically finds himself in the position of responding to simplistic attacks on the sport of hunting. He dislikes having to tangle with people he likes and respects because he understands the reason for their antihunting sentiment: "Many, many good folks just can't stomach the idea of killing wild animals. I know. I used to be one." "But," he continued, "like so many lovers of wildlife, I hadn't understood how those creatures happened to be there in such proliferation." The reason, in Husar's view, is the conservation efforts of hunters. Faced with reduced wildlife abundance due to habitat destruction—because of all the human actions commonly associated with "progress"—and confronted by a chronicle of the passenger pigeon's extinction and the virtual extermination of white-tailed deer east of the Mississippi by 1900, hunters themselves instituted changes because they wanted to save hunting. They agreed to be bound by stringent hunting regulations, to defer hunting in years when game populations are low, to support wildlife agencies through their license fees, and to further fund management efforts through excise taxes on their firearms and ammunition. What they asked for in return was a chance to hunt when conditions are right.

Now there are huge herds of deer in every state and the Giant Canada goose has been brought back from the edge of extinction. In some places, deer and geese feast on crops or graze on lawns and parks and are so numerous they have become a nuisance. Contemporary wildlife management, with the money and restraint of hunters, has promoted the resurgence of many species despite the continuing human assault on wildlife habitat. And hunters participate in wildlife management by harvesting the abundance of game.

Yes, it is true that hunters kill deer and rabbits and pheasants and geese and ducks. And yes, they do hunt grouse and woodcock and prairie chickens and bear. They enjoy the primal nature of the hunt as well as the food they carry home from the field (Husar 1986). Further, Husar asserted, "We even like this food better than the food that is available in stores. We think that animals that spend noble lives foraging as part of nature make more relishing food than the untold unfortunates that never leave the feedlots or cages, that never taste a breath of freedom, that live only for slaughter and consignment to the grocery shelves."

Apart from the importance of nature and sport, the value of tradition and woodland skills, the dollars that hunting brings to the economy, the pronouncements of philosophers on the nobility of the hunt—these considerations aside—Husar wondered why antihunters are so vehemently opposed to his selecting his own venison when there is no outcry against slaughtering millions of domestic animals in commercial meat-packing plants. Even when no game is bagged, hunting lures people outdoors and into a primal contest with nature. Hunters devote considerable money and countless hours toward ensuring that wildlife will continue to be abundant.

Husar argued that if antihunters are successful in eliminating hunting, they will eventually doom the very wildlife they profess to love. In the absence of hunters' efforts, of hunters' fees and taxes, and of the organizations hunters support, the millions now raised every year to preserve wildlife habitat will be lost. With no legal hunting, there will be no justification for wardens to enforce game laws, so protection will cease. Eventually, poachers will kill off much of the game and turn again to shooting eagles, hawks, and songbirds. "We'll have lost everything that we've gained. And Bambi will remain exactly what he is—a humanized character in the storybooks."

Clearly, Husar believed that hunting violates no ethical prohibition; that, in fact, hunting can be an exalting experience. Yet, he was obviously disturbed that hunters do not always behave ethically. In a later article he reported meeting with a group of concerned farmers and hunters from the vicinity of Shabbona State Park in north-central Illinois. These rural people, many of them also hunters, were outraged. They weren't talking about careless or ignorant city hunters, although that is always a problem. They were angry about the actions of friends and neighbors, people they thought should know better (Husar 1987).

Fishing guide and bowhunter Mike McInerney described the problem: "They use airplanes to spook the deer from the park toward other hunters, they chase them with vehicles, they panic the deer and shove them toward lines of waiting gunners. Some of them even shoot the deer out of trucks. It's a bloodbath, not a hunt." Several area farmers confirmed McInerney's assertions. One was on a deer stand when he saw a low-flying plane, then groups of hunters converged to kill the herded deer. "I couldn't believe what I was seeing," he said. Another farmer saw groups of hunters in pickup trucks pushing deer off his property so they could be shot nearby.

Conservation police Sgt. Roy Fitzsimmons, whose district includes this area, had been aware of the complaints for ten years, but was never able to document anything that would stand up in court. Most of these people are "not your low-life poachers. They're mostly medium to wealthy farmers. They all have permits and they all check in their deer." Fitzsimmons also noted that the problem is statewide and often involves hunters who bend the rules on their own lands.

One person interviewed said of the assault-style hunting tactics: "It's illegal, it's immoral, it's got nothing to do with sportsmanship." In fact, such activities are more than unethical; they are illegal. Illinois law prohibits harassing or taking game animals using ground vehicles or airplanes, and shooting from vehicles is strictly forbidden.

Many of the concerned landowners Husar interviewed seemed to feel that their best hope might be peer pressure. In one woman's words, "If they see themselves in print and realize that people they know are upset with them, it should have an effect." Another man was not so sure. "I've heard one of them say that he's heard of folks complaining about a 'bloodbath.' . . . He just said, 'Well, next year I'll get 20 more guys and show 'em a real bloodbath.' "

It is this kind of defiant arrogance—which exceeds legal bounds and mocks sportsmanship—that infuriates the majority of Americans who are nonhunters but not necessarily against hunting. Such arrogance, and the actions it begets, are the greatest threat to the future of hunting.

Several professional wildlife biologists have written on the ethics of hunting. The views of three are summarized here. C. H. D. Clarke, in his essay "Autumn Thoughts of a Hunter," agreed with Albert Schweitzer that the decay of civilization is due to the absence of a proper relationship between humans and other organic life, but Clarke believed that it is "the hunter and angler [who] still cling to strong lines that connect us with the harmonious past" (1958). As a wildlife biologist, Clarke affirmed Schweitzer's reverence for life "only when life is interpreted as being the whole interwoven and interdependent association of plants, animals and soil, and the death that I inflict is right if harmony is maintained." This reverence "does not exclude delight, even in a doomed snowflake, a plucked daisy—or a wild goose headed for the platter." So much for Clarke's view of hunting as a cause of death.

For Clarke, cruelty, the intentional infliction of pain, has nothing to do with the purpose of hunting. Cruelty is a perversion in hunters, as it is in members of the clergy or boilermakers. Hunters must watch for cruel persons who take up the sport. Even early humans feared such cruel persons, as they were likely to offend the spirits of the animals hunted and bring disaster on the tribe. Finally, what of the incidental infliction of pain in hunting? Clarke contended that under conditions of natural predation, "many observations indicate that Nature spares her children fear and pain under such circumstances. David Livingston (1858) remarked on this, after having been himself in the lion's jaws" (425). The goal in shooting is a clean kill; "if it is not achieved, there remains the knowledge that the death of the same animal in toothless old age would not be less painful" (426). Still, there is no justification for needlessly inflicting pain—through ignorance, thoughtlessness, lack of skill, or deliberateness—and the hunters who do so imperil their moral right to hunt.

A short philosophical article by the wildlife biologist Anthony Povilitis (1980) made the point that, within the "naturalist tradition," "the ecological and evolutionary relatedness of living things forms the basis for considering rights." In his view, naturalists view an animal's habitat needs as more fundamental to the issue of rights than abstruse philosophical points. Generally speaking, naturalists recognize "a right to freedom from unnecessary suffering for organisms that have high phylogenetic standing." This right does not, however, necessarily imply a right to life with an associated proscription of hunting or trapping.

In an essay entitled "The Ethics of Hunting and the Antihunting Movement," David R. Klein (1973) suggested that the antihunting sentiment seems to have some of its roots in the association of guns with crime, violence, and war. Substantial segments of society are appalled by these activities and see the gun, even in the hands of a hunter, as symbolizing aggression and destruction.

The popularization of ecology has been accompanied by an emotional and quasi-religious attitude about nature—a kind of pantheism or vitalism—that is often directed toward animals as individuals rather than at populations or ecosystems. Klein noted that this has promoted antikilling sentiments, as has the projection of Judeo-Christian morality onto nature. Human tendencies to anthropomorphize other animals has led to mistaken concepts of good and bad animals. When hunting is mistakenly rationalized within this framework, Klein explained, it may be justified as protecting the good animals—the innocent and defenseless herbivores—from the bad carnivores or by saying that hunting the good ones is in their own interest because it prevents overpopulation and starvation.

"The question of the justification for hunting," according to Klein, "is only part of a much larger question—that of the morality of man's exploitation of other organisms." This exploitation means "any manipulation of other organisms by man which results in altering their ways of life, or in imposing upon them hardship, injury or death." It includes keeping domestic pets, husbandry of farm animals, confinement of wild animals in zoos, the use of animals in experiments, and destruction of wildlife habitat for highways and shopping malls. Hunting is a particularly controversial form of exploitation because it is one of the "blood sports." But consistency demands that hunting be viewed in perspective: it is utilitarian. It serves the interests of humankind.

R. D. Guthrie (1967) maintained that morality and ethics, being human constructs, have to do only with humans and cannot be extended to other organisms. Within this context there is an ethical basis for hunting, but it can be interpreted, according to Klein, only through its effects on humans. Such effects, however, should be evaluated broadly; for example, the immediate recreational returns of a hunting experience should be avoided if hunting a particular species would destroy the opportunity for other people to observe and enjoy it. "Similarly if hunting under certain circumstances fosters disrespect for life and nature or is otherwise degrading to man, it should not be condoned" (Klein 1973). Thus, "there are valid moral and ethical obligations, as well as restraints, associated with hunting, but only those that relate our hunting conduct to ourselves and other humans—other humans living and yet unborn. . . . Each hunting situation should be considered on its own merits, on its total impact on man" (Klein 1973).

Although this justification for hunting may seem too coldly objective, Klein contended that such a rationally based ethics "can provide the basis for a very humane ethic toward the totality of life," and "provides a basis for deep and realistic understanding of life." "Finally it is up to hunters themselves and those who would be advocates of the sport to bring about a re-emphasis on quality in hunting and to return to hunting those high standards which have won it respect in the past" (Klein 1973).

Until recently, most of the opinions on ethical aspects of hunting, vigorously argued by advocates and opponents alike, were the convictions of the philosophical laity. Few of the discussants—whether wildlife biologists or animal-rights activists, hunters or nonhunters—had any real philosophical background for what is essentially an ethical debate.

During the 1970s a number of philosophers interested in environmental affairs began directing their professional capabilities toward their avocational concerns. The outcome has been the emergence of environmental philosophy. Although many practitioners of this new discipline may lack ecological sophistication, or seem woefully naive, wildlife biologists should become acquainted with their work. Environmental ethics will continue to gain stature as a philosophical discipline and will increasingly impinge on the activities of wildlife and natural resource professionals.

Peter Singer's *Animal Liberation* was the first book by a professional philosopher to extend equal moral standing to nonhuman animals (Sumner 1979). Its publication in 1975 prompted controversy among lay persons as well as philosophers and revived a discussion of two categories of questions: Should animals be included within the scope of our moral concern? If so, what kind of standing do they have, and what uses of them—such as hunting and trapping—are permissible? Debate over these questions has also helped to clarify some fundamental issues in ethical theory that are central to the problem. One of these concerns the basis of ethical theories. If moral principles result from contracts or conventions (the "conventional theory"), one might argue that humans neither can nor need to bargain with animals; then, animals can be excluded from moral recognition and can be used as mere things. If, however, moral principles are natural rather than conventional (the "natural theory")—that is, if moral principles are discovered rather than invented—then it is harder to justify the exclusion of animals (Sumner 1979).

According to Cobb (1980), the indifference toward animal welfare in historic Christian teaching should be an embarrassment to any Christian concerned with the humane treatment of animals. This indifference is grounded in the distinction between humans and other creatures that has its basis not in any biblical pronouncement but in the thought of two classical Greek philosophers: Aristotle, who thought that each person is a unique rational being, and Plato, who believed that the soul is immortal (Linzey 1976). The scripture that awarded humans dominion over the remainder of creation has, in Cobb's opinion, been improperly interpreted as a warrant for unlimited exploitation of nature.

From a Christian viewpoint, the category of rights—if it is used at all—must derive from duty (Linzey 1976); that is, if humans have a duty to treat animals humanely, then animals have a corresponding right not to suffer unnecessarily because of human actions. Whether animals have a right to life, and humans a duty not to kill them, is another question. Certain characteristics are used to justify the claim that humans have an intrinsic right to life: the uniqueness of each individual, the ability to anticipate the future (including death), and the strength of social bonds among individuals. If these characteristics are applied universally, they seem to be possessed by some animals as well. There are indications that chimpanzees and porpoises, for example, fulfill these criteria; thus, consistency demands that we recognize their right to life. According to Cobb, the question is not whether animals have rights, but *which* animals have *which* rights?

In a discussion of the morality of hunting, Loftin (1984) contended that many of the arguments used to justify this activity are spurious because only a few game species—generally speaking, the larger herbivores—will overpopulate and degrade their range, so hunters are not needed to replace exterminated predators; crippling losses due to hunting are often significant, which means that many animals will escape to suffer a death as agonizing as death from starvation or predation—and the meat is lost as well; and sport hunters tend to remove the largest and best-conditioned animals, especially if horned or antlered ungulates are the object, so the genetic and behavioral welfare of the population is harmed. Nevertheless, Loftin defended sport hunting on utilitarian grounds: "the loss of sport hunting would . . . mean the loss of a major political pressure group working for the benefit of wildlife through preservation of habitat."

Attempts to resolve the controversy between hunting apologists and their antihunting antagonists have failed, in part, because the participants in this controversy have often not distinguished the various activities labeled "hunting," and treated them separately. This is the perception of Ann Causey (1989), who contended that persons who participate in hunting fall into one of two categories: shooters or sport hunters. "Shooters are those whose ultimate goals do not depend on hunting but can be met in other ways; sport hunters are those who take immense pleasure in the hunt itself and who kill in order to have had an authentic hunting experience." Any discussion of the morality of hunting, as distinguished from the prudence of hunting, should be "restricted to the moral evaluation of the desire of sport hunters to kill for pleasure." "This desire," Causey believed, "can be explained by biological/evolutionary concepts and defended as morally neutral. Neither the animal protectionists nor the utilitarian apologists recognize that violent death is part of nature and that man's desire to participate in it can be both natural and culturally valuable." Utilitarianism, though well-intentioned, is impotent as an ethical defense of hunting because it can judge the prudence, but not the morality, of hunting.

Aldo Leopold is recognized as the father of recent environmental ethics. His "land ethic" has become a modern classic, and may be treated as a paradigm (or prototype) for environmental ethics in general (Callicott 1980). One fundamental, and novel, feature of Leopold's land ethic is the extension of ethical standing not just to wild animals but to other nonhuman natural entities as well. Plants, soils, and waters, for example, are included within his community of ethical beneficiaries (Leopold 1949). Yet Leopold never condemned the hunting of wild animals, nor did he ever personally abandon hunting, even after becoming convinced that his ethical responsibilities encompassed all of nature (Flader 1978). Callicott (1980) has suggested that Leopold may have regarded regulated and disciplined sport hunting as "a form of human/animal behavior not inconsistent with the land ethic as he conceived it." The land ethic is holistic, like the ecological viewpoint that engendered it. Ecology has made it possible to apprehend the "landscape as an articulate unity (without the least hint of mysticism or ineffability)," rather than as a collection of separate objects (1980). The integrity, stability, and beauty of the biotic community is the supreme moral good. All other ethical judgments, in Leopold's view, are derived from this.

The Spanish philosopher José Ortega y Gasset (1972) discussed at length the role of the kill in hunting. He argued that killing, or the possibility of killing, gives authenticity to the hunt. The animal's behavior, and the hunter's responses, both must be based on the conviction that the animal's life is at stake; if it is not, the hunt is a mockery. It is the possibility of a kill that infuses all other parts of a genuine hunt with meaning; the communion with death connects a hunter to life. In Ortega y Gasset's words, "One does not hunt in order to kill; on the contrary, one kills in order to have hunted."

Hidden from public controversy, the hunter undergoes a private turmoil. Ortega y Gasset described the moral dilemma in these words: "Every good hunter is uneasy in the depths of his conscience when faced with the death he is about to inflict on the enchanting animal. He does not have the final and firm conviction that his conduct is correct. But neither . . . is he certain of the opposite."

Figure 3.3. Although Aldo Leopold extended ethical standing to virtually all natural entities—not just wild animals—in his statement of the land ethic he remained a devoted hunter throughout his life. Here, Leopold pauses during a bow hunt along the Rio Gavilan in 1938. (Photo by A. Starker Leopold. Courtesy of the Leopold Papers, University of Wisconsin-Madison Archives, Negative No. X25918.)

## IMPACTS OF HUNTING

The venerable eighteenth-century English lexicographer Samuel Johnson once called hunting "the labor of the savages of North America, but the amusement of the gentlemen of England." As hunting became less a necessity of survival and more a leisure pastime, it began to acquire rituals that emphasize the element of skill while reducing the likelihood of a kill. These rituals preserve some primitive aspects of the experience and invest hunting with the dignity of sport. To ignore them is to become the outdoor gadgeteer Leopold (1966) decried as being devoid of cultural values.

For the sake of convenience, the impacts of hunting are summarized for each of the rather imprecise groups into which hunted animals are often placed. Furbearers are discussed in a later section with trapping.

### *Hunting Impacts on Big Game*

Big game is usually construed as including the artiodactyls, or herbivorous hooved mammals, and certain carnivores—the bears and the largest cats. White-tailed deer (*Odocoileus virginianus*) are the most widely distributed big-game animal in North America, and one of the great success stories of conservation and wildlife management. Estimates suggest there were 24 to 34 million white-tailed deer ranging over most of the continent in 1500 (Downing 1987). During the next three hundred years, numbers declined by 50 to 65 percent, mainly due to massive killing by Native Americans who used deer as an item of trade with European settlers. From 1800 to 1865 some herds rebounded because most Native Americans had been driven out of the East and Europeans had not fully settled the rural areas. However, uncontrolled market shooting and family subsistence hunting between 1850 and 1900 further reduced their numbers to a low of about 300,000 to 500,000, just 1 to 2 percent of the number present before European colonization.

In the late 1800s and early 1900s, remnant herds survived only in sparsely settled areas, inaccessible swamps and rugged mountains, and where they were protected by landowners on large holdings (Downing 1987). Deer numbers did not increase appreciably until the 1930s, when many rural families in the East, Midwest, and South abandoned their small farms and moved to the cities during the Great Depression. The reduction in hunting pressure, and improvement in habitat as abandoned farm fields reverted to weeds and brush, brought an upturn in white-tailed deer abundance. In regions where no remnant herds remained, vacant habitats were gradually repopulated through restocking. Many returning veterans of World War II used provisions of the GI Bill to get college degrees in the relatively new field of wildlife management. These fledgling wildlife personnel were instrumental in reestablishing local herds and learning how to manage them properly. Their efforts led to a resurgence in numbers, so that by the eighties there were at least 14 million white-tailed deer in North America, including some in areas that had never supported them before (Downing 1987).

There has been a similar resurgence in the abundance of other big-game animals from lows in the late 1800s or early 1900s caused by overexploitation. Numbers of pronghorn antelope, elk, and even bison have increased by factors ranging from nearly ten to over thirty; other species, like the North American mountain sheep, are stable or increasing slowly and restricted mainly by suitable habitat (Wildlife Management Institute Staff 1978). Virtually all big-game species are beset by some kind of problem or conflict—overgrazing by domestic livestock, competition from wild horses and burros, fencing that restricts movements or prevents access to traditional ranges, mineral and energy extraction that causes disturbances and destroys habitat, or questionable human management philosophies and land-use policies, to name only a few—but harvest levels due to legal sport hunting are generally very moderate in relation to wildlife abundance.

Big-game species tend to be large and conspicuous resident animals, fairly long-lived, with low to moderate reproductive rates. Deer and the other large ungulate members of the assemblage "often exceed the carrying capacity of their habitats and damage their own food base" (Shaw 1985:153). Management attention has focused on manipulation of abundance to a greater extent than habitat manipulation. Demographic characteristics of populations are monitored using data obtained from animals killed by vehicles on highways and from hunters at check stations. State agencies responsible for management usually concentrate on regulating the geographical distribution of hunting pressure and keeping game numbers within reasonable limits by means of harvesting.

Hunting regulations, particularly with respect to deer, often reflect sociological pressures as well as biological information: hunters fear that liberal regulations will reduce deer numbers permanently (Robinson and Bolen 1984:283). Political coercion imposing very conservative harvest levels, or forcing the retention of "buck laws" so that it is legal to kill only antlered males, can be harmful to populations and habitats alike. There is no evidence, however, that annual harvest levels of 10 to 25 percent, depending upon the species and conditions, are detrimental to the abundance of big game.

## *Hunting Impacts on Upland Game*

Upland game encompasses some smaller mammals, such as the tree squirrel, rabbit, and hare; resident fowl, including the pheasant, turkey, and several kinds of grouse; the various quail; and certain migratory birds, including two favorites of hunters, the woodcock and mourning dove.

Most members of this group are smaller and less conspicuous than big game, short-lived, with fairly high reproductive rates and populations that turn over rather quickly. For this reason, many upland game species can support harvest levels of 40 percent or more. According to Roseberry (1979), maximum sustained yield from the bobwhite quail, America's most popular game bird, occurs at harvest rates of 55 percent per year, but this severely depressed numbers the following spring. An optimum harvest rate of 40 to 45 percent annually was recommended.

The American woodcock, a stocky, long-billed caricature of the other shorebirds, is a resident of woodland swamps and thickets. Its small clutch size, just four eggs, has aroused concern about the extent of hunting mortality the species can safely sustain. Recent estimates suggest that hunting is responsible for only a small proportion of the total annual mortality (Dwyer and Nichols 1982), but there are still no data on the real effect of shooting on woodcock numbers.

It is often thought that habitat resources determine how many animals of a given species can survive in a particular area. The "excess" is presumed to be eliminated by various kinds of mortality. Species with high reproductive rates produce a great overabundance of offspring, few of which will survive to reproduce. This does not, however, imply a clearly defined "harvestable annual surplus." Random environmental events—a spring storm with freezing rain and bitter cold temperatures or a hurricane—often determine demographic parameters of birth, death, and survival. Much of what we may consider to be "surplus reproduction" is dissipated through innate dispersal, which is essential to the survival of species in environments that are temporally and spatially heterogeneous.

Historically, the total annual mortality, which removes each year's "surplus," was thought to be a combination of two or more types of mortality; the magnitude of each type can vary, with higher levels of some kinds compensating for lower levels of others. This is the concept of "intercompensation," or compensatory mortality, which can be traced to Paul Errington's (1956, 1963) studies of muskrat populations on Iowa marshes. The principal causes of muskrat mortality were starvation, disease, and predation by mink.

Roseberry's (1979) research demonstrated that hunting mortality is not completely compensatory, even in species such as the bobwhite that have high reproductive rates. Hunting mortality that depressed game numbers below normal levels is additive. Still, most hunting of upland game does not greatly reduce numbers; abundance in these species seems to respond through enhanced reproduction and reduced mortality, and hunters, responding to diminishing returns, may redirect their efforts to areas of greater game abundance or simply curtail their hunting (Shaw 1985:156–57).

## *Hunting Impacts on Waterfowl*

Waterfowl production in North America is concentrated in the northern "duck factory" areas of the continent. The most important is the "prairie pothole region," the Dakotas and western Minnesota in the United States, and the Prairie Provinces of Manitoba, Saskatchewan, and Alberta in Canada. Although the prairies of Canada and the northern United States comprise only about 10 percent of the waterfowl breeding grounds of North America, they are responsible for more than 50 percent of the yearly crop of ducks (Smith, Stoudt, and Gollop 1964). In 1985, the southerly migrations of these aquatic game birds attracted some 2,703,000 waterfowl hunters in the United States alone (U.S. Fish and Wildlife Service 1988).

Questions about the impact of hunting are particularly pertinent to waterfowl because the same birds are subjected to shooting mortality repeatedly as they migrate from northern breeding grounds to more southerly wintering areas. Of all waterfowl, the mallard duck (*Anas platyrhynchos*) has almost certainly been the object of the most research. The results of intensive studies of mallard population ecology published since the early 1970s have changed the rationale for managing waterfowl in North America.

Until the midseventies a statistically significant positive relationship between estimates of average yearly mortality rates and estimates of average first-year band recovery rates was the scientific basis for waterfowl management. Then, Anderson and Burnham (1976) found that these two statistics had a high sampling correlation, so the procedure was invalid. In fact, analyses using this incorrect methodology would show hunting to be an additive form of mortality even if it were completely compensatory (34–39).

More recently, calculations were made using a general probabilistic model and 47 data sets of adult mallards banded in North America before hunting began (Burnham, White, and Anderson 1984). These calculations supported the likelihood of highly compensatory mortality for adult male mallards, although the evidence for adult female mallards was inconclusive.

A warning from Patterson (1979), however, admonished against using the mallard as a standard for all waterfowl species. With its high reproductive potential and opportunistic habits, the mallard is among the most productive of all North American ducks. Thus, hunting mortality of mallards might be at least partly compensatory.

Patterson rated the diving ducks, such as the redhead (*Aythya americana*) and canvasback (*Aythya valisineria*), as reflecting an adaptive strategy that does not depend on such high reproductive rates. It seems possible that hunting mortality is additive for these species—that shooting may be an added hazard that suppresses numbers well below levels at which compensatory mortality ceases to operate.

The extent of hunting impacts on waterfowl may almost be moot. Over two thousand square kilometers of wetland habitats have been destroyed every year for the past several decades, and half the wetlands in the United States have already been lost (Steinhart 1986a).

One significant resource conflict involving waterfowl and hunting impacts is the drastic decline of geese in Alaska's Yukon-Kuskokwim Delta, a sprawling wildlife breeding ground the size of Kentucky that hosts 100 million birds annually. Over a period of twenty years, cackling Canada geese (*Branta canadensis minima*) declined from 350,000 to 26,000, white-fronted geese (*Anser albifrons*) numbers dropped from 495,000 to about 100,000, and the abundance of both emperor geese (*Philacte canagica*) and black brant (*Branta nigricans*) was down by 50 percent (Steinhart 1986b). Blame has been directed at California sport hunters who kill some of the birds migrating from the delta, at Eskimos who still depend on subsistence hunting for much of their food, and at mining and industrial pollution. Poisoning by ingestion of lead shot may also have contributed, and reduced winter habitat in California is probably an important factor as well. Any management strategy that is successful in arresting the decline of these geese will have to cut across state and cultural lines and impose restraints on all parties concerned.

In the sixties the esteemed wildlife administrator Ernest Swift had harsh words for waterfowlers: "Personally, I cannot generate much sympathy for the plight of the waterfowl hunters, although I deplore the loss of this great American heritage. The waterfowlers have gotten just what they asked for by their indifference, lack of facing realities and wishful dreaming that ducks will annually come out of the northern void regardless of hunting seasons, bag limits and dry periods" (1967:226). His other comments on waterfowl hunting and conservation were also characteristically blunt, but as pertinent today as when they were written. He wrote: "Although the techniques of waterfowl dynamics have greatly improved, integrity to conservation precepts has slipped its G-string to expose a nakedness of lecherous greed" (1967:223).

## TRAPPING—AN OVERVIEW

Trapping is, if anything, even more controversial than hunting, and the debate has been particularly intense in recent years (Mitchell 1982). The term *furbearer* refers to a diverse collection of mammals that grow fur of a quality considered commercially valuable. This group includes such herbivores as the beaver (*Castor canadensis*), muskrat (*Ondatra zibethicus*), and snowshoe hare (*Lepus americanus*), as well as a variety of carnivores that reflect a diversity of ecological adaptations: the wolf (*Canis lupus*), coyote (*Canis latrans*), mountain lion (*Felis concolor*), lynx (*Felis lynx*), black bear (*Ursus americanus*), and Arctic fox (*Alopex lagopus*).

## Historical Notes

When monarchs and nobles dressed for festivities in the late Middle Ages, furs embellished the rich fabrics of their attire and provided a backdrop for their stunning jewels. By the fourteenth and fifteenth centuries, many merchants and master artisans were becoming wealthy and they, too, demanded to be clad in the luxury of furs. Indeed, Chaucer described the merchant thusly: "Upon his heed a Flanndrush bever hat." The fashion of furs spread, and throughout Western Europe this period was characterized by extravagance in dress (Phillips 1961).

Meantime, the poorer classes wore cheap woolens and used whatever skins were available—rabbit or cat, sometimes sheepskin, occasionally deerskin. They were often barefooted and tied rags around their feet in winter. The poor suffered many discomforts because of the shortage of furs and skins. In earlier times, there had been enough wild animals to supply furs even to people of moderate means. By the fourteenth century, however, most of these animals were protected in royal game preserves where commoners were forbidden to hunt; and by the fifteenth century the catch of native fur-bearing animals no longer met the demand (Phillips 1961).

Eastern furs began to reach Western Europe by at least the eleventh century in a trade that was probably begun by the Teutonic knights. Furs came from Scandinavia, from eastern Germany, and from Russia. After a century of heavy trading, fur imports from Russia declined by the end of the 1500s due to reduced numbers of wild furbearers and accompanying high prices. Styles in clothing changed, and woolens, linens, cottons, and silks mostly replaced furs for use in apparel. Yet there remained a demand for furs, and there were fur-bearing animals aplenty in the forests and streams of North America, with Native Americans roaming the continent who could trap them. Soon enough the imperial policies of the French and English monarchies, and the shrewdness of their merchants and industrialists, would promote exchanges of animal pelts for weapons, cheap textiles, and "gaudy finery" from Europe (Phillips 1961).

The first fur traders in North America were engaged in the commercial fishing trade. Although fish were abundant and the European market was good, they inevitably came in contact with the Native Americans, and the advantages of trading were apparent to both. Many

French fishermen became traders as fur returns dwarfed their profits from fishing. These fishermen cum traders had no wish to conquer the continent, however, and they hardly moved inward from the shoreline. It was the search for a short water route to the riches of the Orient that prompted explorations by Jacques Cartier and others in the 1530s that initiated the inland fur trade (Phillips 1961).

Before long the inland fur trade initiated by Cartier became an international business. Within a few years after John Jacob Astor, a young German immigrant, arrived in New York in 1784, he realized the opportunities for wealth in the fur trade while learning the business working for established furriers. By the late 1780s he was no longer a mere peddler, fur trader, or even New York fur dealer; he was competing with London merchants in the world market (Phillips 1961).

With the Louisiana Purchase, Americans gained control of the fur country west of the Mississippi, and the United States promptly began to extend its influence into regions formerly dominated by the French and Canadians. Through his friend DeWitt Clinton, Astor submitted to President Jefferson the idea for a corporation chartered as a monopoly so that Americans would control the fur trade in territories possessed by the United States. Apparently concluding that he could not get a federal charter at the time, Astor applied to the New York legislature for one before hearing from Jefferson. Permission was granted, and the American Fur Company received a charter from the state in 1808 (Phillips 1961).

It was Astor's plan to expand the operations of the American Fur Company into a business empire that reached to the Pacific, but the North West Company of Canada had similar designs. The rivalry between American and Canadian fur traders led to an overt struggle for the Oregon country, and the fur trade influenced the policies of the United States and Great Britain for many years. The struggle for supremacy in the fur trade was an important facet of the economic and political imperialism that guided colonization of more than half the North American continent (Phillips 1961).

Many mountain men and trappers worked for, or were associated with, the American Fur Company, but some were independent and a few even tried to compete with Astor's monopoly. One of these was Robert Campbell (1804–79), who came to the United States from Ireland in 1822. Two years later, a physician in St. Louis diagnosed Campbell's lung problems as consumption and suggested that he go to the Rocky Mountains. Heeding the doctor's advice, young Campbell joined a party of sixty trappers led by Jedediah Smith that left St. Louis in 1825. In 1828 Campbell was included in a smaller party of twelve headed by Jim Bridger, who was off to trap the Crow Indian country of northeastern Wyoming. After four years in the mountains, and now restored to good health, Campbell returned to St. Louis with forty-five packs of beaver pelts that brought $22,476 for the partnership, of which his share was $3,016 (Carter 1983).

Campbell's friendship with William Sublette was apparently cemented at the rendezvous of Pierre's Hole, and the subsequent skirmish with a superior force of Blackfeet in which Sublette was seriously wounded. Upon their return to St. Louis the firm of Sublette and Campbell was established in 1833, a partnership that lasted until 1842. It is not clear whether the partners had actually hoped to compete successfully with the American Fur Company; however, the eventual outcome was that Astor's monopoly paid handsomely to abate their nuisance. Campbell spent his later years as a successful merchant and financier in St. Louis, continuing to buy furs and supply trappers until the end of his life (Carter 1983).

The pattern of exploitation by mountain men, trappers, and Native Americans was so successful that the beaver was practically extirpated. By the early 1900s, beaver colonies remained only in remote and isolated areas of North America. The estimated 60 million beaver that existed before European colonization had been reduced to only about one hundred thousand by 1900 (Hill 1987).

The first efforts to restore beaver to their former range began with small releases of live-trapped animals in New York in 1904 and 1920, in California in 1924, and in Missouri in 1928. Similar programs followed in other states, often supported by Federal Aid in Wildlife Restoration funds made available through provisions of the Pittman-Robertson Act (Hill 1987).

Restoration of the beaver enjoyed great public support. Beavers at once embodied a historical mystique associated with the early days of North American exploration, a flavor of rural America, and a valuable commodity during and just after the Great Depression. Pelt prices had increased to thirty dollars, which was a considerable sum in those years (Hill 1987).

Even earlier, by the end of the World War I, beaver abundance had increased to astonishing levels in parts of the Great Lakes region and mountain areas of the West, although this was not widely known. As a few beaver pelts began to appear in the markets a demand was created, and beaver coats became as much a status symbol as beaver hats had been a century earlier. Beaver were still protected by closed seasons, however, which was the impetus for an illegal fur trade during the twenties and thirties "far more extensive than can be imagined; it was secretive, complex, and often as sinister as rum running" (Swift 1967:25). The financial incentives attracted backwoods trappers, fur bootleggers, purportedly respectable village businessmen, dishonest public officials, and members of notorious crime syndicates. Involvement, by way of many loosely knit networks, extended from the Rocky Mountains to New York City. Often, the same contacts that brought Prohibition liquor from the big cities to country towns funneled illegal furs back to the cities (Swift 1967).

## *Attitudes toward Trapping*

John Gentile (1987), in a study on attitudes toward trapping, identified four historical periods in the evolution of antitrapping sentiment. During the first of four historical periods, the Early Years (1890–1924), identified by Gentile antitrapping sentiment was not widespread. Before 1925, the strategy used by opponents of trapping was to promote boycotts of trapped furs. There was little discussion of alternative types of traps and only sporadic attempts to legislate requirements for humane trapping methods. Virtually all the antitrapping effort was directed at the fur industry rather than at trappers and leg-hold traps.

He further noted that in the early 1900s, there was a pervasive attitude that state governments were not giving fur resources the attention they deserved. W. P. Taylor (1913) pointed to the value of furbearing animals and indicated some factors that had led to reductions in their numbers. His advice was to institute regulations on trapping that would protect the fur animals. But according to Gentile, "In response, some states began adopting regulations to protect furbearer populations. However, these efforts were not adequate to prevent declining populations, primarily because open seasons were too long and existing laws were not being enforced." Fur animals were being taken in the early fall and during the breeding season, when the fur was almost worthless. This was apparent from "the fact that far too many pelts [reaching] the raw-fur markets [fell] into the unprofitable class" (Ashbrook 1925).

Gentile classified 1925 to 1939 as the Idealistic Phase. During this period the first organized efforts to reform trapping began with the formation of the Anti–Steel-Trap League in 1925. This group was not founded to stop all trapping, but rather to ban leg-hold traps, which members felt were unethical. The newsletter published by the ASTL "specialized in lurid accounts of stray pets caught in steel traps as well as virulent attacks on traditional conservation groups like the National Association of Audubon Societies" (Reiger 1978). As Gentile observed, the ASTL blamed the general public rather than trappers, because the public condoned such cruelty as the leg-hold trap for the sake of vanity.

According to E. J. Dailey, the American Trappers Association's first president, substantial—and even more effective—antitrapping sentiment was generated during the period by "rich fox and 'coon hunters' organizations" (Reiger 1978). Opposition to trapping by these groups was based on the belief that any hound not returning with the pack was caught in a leg-hold trap and on an apprehension that the trapping of foxes and raccoons might diminish the numbers of these animals for their own hunting recreation.

The Anti–Steel-Trap League achieved some successes during the Idealistic Phase as South Carolina (1927), Georgia (1929), Massachusetts (1930), and Kentucky (1938) all banned the leg-hold trap. Among other developments during this time, the Society for the Prevention of Cruelty to Animals, the National Association of the Fur Industry, and the American Humane Association all offered prize money for development of an alternative trapping device that was humane, yet comparable to the leg-hold trap in weight, durability, and cost (Gentile 1987).

Probably the most important outcome of the legislative and alternative-trap efforts was an increase in trapping regulations. By 1939, all of the forty-eight states except Washington had established trapping seasons or restrictions on the size and type of trap. Also adopted were regulations covering daily visits to trap lines, trap locations, name tags on traps, permission from landowners, and trapping reports. Leg-hold trap opponents agreed that these were good measures, but they also feared that the requirements were intended to appease opponents of trapping while avoiding the humane issue.

Gentile called the years from 1940 to 1967 the Institutional Phase. In the early forties opposition to trapping nearly ceased and the leg-hold trap bans that existed were being reconsidered; by 1948 all statewide trapping bans had been rescinded. Among the explanations advanced to account for reduced antitrapping sentiment were that the combined influence of the Great Depression and World War II had the effect of emphasizing the needs of people, so that concern for animal welfare was accorded a lower priority (Reiger 1978; Kellert and Westervelt 1981), and that domestic fur prices increased during the war years as the availability of foreign imports decreased, which promoted interest in trapping and gave a greater voice in trapping policy to trappers themselves ("Furs and the War" 1942).

These two points notwithstanding, Niven (1963) summarized six reasons for reduced antitrapping efforts during the forties: trapping was part of the American way of life; trapping was the basis of the fur industry; trapping was one of the oldest American industries; trapping protected crops and small livestock from predation by wild furbearers; trapping helped satisfy the public demand for furs; and there was no substitute for the steel trap.

After so many legislative defeats, opponents of trapping had to acknowledge the effectiveness of their opposition. They were doing battle not only with a well-organized trappers' association but also with American consumers and a fur industry that was an important part of the national economy. In 1950, the director of the American Humane Association admitted defeat and attributed their failure to the lack of a humane and suitable trap. Thus, humane trapping advocates resorted to a strategy of influencing trapping regulations (Gentile 1987).

During the Modern Phase (1968–86) the antitrapping movement saw a revival after having been dormant for forty years. In the seventies, humane groups were discouraged with their regulatory strategy—they viewed trapping regulations as inconsistent, unenforced, and designed to benefit trappers—and also concerned about a shift in fur fashions from ranch-raised, short-haired animals to such long-haired wild furbearers as red fox (*Vulpes vulpes*), coyote (*Canis latrans*), and raccoon (*Procyon lotor*).

State agencies reduced their furbearer management programs in the sixties because of decreased trapper participation and lower license sales. This also had the effect of reducing regulatory control over trapping. As a consequence, humane sympathizers saw the regulatory process as failing to address their concerns. Their response was to resurrect the legislative strategy.

Gentile commented that in the years since 1968 more than 360 antitrapping bills have been introduced at all levels of government in the United States—a forty-fold increase over the preceding twenty-eight years. Of these legislative actions, approximately 50 percent were introduced at the state level, about 30 percent at the local level, and nearly 20 percent at the national level. Statewide actions against trapping have been attempted in thirty-three states since 1968, and as of 1986, seven states (Connecticut, Florida, Maryland, Massachusetts, South Carolina, New Jersey, and Tennessee) have banned the leg-hold trap.

Concluding his analysis of the evolution of antihunting sentiment, Gentile noted that the protrapping faction appears to be better organized than its counterpart. The Wildlife Legislative Fund of America, the principal proponent of trapping, has several brief policy statements that tend to unite diverse groups in support of trapping. Perhaps the most successful strategy of protrappers has been to portray their adversaries as being opposed to hunting and fishing as well, thus garnering support from other groups that use wildlife consumptively. The antitrapping segment is made up of a spectrum of groups ranging from those that oppose only inhumane trapping to organizations opposed to any use of animals. These diverse groups have often worked against each other, leading to the repeated defeat of antitrapping legislation and a public perception that the humane movement is inept and lacks merit.

A newly emerging development of potential significance is the animal rights issue. The first American law protecting animals was passed in New York in 1866 (Niven 1963:108). This law applied to domestic animals, but it set a precedent in that animals were no longer considered mere property—they had legal rights. The philosophy underlying the humane movement has always been that animals have rights, although the use of this idea to combat trapping is new (Gentile 1987). This tactic might eventually provide a common focus for uniting all humane groups, and could have ramifications for hunting and wildlife management as well.

Based on conversations about the status of leg-hold trap legislation with officials from Ohio and South Carolina, Reiger (1978) commented that the cruelty of the leg-hold trap did not seem to be the primary force shaping antitrapping attitudes. Instead, he believed "the capture of non-target species is the Achilles' heel of trapping." Although an experienced professional trapper rarely takes a house cat or pet dog, Reiger noted that youths playing Davy Crockett are likely to do just that. Many states allow residents under sixteen years of age to trap without a license. In Reiger's view, the ideal would be to prevent prospective trappers from trapping until they are responsible, competent, and have been certified.

Attitudes toward trapping in the United States were investigated by Kellert (1981), who used a survey questionnaire. As one might expect, attitudes toward leg-hold traps depended on whether or not the respondent used them. Only 19 percent of the general public responding to the survey agreed with the proposition that there is nothing wrong with the use of steel traps; however, 96 percent of the trappers surveyed agreed with this thesis. In reporting these findings, Kellert expressed the unsubstantiated opinion that trapping cannot be inhumane because trappers know what they are talking about.

## *Ecology of Trapping*

Several biological, economic, and social arguments are frequently advanced to justify fur-trapping. The biological rationale is that trapping is the most practical way of harvesting a renewable resource that would otherwise be lost to natural mortality. The basis for this view is that wild animals can, and often do, produce more offspring than their habitat can support, and this surplus cannot be stockpiled indefinitely. Arlen Todd (1981) looked at furbearer population ecology in the northern Boreal Region of North America to evaluate the common biological arguments for trapping. Protectionists often contend that trapping, hunting, or management of wildlife is unnecessary and cannot be justified in wilderness regions because of the "balance of nature." Todd considered the balance of nature concept to be valid, but insisted that we realize there is not a fixed or static balance. A dynamic balance may entail drastic fluctuations in animal numbers around a long-term mean level, with declines often precipitated by disease or mass starvation. Environmental changes may produce a new balance rather than restoring a former one, so even dynamic balances should not be considered permanent. By the time there is a decline in animal abundance, long-lasting habitat damage has often occurred, which may result in the long-term suppression of numbers for some species (Todd 1981).

The short-term impact of trapping is the reduction of furbearer numbers. However, wise management dictates that only the surplus should be removed. Since trapping mortality is intended to substitute for natural mortality, trapping at optimal levels may not reduce the average number of animals (Todd 1981). The long-term impact of trapping may actually be positive. Some of the herbivorous furbearers are more abundant when subjected to sustained-yield harvesting than they are when not trapped. Here, trapping prevents numbers from reaching such high levels that "eat-outs" occur. Large numbers of plant-eating animals have the capacity to virtually destroy their habitat before the resulting food shortage causes a population "crash" (Todd 1981). For example, in Louisiana coastal marshes, extensive "eat-outs" by muskrats, where they are underharvested, often result in areas being completely denuded of vegetation. These marshes will not support muskrats again for a very long time unless the areas are artificially drained or burned (Todd 1981). Similarly, on marshes in northern states and Canada, die-offs caused by disease can nearly annihilate overabundant muskrats. This can also result in long-term suppression of muskrat numbers because bacterial contamination of the water and mud often causes recurring epidemics (Todd 1981).

Beaver are generally most abundant in forested areas dominated by early-succession vegetation, particularly aspen, due to periodic forest fires or logging. Plant succession is usually accompanied by reduced beaver numbers; however, beaver tend to accelerate forest succession by selectively cutting aspen trees. Since an overabundance of beaver virtually destroys its habitat, management aims at retaining early stages of succession and harvesting surplus beaver to maintain a balance with its food supply. The intent of optimal exploitation is to sustain, or even increase, average long-term beaver numbers by keeping the animal from destroying its own habitat (Todd 1981).

Since the muskrat and beaver are integral components of their respective wetland ecosystems, it is desirable to maintain numbers of these furbearers at optimal levels. Ecological benefits of wetlands include flood control, water storage and purification, aquifer recharge, and habitat for other wildlife. One might argue that fur-trapping can contribute to the stability of ecosystems, even in some wilderness areas. Furthermore, optimal numbers will tend to minimize dispersal movements from wilderness to settled areas, and thus reduce land-use conflicts between wildlife and people (Todd 1981).

Carnivorous furbearers are predators, and "predator management" is a complex and controversial topic. There are two common arguments in favor of reducing predator numbers: minimizing depredations on livestock, and minimizing predator dispersal and the risk that diseases will be spread into settled areas. Although acknowledging that carnivore reductions would have little effect on continent-wide damage levels to crops and livestock, Todd (1981) nevertheless believed systematic harvests (by fur-trapping or recreational hunting) in boreal wilderness areas to be a sound preventative measure. Specifically, he felt that reducing wolf and bear levels in boreal wilderness forests immediately adjacent to settled areas would reduce damage and conflicts caused by these predators.

## *Economics of Trapping*

There is one particularly significant economic difference between the trapping of fur-bearing animals and hunting of game animals. "Harvest of furbearers involves commercial motives because the hides of these animals, unlike the meat from game species, can legally be sold on the free market" (Shaw 1985:164).

This poses a unique problem for wildlife management biologists, since trapping pressure often reflects the market price of pelts from a particular species. Changes in pelt prices can be substantial and often are quite independent of abundance of the species sought by trappers. This makes it difficult to protect a species for which numbers are low when pelt prices are high. Conversely, it is just as difficult to promote harvesting to reduce numbers of an abundant species when pelt prices are very low (Shaw 1985).

Between 1976 and 1980 the average annual harvest value of furs and skins from wild North American mammals and reptiles was approximately $176 million—$122 million from animals harvested in the United States and $54 million (in U.S. dollars) from animals taken in Canada. Economically, the top two species, raccoon and muskrat, were both high-volume species with harvests numbering in the millions each year. The annual muskrat harvest was more than double that of the raccoon, but the raccoon pelt was more valuable. Consequently, raccoon pelts are economically preeminent in the United States and in North America as a whole. Between 1976 and 1980 an average of about 3 million raccoons, with a value exceeding $54 million, were harvested each year (Prescott-Allen and Prescott-Allen 1986).

Lynx and bobcat are considered medium-volume, high-value species, and the economic importance of both have increased dramatically in the last few years. Lynx fur is more durable and more valuable than bobcat, and is now considered to be a high-style fur. Bobcat pelts seldom brought more than ten dollars each prior to 1970, but now sometimes sell for as much as three hundred to four hundred dollars; lynx pelts are worth twice as much. These increased prices reflect a shift to the smaller cats, beginning in the early seventies, as overexploitation threatened the survival of many of the big cats in Asia and India (Prescott-Allen and Prescott-Allen 1986).

Public opinion has always been a potent economic force, creating markets for some furs and curtailing markets for others. The public outcry against the killing of harp seal (*Pagophilus groenlandicus*) pups in the early eighties prompted the European Economic Community to impose a ban on furskin imports of this species and the hooded seal (*Cystophora cristata*). Since the EEC countries were the principal markets for harp and hooded seal products, this ban virtually ended trade in their fur and leather (Prescott-Allen and Prescott-Allen 1986).

A survey conducted by Boddicker (1981) revealed that the average American trapper in the late seventies spent about sixty days a year trapping, used fifty-six leg-hold traps or snares, and caught 112 animals—mainly muskrat (*Ondatra zibethicus*), raccoon (*Procyon lotor*), and red fox (*Vulpes vulpes*). The average profit from the sale of furs was $1,097 after expenses of $499 were deducted. This return represented nearly 18 percent of an annual income of approximately $11,000. Maximum trapping receipts reported for one person were $10,144 in 1977–78 and $12,285 in 1978–79. Although most trappers maintained that the income from trapping was important to them, only 6 percent indicated that money was the major reason they trapped.

On a national basis, the total value of the wild fur trade in the

United States in 1977 was $273 million. The most valuable pelts were those of the lynx (*Lynx canadensis*) and gray wolf (*Canis lupus*), at $219 and $200, respectively; but the raccoon (*Procyon lotor*), with a pelt worth only $20, accounted for $99.6 million, or about 48 percent of the fur receipts from wild-trapped animals (Nilsson 1980). Only seven species of furbearers—bobcat (*Lynx rufus*), coyote (*Canis latrans*), gray fox (*Vulpes cinereoargenteus*), red fox (*Vulpes vulpes*), muskrat (*Ondatra zibethicus*), nutria (*Myocastor coypus*), and raccoon (*Procyon lotor*)—were responsible for over 90 percent of the value of furs from the twenty-five species reported (Nilsson 1980).

A survey by the U.S. Fish and Wildlife Service (1988) indicated the extent of participation in trapping in 1985, but gave no estimates of economic value. Total trappers numbered 508,000, of which 316,000 (62 percent) trapped for sport and 162,000 (32 percent) trapped for income. The remaining 6 percent did not specify why they trapped. Total trapping days approximated 11,508,000, an average of 23 days per trapper.

The relationship between economic and recreational aspects of trapping is ambiguous—or trappers themselves are unclear about their motives. As Boddicker (1981) noted, most trappers maintained that the income from trapping was important, but only 6 percent indicated that money was the major reason they trapped. This view is inconsistent with Keith's (1963) observation that furbearer harvests quickly decline when pelt prices drop. Ernest Swift wrote: "Trapping has always been a cold-blooded commercial business" (1967:25). We might soften this appraisal by suggesting that the motivation for trapping has always been monetary, but with the added attractions of getting outdoors, of adventure, of freedom from life's normal confinements, and of testing one's skills in nature.

## *Concluding Comments*

In a discussion of furbearer management and trapping, Neil Payne (1980) remarked that the management and harvest of furbearers is just as proper as the management and harvest of domestic livestock. In today's society, neither livestock nor wildlife is essential for food or clothing; plants can provide both. However, the use of wild natural fur, a renewable resource, could reduce the demand for synthetic fur made from petroleum, which is increasingly scarce and expensive.

Payne further noted that society has a responsibility to maintain wildlife for future generations as part of our natural heritage. Management of wildlife is necessary in most areas because of the heavy demands that humans make on the environment. Hunting can be a useful tool in managing many species, but it is relatively ineffective for most fur-bearing animals due to their secretive behavior. Trapping is the best alternative for harvesting furbearers.

In a short essay prompted by Todd's (1981) discussion of fur-trapping in boreal wilderness regions, Roger Powell (1982) pointed to what he believed to be a major problem within the trapping/antitrapping and hunting/antihunting debates. Wildlife biologists often make statements in support of hunting or trapping using so-called ecological arguments. Opponents of these activities counter with statements of their own, also relying on ecological arguments. In Powell's view, what both sides are really doing "is presenting arguments based on human value judgements they have made from ecological information."

In Powell's view, ecological information has no inherent value content; it does not imply that a condition or action is good or bad. Whether hunting or trapping will stabilize, destabilize, or exterminate a population is value-neutral information about a species in a given area. It is people who make value judgments—about how they want a particular population treated and indeed whether they want that population to be manipulated or free from human interference. Persons wishing to use ecological information in discussions about hunting or trapping should understand that this information is being used as a basis for human value judgments, and that the disagreements are about those judgments. There are no ecological arguments, only arguments between people.

PERSPECTIVE

## Leopold's Land Ethic and Western Philosophy

Some Oriental philosophies embrace nature and accord ethical standing to nonhuman natural entities. Taoism, for example, teaches that everything has equivalent significance; humans have no special status. Human beings and other natural things, whether animate or not, are equally invested with being and value (Ip 1983).

Traditional Western systems of ethics, both popular and philosophical, have generally not included nonhuman beings—and certainly not natural objects—within the ethical compact (Callicott 1980). Nevertheless, as Aldo Leopold (1949) pointed out, the history of morality in Western civilization has been the record of continually expanding ethical standing to include ever broader categories of entities and relationships. The holistic "land ethic," with its appeal to the court of ecological integrity and stability, is the logical outcome of what he regarded as "the ethical sequence" (1966). Leopold's land ethic extended ethical standing not just to wild animals, but to virtually all natural entities. Plants, soils and waters, rocks and mountains are all included within the community of ethical beneficiaries. Leopold used poetic language to express an ecological maxim that carries the force of a moral imperative: "Only the mountain has lived long enough to listen objectively to the howl of a wolf."

There have been other philosophers in the history of Western thought who recognized nonhuman beings as having ethical rights (Callicott 1980). Pythagoras, the Greek philosopher and mathematician who died about 497 B.C., taught the kinship of beasts and humankind (Burnet 1957). His doctrine of transmigration held that the human soul is immortal and, at death, enters into the body of an animal (Robinson 1968). Thus, he considered that killing animals for food was murder, and eating animal flesh was forbidden as a kind of cannibalism.

Empedocles of Acragas (fifth century B.C.) was another early Greek philosopher who regarded animals as human kin (Burnet 1957). He, too, thought that the soul is immortal, and believed that at death the soul enters a new body—human, plant, or animal (Robinson 1968). In Empedocles' view, killing an animal was parricide.

In the Middle Ages, St. Francis of Assisi (1181–1226) had a celebrated, almost mythological, relationship with animals and called all creatures his "brothers" and "sisters." St. Francis also seems to have believed in the animal soul (Callicott 1980), and there is a legend that he preached to the birds.

The possibility of the animal soul is a common idea that has been repeated throughout history. Animals were even thought to have religious instincts: Psalm 148 proclaimed that all creatures praise the Lord, even "beasts and all cattle; creeping things and flying fowl."

During the Renaissance the rational soul was often cited as distinguishing humanity from animals. Yet at a popular level, religion has never been considered inaccessible to animals (Thomas 1983). There were hints of popular belief in a kind of transmigration of souls that recalls similar ideas in early Greek philosophy. Fishermen sometimes considered seagulls to be the spirits of dead sailors (Armstrong 1958). Some of the Neo-Platonists of the Renaissance also revived this doctrine of "metempsychosis," which had been taught by Pythagoras and Plato (Thomas 1983).

In the modern era, the English jurist and utilitarian philosopher Jeremy Bentham (1748–1832) defined ethics as "the art of directing men's actions to the production of the greatest possible quantity of happiness," and he indicated that animals as well as human beings "are susceptible of happiness" (1907:310). Bentham did not oppose the killing of animals for food, because their death is usually speedier and less painful than they would suffer under natural conditions; but he did not believe they should be tormented or have to suffer.

His most telling point, however, was that the boundary between humans and other animal species does not seem relevant to morality. It is not the "faculty of reason" or the "faculty of discourse" that is uniquely relevant to morality. Under either of these criteria many animals would be more rational than human infants, the brain-damaged, and the congenitally disabled. For Bentham "the question is not, Can they *reason?* nor, Can they *talk?* but, Can they *suffer?*" (1907:311).

The distinctive feature of Leopold's environmental ethic is its holistic vision: "the moral worth of individuals (including . . . human individuals) is relative, to be assessed in accordance with the particular relation of each to the collective which Leopold called 'land' " (Callicott 1980:327). Yet Callicott pointed out that there is a precedent for Leopold's view in Western ethics: the moral and social philosophy of Plato. It is true Plato never developed anything resembling an environmental ethic, nor did he ever reach an ecological view of nature. But Plato (1985) did insist that good for the whole takes precedence over benefits to individuals. In book 5 of *The Republic* he stated that "the best city is one whose situation is most like that of an individual human being." Callicott (1980) rendered this passage as "the best governed state most nearly resembles an organism." (462D), and "Can a city know any greater evil than to be divided, to be many instead of one? Can there be any greater good than what binds the city together?" (462B).

From the perspective of naturalists and evolutionary biologists, there is ample justification for including animals within the ethical compact. It is simply that to do so is an ethical implication of evolutionary theory. Charles Darwin claimed that "there is no fundamental difference between man and the higher mammals in their mental faculties." Recent biological studies, at levels of organization ranging from the molecular through the organismal, increasingly support this pronouncement. Why, then, is there so much resistance to including animals, much less all of nature, within the community of ethical beneficiaries? As Darwin suggested, "Animals whom we have made our slaves we do not like to consider our equals" (Gruber and Barrett 1974:447).

## PERSPECTIVE

## The Foundations of Backwoods Hunting in Colonial America

In their book *The American Backwoods Frontier: An Ethnic and Ecological Interpretation,* the cultural geographers Terry Jordan and Matti Kaups (1989) documented the thesis that colonial Finnish immigrants played a highly significant role in shaping the backwoods colonization culture that spread across the forested regions of North America.

Their research effort began when Jordan set out to test the widely accepted, but unproven, notion that the American notched-log construction of log cabin fame had a Germanic ethnic basis and originated in Central Europe. To his surprise, Jordan found very little evidence of such an influence. Puzzled,

he directed his attention toward Scandinavia to examine the hypothesis, long since discarded, that settlers of the short-lived New Sweden colony on the Delaware River introduced log construction to America. He was unexpectedly rewarded to find the techniques and forms associated with American notched-log buildings in a Finnish ethnic region called the Finnskog on the border between Sweden and Norway. Significantly, immigrants from this district were prominent among the settlers of the New Sweden colony.

American backwoods pioneers knew they were distinctive. Pioneers on the Pennsylvania frontier in the 1720s preferred to be known as "the Back Inhabiters" or "borderers." By the 1780s their favored appellation was "backwoods men." Though the backwoods pioneers were not highly regarded—they were often depicted as "shiftless, lazy, dirty, drunken, ignorant, and sinful"—their system of colonization was stunningly successful: they opened the continent to settlement and laid the foundations for an independence of thought and action we now consider to be characteristically American.

Native plants and wildlife constituted a resource base for the backwoods pioneers that was at least as important as timber and tillable soil. Thus, hunting was an essential element in the diversified economy of these backwoods people, and the rifle has been rightly noted as an important adaptive key to midland America forest colonization.

Although most colonies on the eastern seaboard were heavily involved with trading of furs and skins, the actual hunting was generally done by Native Americans. "As late as the Proclamation of 1763, the British crown was concerned to protect and preserve Indian territorial rights in the North American interior, in order not to disrupt the fur trade" (211). Only in the Delaware Valley did European settlers do much hunting and rely on it for part of their livelihood.

The reason colonists did not engage in subsistence hunting was a consequence of their historical backgrounds. Most immigrants came from countries where commoners had long been denied the right to hunt and bear arms. Even British Highlanders, the Scotch-Irish and Welsh, were no longer hunters by the 1600s, and most of the English could refer only to tales of Robin Hood poaching in the royal forests hundreds of years before that. French, Dutch, and German immigrants likewise had no recent hunting tradition.

The only European commoners who possessed rifle-hunting skills upon their arrival in colonial America were the Finns of New Sweden. Hunting was a traditional activity of backcountry Finnish people, who still lived the life of the chase. In fact, the emigration of Savo-Karelian Finns from Sweden to colonial America "was prompted in part by their habitual violation of royal, Germanic game laws, which had been instituted in an attempt to curtail the large-scale hunting the Finns had brought to Scandanavia" (213).

Even the skin clothing of American backwoods settlers likely had its origin with the Finns of the New Sweden colony. Although such attire is usually assumed to have been adopted from the Native Americans—as suggested, for example, by the Delaware Algonquian word *moccasin*—it is noteworthy that the Savo-Karelian Finns had a long tradition of skin clothing and moccasin-type shoes. Hence, it is quite possible that the backwoods buckskin apparel developed in the Delaware Valley was a combination of Finnish and Native American styles and techniques.

According to surviving accounts, Finns in Scandanavia as well as backwoods Americans held bear hunting in the highest regard—because the animal was a dangerous adversary, because they preyed on open-range livestock, and because of a fondness for bear steaks. Neither Savo-Karelian hunters in northern Europe nor their American counterparts were highly specialized hunters, but the preferred game of both were bear and deer. Even such small game as squirrels were a fairly important food source for Finns in Europe as for American backwoods settlers, but the honored hunters of northern Europe and frontier America were those who killed many bears, moose, or deer.

Most backwoods Americans hunted with rifles, though few were able to afford the famous Kentucky long rifle of popular lore. The majority of rifles used were probably of a long-barreled type fired by a flintlock. Savo-Karelian Finns, while still in Europe, were likewise rifle hunters using flintlock weapons. Beyond that, they arrived in America knowing how to mine surface deposits of iron ore, mold their own bullets, and fashion firearms at backwoods forges. While hunting equipment was similar wherever flintlock rifles were used, the similarities between Fenno-Scandian and backwoods American paraphernalia extended even to the position of various accessories on the shoulder strap.

In seeking to explain the roots of some environmental problems in present-day America, we might look to the colonization practices of the backwoods frontier culture for clues. In backwoods society, good hunters were greatly admired, and their skill was largely measured by the size of the kill. Davy Crockett, for example, boasted of having killed 58 bears during one fall and winter, and Texas pioneer Martin Bailey claimed to have killed 1,500 deer in just four years, saving only their skins.

The boastful, wasteful American backwoods hunter has a model in the Scandanavians and Finns of northern Europe. By the 1630s, Savo-Karelian Finns had incurred the wrath of officials by shooting moose solely for their hides, leaving the rest to rot. In fact, the Finns' lack of conservation in hunting contributed to their deportation to colonial America. There the same practices continued without interruption. Ironically, the Rambo-like actions of some contemporary American hunters, whose hunting tactics are really closer to assault-style warfare, have a prototype in a real person. In the 1700s, Mauntz Rambo, who lived above the falls of the Schuylkill River near Swede's Ford in eastern Pennsylvania, bore the title "celebrated hunter" as he had "killed numerous deer in the neighbourhood" and once even "shot a panther" (229).

## SUGGESTED READING

Clarke, C. H. D. 1958. "Autumn Thoughts of a Hunter." *Journal of Wildlife Management* 22:420–27. Philosophical reflections on hunting by a respected wildlife biologist.

Elman, R., and D. Seybold, eds. 1985. *Seasons of the Hunter.* New York: Alfred A. Knopf. 233 pages. A collection that evokes much of the hunting experience in twenty short stories. Captures the moods and contradictions of hunting without evading the dilemma of the contemporary hunter.

Leopold, A. 1982. *A Sand County Almanac, with Essays on Conservation from Round River.* New York: Ballantine Books. In Leopold's words, "There are some who can live without wild things, and some who cannot. These essays are the delights and dilemmas of one who cannot." This is a classic that everyone should enjoy and ponder.

# Nonconsumptive Values of Wildlife 4

The term *nongame* has been called a nondefinition, but the word is not simply meaningless. Rainer Brocke (1979) suggested it could conceivably lead to a situation in which wildlife species are "parcelled out among competing interest groups," with game animals being assigned to hunters and trappers, while nongame wildlife is allocated to observers and photographers.

The word *nonconsumptive* is likewise unsatisfactory because it is misleading. Many nonconsumptive uses of wildlife are actually consumptive in the sense that these activities have adverse impacts. They may affect behavior (through disturbance), alter habitat (for better viewing or photographing), change feeding patterns (through discarded food items or harassment), degrade habitat (by trampling), increase mortality (through nest abandonment, separation of young from mothers, or vehicular collisions), increase vulnerability to poaching (due to habituation), and place greater energy demands on animals (by disrupting feeding or causing animals to flush). The effects of nonconsumptive recreation on wildlife were reviewed by Boyle and Samson, who challenged conservationists "to identify recreational impacts on wildlife, establish priorities for management, and implement schemes to conserve wildlife resources while providing for increasing use-demands of recreationists" (1985). I still use the terms *nongame* and *nonconsumptive,* despite their difficulties, because they are convenient and most alternatives are unwieldy or unsuitable.

Persons whose interest in wildlife is directed toward nongame animals, or nonconsumptive uses of all species, should be aware of the perpetual debt they owe to hunters. Hunters were responsible for the origins of American conservation, and they can claim legitimate credit for many of the activities and programs that have benefited wildlife and preserved habitats (Reiger 1986).

Hunters must realize, however, that they are no longer the exclusive custodians of wildlife and be willing to accept a new role, one in which a solicitude for wildlife and the responsibility for wildlife conservation is shared with a variety of interest groups. Some of these other groups have a focus that may be inimical to the consumptive recreational pursuits of sportsmen, yet all have a common concern for the welfare of wildlife species and habitats.

Several studies in the 1970s examined the relative importance of consumptive and nonconsumptive uses of wildlife to the public and to hunters (Arthur and Wilson 1979). Ratings of the perceived importance of six wildlife uses showed that all of the nonconsumptive uses were valued more than any consumptive use by pro- and antihunting respondents alike. When survey participants were asked to divide 100 points among three uses—hunting, knowing that animals exist, and viewing (in person or in pictures)—to reflect their relative enjoyment of each use, even prohunting respondents valued nonconsumptive uses much more highly. Viewing was awarded 50 points; knowing animals exist received 33 points; and hunting was given just 16 points. Hunters in general expressed relatively greater interest in viewing wildlife and enjoying wildlife habitats than in bagging game or filling their limit and would willingly trade lower bag limits for the continued availability of these opportunities (Arthur and Wilson 1979).

Reviewing their findings, Arthur and Wilson concluded that the public valued and enjoyed all nonconsumptive wildlife uses more than any consumptive use; that hunters considered the experience of natural environments, and the companionship of others with similar interests, to be the major determinants of user-satisfaction; and that public interests generally paralleled hunters' interests in that both groups were concerned with protecting wildlife habitats and providing sanctuaries to assure the existence of a variety of species.

In 1966, R. T. King specified several categories of wildlife values: commercial; recreational; biotic; scientific, philosophical, and educational; aesthetic; social; and negative. The first two have obvious consumptive as well as nonconsumptive aspects.

## RECREATIONAL VALUE

Recreation refers to activities that create us anew, that restore and refresh us. Few pastimes are more thoroughly invigorating than those associated with wildlife. The economic and recreational values of hunting are impressive, but the corresponding impact of nonconsumptive wildlife-related recreation is even greater.

In 1985, 109.6 million persons—about 61 percent of all Americans age sixteen and over—participated in nonconsumptive wildlife-related recreation. Some 16 percent of adult Americans (29.3 million persons) engaged in what the U.S. Fish and Wildlife Service (1988) calls *primary nonresidential activities*—trips or outings of one mile or more to observe, photograph, or feed wildlife. Fully 58 percent of the adult population (105.3 million persons) were involved in *primary residential actions*—activities around home whose main purpose is wildlife-related: wildlife observation or identification; wildlife photography; feeding wildlife on a regular basis; maintaining natural areas to benefit wildlife; maintaining plantings to benefit wildlife; or visiting public parks within one mile of home to observe, photograph, or feed wildlife. Included among the nonconsumptive residential recreationists were 82.5 million persons who feed wild birds on a regular basis, 60.9 million bird-watchers, and 18 million wildlife photographers (U.S. Fish and Wildlife Service 1988).

The economic impact is equally impressive. Nonconsumptive wildlife-related recreationists spent approximately $14.3 billion on their nonconsumptive activities in 1985, an average of $106 per participant. A total of $3.6 billion was spent for such nonconsumptive equipment as field guides, birdseed, and binoculars (U.S. Fish and Wildlife Service 1988).

Projections by Shaw and Mangun (1984) for the year 2000 suggest that nonconsumptive wildlife use will probably increase at a faster rate (20.6 percent) than hunting (16.7 percent) from 1980 levels. Although all wildlife-oriented recreation is expected to increase at a slower rate than growth of the general population, an additional 19,238,000 nonconsumptive wildlife users is forecasted for the year 2000 relative to 1980 participation levels.

One of the fastest growing wildlife-related recreational activities in North America is bird-watching. In 1985, over 49.8 million adults participated in this activity in the United States alone (U.S. Fish and Wildlife Service 1988). In Canada, at least 13 percent of the population annually takes trips especially to observe, photograph, or study birds (Jacquemot and Filion 1987). Birding results in economic expenditures conservatively estimated to exceed $20 billion a year in North America (Hvenegaard, Butler, and Krystofiak 1989).

In this context, Glen Hvenegaard and his colleagues (1989) interviewed 603 randomly selected birders at Point Pelee National Park, Ontario—one of the premier locations in the world for observing the spring migration of songbirds—during the peak birding season in May 1987. They also interviewed representatives of 183 businesses in the

Figure 4.1. According to a U.S. Fish and Wildlife Service survey, 134.7 million Americans sixteen years of age and older observed, photographed, or fed fish or wildlife in 1985. (Photo by the author.)

Leamington community near Point Pelee, including virtually all the facilities and services that birders frequent during their stay.

Expenditures of birders at Point Pelee were estimated at $3.8 million for May and $5.4 million for all of 1987. During May, the average birder spent about $224 a trip, or $66 per day of birding at Point Pelee. Local expenditures reported by birders visiting the Leamington vicinity amounted to $2.1 million in May, and were estimated at $3.2 million for the whole year.

When asked, "What is the most your costs on this trip could have risen before deciding not to come birding at Point Pelee?" 75 percent of respondents said their expenses could have doubled. Responses to this hypothetical question were used to estimate the net economic value of a Point Pelee birding experience. The average was $256 per trip, or $76 a day, and totalled $4.1 million for May birding trips to Point Pelee or $6.3 million for 1987.

These researchers concluded that "the rapid expansion of bird watching and other forms of wildlife tourism throughout much of the world is making a substantial contribution in economic terms that we are only now beginning to measure. Such tangible benefits associated with parks and wildlife areas are providing sound incentives for protection of landscapes and species, especially when threats are derived from alternative resource uses that are traditionally measured in the marketplace."

Questionnaires are sometimes used to assess preferences for wildlife-related recreation by nonconsumptive users. One portion of a study of municipal conservation commissioners in Massachusetts sought to determine their preferences for nonconsumptive wildlife-related activities (Gray, Larson, and Braunhardt 1979). This survey population was selected for two reasons: first, there were no special qualifications for conservation commission membership, so members were thought to represent a cross section of concerned lay persons actively involved in positions of conservation authority and leadership at a local level; and second, it seemed likely that the preferences of commission members might be translated into land acquisition for wildlife habitat by the municipalities they represented. The findings of the study suggested that these persons, who represented the lay leadership of official conservation programs in a largely urban state, were most interested in activities related to viewing wildlife, hobby nature study, and wildlife photography (see Table 4.1).

Another part of this study examined the extent to which wildlife considerations actually influenced the acquisition of conservation land by the municipal conservation commissions surveyed. The findings indicated that land was acquired for a variety of reasons, but principally for general recreation and water quality. Despite their professed interest in wildlife, there was little evidence that conservation commission members used their authority to acquire conservation land specifically to preserve wildlife habitat.

Several provisions might enable local conservation commissions to function more effectively to preserve habitat for nonconsumptive wildlife-related recreation, as well as critical habitat areas for threatened species. Such provisions might include special training for commissioners, furnishing expert technical assistance, and eligibility criteria for the selection of commission members.

## SCIENTIFIC VALUE

In an environmental impact assessment, a knowledge of ecological relationships may allow field biologists to identify a species, or more often a set of species, that can serve as an ecological indicator to environmental conditions (Ward 1978).

Wildlife habitat evaluation is frequently based on the condition of individual animals that serve as indirect indicators of habitat quality. Physical characteristics, such as animal weight, antler size, amount of kidney fat, condition of the femur bone marrow, parasite levels, and

Table 4.1. Preferences among nonconsumptive wildlife-related activities by municipal conservation commissioners in Massachusetts in 1974.

| Rank | Activity | Preference score |
|---|---|---|
| 1 | Bird observation | 3.6 |
| 2 | Hobby nature study | 2.6 |
| 3 | Mammal observation | 2.5 |
| 4 | Wildlife photography | 1.3 |
| 5 | Amphibian and reptile observation | 0.9 |
| 6 | Bird study | 0.5 |
| 7 | Sketching or painting wildlife | 0.4 |
| 8 | Mammal study | 0.2 |
| 9 | Amphibian and reptile study | 0.1 |
| 10 | Hobby taxidermy | 0.1 |
| 11 | Other[a] | 3.9 |

Source: Reprinted by permission of the publishers from "Urban Conservation Leadership and the Wildlife Resource" by Gary G. Gray, Joseph S. Larson, and Denise A. Braunhardt, *Urban Ecology,* 4 (May 1979): 3. © by Elsevier Science Publishers.

[a] This category represents the combined total for all other activities respondents listed.

assays of blood samples, reveal an animal's nutritional condition and indirectly indicate habitat quality (see Shaw 1985).

Radionuclides and persistent insecticides, such as DDT and dieldrin, do not break down quickly into relatively harmless by-products. Therefore, these substances may enter ecological cycles, be distributed throughout ecosystems, and concentrate in the tissues of animals at the top of food chains (Woodwell 1967). Pesticides affect wildlife populations by depressing reproductive performance and reducing survival. Peregrine falcons became endangered largely because of reproductive problems, especially reduced eggshell thickness, caused by ingestion of DDT; Hickey and Anderson (1968) showed that weights of peregrine eggshells in some parts of North America declined as much as 26 percent after DDT use became widespread. The use of selected wildlife species—particularly raptors and other predators at the top of food chains—to monitor environmental conditions may alert us to environmental problems before they become insolvable.

The pursuit of knowledge about wildlife often generates information of direct use to humans; for example, studies of the sea urchin helped us comprehend human embryological development; a desert toad has been used for the early determination of pregnancy; the rhesus monkey has contributed to our understanding of human blood groups; deer antlers have provided a means for measuring radioactive contamination of natural environments; the armadillo furnishes us with an animal model for studies of leprosy (Dasmann 1981). The list of wildlife's scientific values is long and impressive.

Currently, one of the fundamental wildlife and conservation problems is the loss of biodiversity. Biodiversity refers to "the variety of the world's organisms, including their genetic diversity and the assemblages they form" (Reid and Miller 1989). We can think of biodiversity as a general term for the natural biological wealth that underlies human life and well-being. Perhaps one-quarter of all species present in the mideighties may be extinct by 2015 or soon thereafter (Raven 1988). Species of known value, and others having potential future value, for foods, medicines, or industrial products are rapidly disappearing.

Patterns of species distribution show that closed tropical forests, those with a continuous tree canopy, apparently contain over half the world's species although they cover only 7 percent of the land surface (Reid and Miller 1989). These species are particularly vulnerable in developing countries where economic development is predicated on destruction of tropical forests. Yet, even the United States has caused direct destruction of tropical forests in Hawaii, where they have been sacrificed for pineapple and sugarcane plantations and geothermal development.

## EDUCATIONAL VALUE

People have been captivated by the "awesome beauty and intriguing nature of wildlife" throughout the ages. This is no less true in today's mass media world as evidenced by the "enduring popularity of such television programs as 'Wild Kingdom'. . . and countless other wildlife documentaries" (Hair and Pomerantz 1987). There is a nineteenth-century precedent for this public interest in mass media representations of wildlife: the subscriptions Alexander Wilson and John Audubon each sold for their respective series of volumes portraying American birds.

The fascination people have for wildlife is especially valuable because it fosters a consideration of the natural world. Conservation organizations concerned with public education use the attraction of wildlife, through such magazines as *National Wildlife,* as a vehicle for exposing readers to articles on natural resource conservation and a wide range of environmental problems, such as air and water pollution, soil erosion, and toxic wastes (Hair and Pomerantz 1987).

Two different studies indicated that reading wildlife magazines increased the environmental knowledge of young people. Fifth-grade students had a greater knowledge of animals, plants, and ecological concepts after a three-month exposure to *Ranger Rick* (a children's nature magazine published by the National Wildlife Federation) (Pomerantz 1985); and ninth-graders who read *National Wildlife* magazine demonstrated a greater understanding of the marine environment than those who did not (Fortner and Mayer 1983).

Most children who read *Ranger Rick* magazine indicated that they were mainly interested in the animal stories, but subscribers had more positive conservation attitudes than nonsubscribers. Obviously, children learned more from reading the magazine than just information about wildlife. "The broader educational value of *Ranger Rick* was also shown by the fact that 76 percent of the subscribers who responded to a national survey indicated *Ranger Rick* helped them with their schoolwork" (Pomerantz 1985).

The educational value of wildlife is that wildlife can teach us more than just facts about animals. Wildlife can create interest in—and motivation to act—on broader environmental problems (Hair and Pomerantz 1987). The earliest education was a wildlife-related environmental education: the survival of prehistoric humans depended upon their understanding of the environment (LaHart and Tillis 1974). The human-wildlife relationship is deeply ingrained in all societies. The secret sign of the early Christians, for example, was not a cross; it was a fish. Today, wildlife is perhaps the most universal symbol for the environment (Schoenfeld 1978). "The ultimate purpose of wildlife conservation . . . is more than a concern for wildlife per se. Exposure to wildlife can be a doorway to ecological understanding. Conserving wildlife demonstrates the totality of our relationships with people and land" (Schoenfeld 1978:483).

## AESTHETIC VALUE

"Subsistence and commercial uses of wildlife were long taken for granted, and exploiting them required no particular philosophic insight. . . . Yet, from the first, professionals in the field have agreed with unusual consistency: The greatest significance of wild living things is aesthetic or environmental rather than exploitative" (Allen 1978).

Holmes Rolston III (1986) described four ways in which wildlife is valued aesthetically. First, wild lives are spontaneous form in motion. Unlike art in museums or a scenic vista, animals move. Their movements are self-actuated and spontaneous—not the motion of wildflowers swaying in the breeze nor the programmed action of most performing arts. There is a rhythmic beauty in the symmetrical dy-

Figure 4.2. Aesthetic aspects of wildlife have been recognized by virtually all cultures throughout history. This bronze poletop from Mongolia, sixth-fifth century B.C., features the likeness of an antelope or, more likely, an ibex. (Mongolian, Ordos Steppe region, Poletop with Antelope [Ibex?], bronze, 6th-5th century B.C., ht.: 17.7 x w.: 9.5 cm, Lucy Maud Buckingham Collection, 1937.326. Photograph by Robert Hashimoto. Photograph © 1991, The Art Institute of Chicago. All Rights Reserved.)

namics of a gazelle on the run, an eagle in flight, or a slithering snake. There is an air of anticipation at the redtail hawk perched high on a limb or the fox investigating a scent in the meadow. There is surprise at the unexpected encounter with a bobcat in the hollow. Pets or zoo animals can never replace the aesthetic experience of wildlife: their motion has been captured and tamed. Agricultural environments offer less pleasure than wilderness—a cow is never as exciting as a deer—but small woodlots and overgrown fencerows enrich the rural landscape with the movements of rabbits and bobwhites. The spontaneous motion of wildlife stirs human emotions and raises our quality of life.

Second, wild animals are kindred yet alien sentient life. Mountains and rivers are objects, and even the pines and oaks lack sentience; but higher animals are subjects—there is a "somebody" behind the fur or feathers. I see the bighorn and the bighorn also sees me. This sets up a reciprocity that heightens the aesthetic experience. The chipmunk scratches; the mallard dozes in the sun; the jay defends its territory; the plover deceives a predator with its "broken wing" act. Humans know analogues of these experiences, so there is a kinship. Yet, the lives of wild creatures are wild, spontaneous, and beyond complete human management. "They have subtleties of cognition and decision that humans do not, as when by echolocation a bat recognizes its own sonar and sees a mosquito with it. . . . One form of life [namely, human beings] seeks to understand another, and this transvaluing brings aesthetic richness and creativity" (Rolston 1986).

Third, wild animals struggle to actualize their potential. There is a struggle behind the motion and the sentience. A wild animal's freedom entails the possibility of success or failure in coping with its environment. A scenic vista cannot fail because nothing is attempted, but a wild animal can be better or worse off than others of its kind. The bull elk with a large rack, an adult bald eagle, and the full-curl ram all excite us more than immatures of their species. They are commanding because each has succeeded in making the ideal real. Perhaps admirers of wildlife do, as a critic might charge, overlook as much as they see—the bison that are shedding and dirty, the hawk with missing feathers, the diseased and scarred marmot. "Every wild life is marred by the rips and tears of time and eventually destroyed by them. But none of the losers and seldom even the blemished show up on the covers of *National Wildlife* or in the Audubon guides." Still, our aesthetic appreciation need not be limited only to the successful or the ideal. "The admirer of wildlife can enjoy the conflict and resolution in the concrete particular expression of an individual life. The weatherbeaten elk are not ugly, not unless endurance is incompetence." If we accept nature on its own terms, the genetic code for each species is carried out in the struggle for life, "and this is heroic and exciting even in its failures. The struggle between ideal and real adds to the aesthetic experience" (Rolston 1986).

Fourth, wild lives are used as symbols in human culture. The bald eagle is portrayed in the presidential seal and expresses "freedom, power, grace, lofty alertness." States have also adopted animal symbols; for instance, Colorado has selected the bighorn sheep. The names of sports teams are often those of animals (Wolf Pack, Falcons, Rams), as are the model names of automobiles (Cougar, Skylark, Rabbit). "We elevate into symbolism something of the competence, the integrity, the character of the wild life." Wild lives also lend to our mobile, rootless culture a sense of attachment to landscape, locale, and place. Even when the human environment displaces the natural one, we assign place names that evoke memories of the natural world. "We name a street Mockingbird Lane, or a summer home is more romantic if it lies up Fox Hollow." And wild lives add interest and diversity to human culture—in the Audubon calendar on the kitchen wall or the butterfly pattern in the curtains, in the painting of a hunting scene on the executive's office wall, and the yard landscaped to attract cardinals and squirrels. Wild lives have value as decoration, and for the color and interest the animals themselves provide, but there is also a symbolic meaning: "Wild lives can become symbols of characteristics we value in our human lives" (Rolston 1986).

After pondering the mating dance of the woodcock, Aldo Leopold concluded, "The woodcock is a living refutation of the theory that the utility of a game bird is to serve as a target, or to pose gracefully on a slice of toast. No one would rather hunt woodcock in October than I, but since learning of the sky dance I find myself calling one or two birds enough. I must be sure that, come April, there will be no dearth of dancers in the sunset sky" (1949:34). As much as wild lives have sustained human material needs and economic interests, we can now admit without embarrassment that wildlife is most meaningful when it nurtures the human spirit.

## ECOLOGICAL VALUE

Basic ecological processes involve all organisms—plants, animals, fungi, protists, and bacteria. Although wildlife is the most conspicuous form of animal life, it probably comprises much less than 1 percent of the biomass—the total weight of all living material—in most ecosystems. Its presence is nonetheless critical; for example, Grant (1974) concluded that the functional role of small mammals in grassland ecosystems is to regulate the rate of mineral cycling. Wildlife has innumerable other ecological values—pollination of plants (by hummingbirds, fruit-eating bats, and other small nectivorous mammals); dispersal of seeds and other plant propagules (by many birds and mammals); assistance with germination (by mammals gnawing hard-shelled seeds or the passage of seeds through digestive tracts of mammals or birds); enhancing soil aeration and fertility (by tunneling rodents and larger burrowing mammals) (Talbot 1987).

The loss of biodiversity also affects many ecosystem "services," including such processes as the regulation of water discharge and the absorption and breakdown of pollutants, which are being compromised as ecosystems lose component species and natural habitats are converted to other land uses (Reid and Miller 1989). Even the earth's basic biogeochemical cycles, which circulate water, oxygen, carbon dioxide, and nutrients to living organisms, are being affected.

The stability of whole biotic communities may depend upon the activities of a single critical, or keystone (Krebs 1988), species: digging by East African elephants and American alligators exposes or maintains water holes that support many species during dry seasons; dam building by beavers restores degraded wetland habitats by dispersing the water and current (thus controlling erosion and sedimentation and raising the water table), with rapid and favorable responses by vegetation and other wildlife (Apple 1985); and sea otter predation on Aleutian Island sea urchins apparently controls sea urchin numbers and prevents them from destroying kelp beds that support much other marine life (Estes, Smith, and Palmisano 1978; Estes, Jamieson, and Rodes 1982).

## NEGATIVE VALUES

When considering wildlife values the natural presumption is to think of all such values as being positive. Many, in fact, are not. Negative economic values include "the costs of wildlife damages to crops and other property and the costs of controlling those damages. Where these values can be expressed in dollars, they should be subtracted from the total commercial and recreational value of the wildlife resource" (Bailey 1984:43). Other examples include browsing or gnawing that kills seedling trees, consumption of orchard fruit and damage to trees, consumption and fouling of standing or stored agricultural crops and livestock forage, nuisance noise and concentrations of feces, predation on livestock, and the costs of labor and materials needed to avert or control these damages (Bailey 1984).

Most wildlife problems resulting in negative values have an economic component, but these problems are not limited to the monetary cost of damage control or replacement. Other problems were noted by Smith (1974) and include *structural damage* due to rodents gnawing on telephone cables or dwellings and woodpeckers damaging house siding and utility poles; *ornamental plant and landscape damage* caused by mole tunnels, rodents and lagomorphs girdling trees, and wildfowl droppings on lawns and beaches; *aesthetic degradation* of urban environments by rats and pigeons and the maddening noise and putrid odor often produced by concentrations of roosting birds; *human safety problems* caused by alligators in Florida backyards, coyotes in suburban Los Angeles, and deer-vehicle collisions virtually everywhere; and *disease transmission* of sylvatic zoonoses—infections naturally transmitted between wild animals and humans—including viral infections such as rabies and Colorado tick fever, rickettsial infections like Rocky Mountain spotted fever, bacterial infections such as anthrax and plague, fungal infections like ringworm, protozoan infections such as toxoplasmosis, helminth infections including hydatid disease and trichinosis, and arthropod infections like scabies, to name only a few of the best known and most common maladies.

In addition, wildlife are frequently responsible for accidents involving humans. In the spring of 1912, Cal Rogers became the first person reported killed in an aircraft crash caused by a bird (Solman 1974). There have been numerous others since. One of the most spectacular occurred when a flock of starlings rose in front of an aircraft climbing after take-off from Boston's Logan Airport in 1960. The resulting crash killed more than sixty people (Solman 1974).

Ever-growing multitudes of humans continue to encroach on wildlife habitat and interact with wild animals in ways that cause problems or conflicts. From a human perspective these interactions constitute negative values of wildlife.

## DEFINING SOCIAL VALUES

Throughout this chapter the term *values* has been used as if its meaning is clear. In fact, there is considerable ambiguity attached to the word (Shaw and Zube 1980; Steinhoff 1980). Two meanings were distinguished by Steinhoff (1980): "an attitude which results in the value of a thing," and "its worth in relation to other things"—what might be called attitudinal value and comparative value, respectively. These have also been called "held value" and "assigned value" (Brown 1984).

Another usage of *value* has to do with the relative importance of values. Clearly, people differ in the relative importance they place on various values (Brown and Manfredo 1987). To some, a parcel of land would be more important in its natural state as a seasonal wetland; to others, the same land would be more valuable as cultivated farmland.

A third kind of values is intrinsic. They are not assigned by humans, but rather are inherent in things or in relationships (Rolston 1983). Ecological values, for example, exist "apart from human experience." They "are independent of human perception and preference," and are therefore only relevant to a consideration of social values "when humans incorporate them into their preference realm" (Brown and Manfredo 1987:13–14).

Economic values aside, we can identify four kinds of social values: *cultural* ("about the ideas and thoughts that make up a culture"), *societal* ("relating to social relationships among people"), *psychological* ("perceived to enhance personal well-being"), and *physiological* (related "to improving health and functioning of the human body") (Brown and Manfredo 1987:15–16).

Each of these kinds of social values can, or does, have some relation to wildlife—cultural value because wildlife could be given moral and legal standing, and human actions regulated accordingly; social value because family togetherness, fostered through wildlife-related recreation, might be considered beneficial; psychological value because studying wildlife presumably leads to greater knowledge of the natural world, which is usually considered worthwhile; and physiological value because wildlife-related outdoor pursuits are thought to enhance health through exercise and reduction of stress (Brown and Manfredo 1987).

Economic valuation of wildlife is limiting because the array of relevant attitudinal values is not ordinarily represented. Therefore, noneconomic valuation is important in wildlife and resource planning. The issue of attitudinal, or held, values is directly relevant to goal-setting processes—because what we want is often based on attitudinal values, which imply goodness (Bambi deer) or badness (wily wolf)—and may be instrumental in setting funding or management priorities. Valuation of wildlife is rudimentary at best, and much additional effort is needed to clarify how and what we should value in wildlife (Brown and Manfredo 1987).

PERSPECTIVE

## A Crosswise Look at Species Valuation: What Good Are Humans, Anyway?

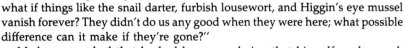

In his natural history of the Mississippi River, John Madson (1985) wrote about a bivalve called the Higgin's eye pearly mussel. The Higgin's eye seems to prefer deeper parts of large rivers where turbulence and oxygen content are both high, and this endangered species is apparently found only in the drainage of the upper Mississippi north of the mouth of the Missouri.

A reader of Madson's local newspaper wrote to the editor expressing a common view: "So what if things like the snail darter, furbish lousewort, and Higgin's eye mussel vanish forever? They didn't do us any good when they were here; what possible difference can it make if they're gone?"

Madson remarked that he had been wondering that himself, and mused: "But then, what is modern man good for? Of all earth's creatures he is unique in not being good for anything. He is equally unique in being bad for almost everything. No other critter can make that claim. The sad truth is, our lovely little planet can no longer afford us. We are Earth's only bad habit, one that started out harmless enough a few million years back, but which has become a major vice" (99).

The Higgin's eye mussel, on the other hand, really is useful. It "helps stabilize the streambed in which it lives; it filters and clarifies water that passes through it, straining out suspended materials and converting tiny organisms to tissue that can be used, in turn, by such higher forms as fish, otters, muskrats, waterfowl, and crawdads. I can't do those things; I tear at the riverbeds, poison the food chain, and corrupt the waters that sustain me. All that is bad enough. But the real blow to my lordly pride is the knowledge that while the mussel can make a pearl, the best I can do is gallstones" (100).

We often ask, with respect to other species, "What good are they, anyway?" as though the absence of a prompt and satisfactory answer is sufficient reason to justify our extinguishing a life-form with an evolutionary lineage more ancient than our own. Can anyone looking at a crowded suburban shopping mall on a Saturday afternoon really explain the value of human hordes that have buried productive prairies, forests, and wetlands under a mantle of concrete? From an ecosystem perspective, "What good are humans, anyway?"

---

## SUGGESTED READING

Swift, E. F. 1967. *A Conservation Saga.* Washington, D.C.: National Wildlife Federation. 264 pages. The observations and opinions of one who has seen and lived it all, from backwoods conservation warden in the Roaring Twenties to respected wildlife administrator, and whose career was devoted to promoting the wise use and management of natural resources.

Thomas, K. 1983. *Man and the Natural World: A History of the Modern Sensibility.* New York: Pantheon Books. 426 pages. Provides a background for our present-day concern about human relationships with wild nature by tracing the changes, between 1500 and 1800, "in the way in which men and women, at all social levels, perceived and classified the natural world around them."

# Attitudes and Preferences for Wildlife

# 5

The previous two chapters considered the value and importance of wildlife for a variety of economic, social-psychological, and biological purposes. In fact, the question of wildlife's value is moot: life itself would not be possible without the complex interactions of matter and energy of which wildlife is an integral part. Yet even this most basic wildlife value seems to be beyond the comprehension of the majority of people. Apparently most members of society have little concern for more than a few species, doubt that wild animals are really related to human well-being, and are skeptical about the range of values claimed for wildlife (Kellert 1987).

## DEVELOPMENT OF WILDLIFE ATTITUDES

In a discussion of childhood education about wildlife and environmental topics, Hair and Pomerantz (1987) traced the development of attitudes toward wildlife. This section is largely based on their comments.

Some researchers contend that the foundations of attitudes toward the environment are laid during early childhood (Miller 1975) and that attitudes, preferences, beliefs, and values developed during youth govern human behavior throughout adult life (More 1977). Other studies strongly suggest that early childhood is a critical period in the development of cognitive abilities for environmental knowledge (Chemers and Altman 1977).

According to Moore, from about eight to twelve years of age "children have their deepest and most extensive relationships with the outdoors," and "interaction with nature on a large scale reaches its highest level of behavioral significance" (1977:208). To a large extent, these interactions are reinforced by books and stories that emphasize personal relationships between young persons and animals, many of which attribute human qualities and characteristics to animals. There is no evidence that this anthropomorphization of animals leads to misconceptions about animals and the natural world. Indeed, subscribers to the National Wildlife Federation's *Ranger Rick* children's magazine had more realistic perceptions of animal behavior than youngsters who did not read the magazine (Pomerantz 1985).

To further understand the development of children's perceptions of the environment, Rejeski (1982) used an approach based on Piaget's stages of cognitive development in children (Ripple, Biehler, and Jaquish 1982). Rejeski concluded that children are not able to discern the effect of human actions on the environment until age nine or ten, and they do not begin to understand ecosystem concepts until they are thirteen or fourteen.

Rejeski's findings were corroborated by Kellert and Westervelt (1983), who showed that children ages seven to ten (grades two to five) were the least informed about animals, and the most exploitive toward them, of three age groups studied. From age ten to thirteen (grades five to eight), children's factual knowledge of animals increased dramatically. Adolescents thirteen to sixteen years old (grades eight to eleven) were more interested in animals for ecological, moral, and naturalistic reasons.

Thus, the middle group seems to provide the greatest opportunity for imparting knowledge about the environment. Environmental educators need to be aware of these findings and target this age group for educational programs that encourage young people to assess environmental situations objectively and develop skills for dealing with environmental problems (Hair and Pomerantz 1987).

In present-day urban society, children often have their first contact with wildlife through children's books. Since these books are sold in the marketplace, Thomas More (1977, 1979b) thought that the number of books about a specific animal might be an indicator of that animal's popularity. Therefore, he categorized children's stories about animals using the title index of *Children's Books in Print.* Individual animals were grouped by scientific classification, and the entire animal kingdom was covered (so no distinction was made between domestic animals and wildlife). He found that 13 percent of the children's books in print in 1972 included the name of one or more animals in the title. More than 62 percent of the animals mentioned in the titles were mammals, with birds accounting for another 18 percent. Horses, dogs, and cats were mentioned most often in titles, with bears being the wild animal most often listed. A list of the twenty-five animals most often appearing in book titles included such diverse creatures as ants, bees, baboons, frogs, mice, owls, turtles, and whales. In conclusion, More (1977, 1979b) suggested that wildlife professionals should communicate with librarians and educators so that children are better able to understand wildlife and have realistic impressions of them.

Our current environmental leaders are proof of the impact of early and repeated exposure to the natural world. A survey of the early life experiences of today's environmental leaders indicated that thirty of the forty-five who responded vividly recalled outdoor experiences as a major factor influencing their choice of professions (Tanner 1980).

## THE WILDLIFE ATTITUDE AND VALUES SCALE: USING VALUES INFORMATION IN MANAGEMENT

A Wildlife Attitudes and Values Scale (WAVS) was developed by human dimensions researchers at Cornell University to gather data about social values of wildlife not related to economics. Their goal was to develop a standardized measure of values that could be incorporated into a variety of questionnaires, would be relevant to various management issues and audiences, and would provide useful information to wildlife managers (Purdy and Decker 1989).

People's attitudes were selected as the basis of measurement for the WAVS because they were thought to be indicators of broadly integrated feelings, beliefs, and values held by individuals (Kellert 1980b). The researchers believed that this type of values assessment would be most useful to wildlife personnel in New York, and would be most applicable to the issues and audiences for which they anticipated using the scale. The scale was tested in mail surveys of public attitudes toward wildlife in which respondents were asked to rate the importance of each attitude statement on a five-point scale from strongly agree to strongly disagree. Results suggested three broad groups of attitudes: traditional-conservation attitudes, societal-benefits attitudes, and problem-acceptance attitudes (Purdy and Decker 1989).

*Traditional-conservation attitudes* were related to statements about whether respondents felt it was important to them personally to hunt game animals for recreation, to hunt game animals for food, to trap for the sale of furs or pelts, to have game animals managed for an annual harvest without harming the future of the population, and to have local economies benefit from the sale of goods and services related to wildlife recreation. *Societal-benefits attitudes* were related to statements about whether respondents felt it was important to them personally to talk about wildlife with family and friends, to observe or photograph wildlife, to see representations of wildlife (in books, movies, paintings, or photos), to express opinions about wildlife and management of wildlife to public officials or officers of private conservation organizations, to appreciate wildlife's role in the natural environment, to have wildlife included in educational materials related to nature, to know that wildlife exists in nature, to consider the presence of wildlife as a sign of environmental quality, and to understand more about the behavior of wildlife. *Problem-acceptance attitudes* were related to statements about whether respondents felt it was important to them personally to tolerate most levels of property damage by wildlife, to tolerate most wildlife nuisance problems, to tolerate the ordinary personal safety hazards associated with some wildlife, and to tolerate the ordinary risk of disease transmission from wildlife to humans or domestic animals (Purdy and Decker 1989).

The scale was subsequently used to assess the wildlife values of almost seven thousand people representing ten separate audiences. Factor analysis was used to determine which statements were associated with each of the attitude groups identified in the earlier studies. In general, statements that were expected to characterize those groups did so at least 70 percent of the time. In over half of the studies, however, statements related to societal-benefits attitudes were better explained by introducing two subgroups distinguishing *social-significance* and *ecological-significance* components (Purdy and Decker 1989).

Several studies showed how the Wildlife Attitudes and Values Scale can be used. In one, Decker and Gavin (1987) looked at the attitudes and experiences of residential property owners in the vicinity of Seatuck National Wildlife Refuge on Long Island with respect to a small herd of deer that moves between the refuge and neighboring residential properties. Property owners were asked to complete the WAVS as part of a mail-questionnaire survey. Responses indicated that residents having contact with the deer herd generally expressed positive attitudes about the presence of deer in their neighborhood; the majority enjoyed the deer and considered them an aesthetic resource. Although residents' enthusiasm for deer was tempered by deer damage to ornamental plantings and gardens and concerns about Lyme disease (transmitted by the deer tick) nearly three-quarters of the residents surveyed wanted deer numbers in the neighborhood maintained at current levels or increased.

Residents who were concerned about plant damage and Lyme disease were more likely to want fewer deer, suggesting that if such concerns became widespread the preference might favor a decrease in deer numbers. This could present wildlife management personnel with a problem, since Islip residents generally had a negative view of hunting.

Thus, a nontraditional approach to deer population management, or an effective educational effort preceding a hunt, would probably be necessary if deer numbers ever had to be reduced.

The Wildlife Attitude and Values Scale was also used in surveys of 1978 and 1983 graduates of New York's Hunter Training Course to help understand how wildlife values are related to people's reasons for hunting. Findings showed that hunters consistently emphasized societal-benefits values over values related to traditional conservation. Thus, labeling hunters' values of wildlife solely as "consumptive" was considered simplistic and misleading. Hunters' positive attitudes about the ecological and social significance of wildlife illustrated the importance of their nonconsumptive interests and might provide a basis for expanded programs that would benefit both hunters and nonhunters (Connelly, Deckers, and Brown 1985).

## A TYPOLOGY OF WILDLIFE ATTITUDES

A typology, or classification, of attitudes toward animals was developed by Kellert (1980a) to study wildlife values from a conceptual and methodological approach. His study uncovered numerous pieces of information about human interactions with wildlife. One major purpose was to better understand competing wildlife values in the United States and to get a better idea of attitudes toward animal-related conflicts.

The attitudes Kellert identified "primarily describe basic perceptions rather than behaviors." Furthermore, he cautioned that attitudes not be associated with individuals—that is, "attitudes may describe elements of a person's perception, but rarely will all of an individual's actions be explained by just one attitude" (32). Finally, attitudes may change over time as persons experience different life situations, but there is a certain amount of attitude stability in nearly everyone.

This typology of wildlife attitudes was initially developed from analyzing responses from open-ended interviews with a group of individuals directly involved with animals. The group was rather small, but represented a wide range of people. The typology was modified during a later study of national attitudes toward animals. The ten attitudes toward animals he identified are briefly defined and described in Table 5.1.

## ATTITUDES TOWARD WILDLIFE

In a later study, sponsored by the U.S. Fish and Wildlife Service, numerical scales were developed—based on a total of sixty-five questions—for each of the ten attitudes distinguished in the typology of

Table 5.1. A typology of attitudes toward animals.

| Attitude | Brief description |
|---|---|
| Naturalistic | Primary interest in wildlife and the outdoors; animals provide context and meaning for activities in natural settings |
| Ecologistic | Primary concern for the environment as a system; emphasis on wildlife interactions with other species and the ecosystem |
| Humanistic | Primary interest and affection for individual animals, especially pets; wildlife focus on large, attractive animals |
| Moralistic | Primary concern for ethically correct treatment of animals; strongly opposes exploitation of and cruelty toward animals |
| Scientistic | Primary interest in studying and/or observing the physical attributes and biological functioning of animals |
| Aesthetic | Primary interest in artistic and symbolic features of animals |
| Utilitarian | Primary concern for practical and material values of animals |
| Dominionistic | Primary satisfactions derived from mastery and control over animals, typically in a sporting context (such as hunting) |
| Negativistic | Primary orientation is an active avoidance of animals due to fear or dislike |
| Neutralistic | Primary orientation is a passive avoidance of animals due to indifference |

Source: Kellert 1980a, 1980b.

attitudes toward animals. For some items, respondents were able to indicate the strength of their response (for example, strongly versus slightly agree/disagree) to a question. Thus, the smallest scale (ecologistic) consisted of four questions with scale values ranging from 0 to 11, whereas the largest scale (utilitarian) was made up of thirteen questions with scale values from 0 to 27.

The relative frequency of attitudes was assessed in a national survey by first standardizing the scale score distribution frequencies for each attitude and then using the resulting frequency curves and regression figures to estimate the relative "popularity" of each attitude. A particular score on one attitude scale cannot be equated with a similar score on another scale. Nevertheless, the procedure yielded a rough indication of the relative frequency of a particular attitude in the American population. The estimated proportion of the population strongly oriented toward each of these attitudes is indicated in Table 5.2.

The results of this survey suggest that the most common attitudes toward animals held by Americans are the humanistic, moralistic, utilitarian, and neutralistic. These attitudes can be subsumed under two broad—and conflicting—perceptions of animals. The first is a clash of the moralistic and utilitarian attitudes around the theme of "human

Table 5.2. Attitudes toward wildlife by Americans based on a 1978 survey.

| Attitude | Strongly oriented toward (est. %)[a] | Common behavioral expressions |
|---|---|---|
| Naturalistic | 10 | Backpacking, nature study, sport hunting |
| Ecologistic | 7 | Ecological study, conservation activism |
| Humanistic | 35 | Pet ownership, casual zoo visitation |
| Moralistic | 20 | Animal welfare organization memberships |
| Scientistic | 1 | Scientific study, hobby nature study |
| Aesthetic | 15 | Nature appreciation, collecting wildlife art |
| Utilitarian | 20 | Meat hunting, trapping |
| Dominionistic | 3 | Trophy hunting, animal spectator sports |
| Negativistic | 2 | Animal cruelty, fear of animals |
| Neutralistic | 35 | Avoidance of animals |

Source: Kellert 1980b, table 1.

[a] Totals more than 100 percent because persons can be strongly oriented toward more than one attitude.

exploitation of animals," with the moralistic attitude opposing exploitive uses of animals involving presumed suffering and death (including hunting, trapping, and whaling) and the utilitarian endorsing such uses if there is a significant benefit to humans. The other perception of animals is a conflict of the neutralistic and humanistic attitudes around the theme of "affection for animals." The neutralistic attitude is characterized by an avoidance of animals while the humanistic is associated with an intense emotional attachment to them (Kellert 1980a, 1980b).

Attitudes were examined for a number of demographic groups (age, gender, education, income, etc.) and animal activity groups (hunters, bird-watchers, backpackers, zoo visitors, etc.) in American society. The group that ranked highest and lowest on each attitude scale is indicated in Table 5.3, and the animal activity group ranking highest and lowest on each attitude scale is shown in Table 5.4.

Several findings of Kellert's study seem particularly notable. Alaska residents ranked high on the naturalistic and ecologistic scales but ranked low on the utilitarian scale. This suggests that they may be more concerned with protecting wildlife and natural habitats than the news media often implies with its concentration on Native American subsistence hunting. Attending zoos may be more of a recreational outlet than a reflection of an interest in wildlife conservation because of the relatively low ranking of zoo visitors on the ecologistic scale. Bird-watchers ranked low on the humanistic scale, which implies that they are not interested in individual animals or in a personal relationship with animals. People with a scientific interest in animals ranked

Table 5.3. Attitude toward wildlife by demographic group based on a 1978 survey.

| Attitude | Demographic group with Highest rank (score[a]) | Demographic group with Lowest rank (score[a]) |
|---|---|---|
| Naturalistic | Alaska residence (4.6) | Less than 6th grade (1.2) |
| Ecologistic | Ph.D. education (5.3) | Less than 6th grade (2.2) |
| Humanistic | Age 18–25 (4.8) | Less than 6th grade (2.3) |
| Moralistic | Pacific region (7.5) | Less than 500 population (3.2) |
| Scientistic | Ph.D. education (1.9) | Less than 6th grade; age 75+ years (0.4) |
| Aesthetic | — | — |
| Utilitarian | Farming (8.5) | Ph.D. education (3.8) |
| Dominionistic | Farming; Law/M.D. (2.7) | Pacific; Ph.D.; female (1.5) |
| Negativistic | Less than 6th grade (6.4) | Ph.D. education (2.2) |
| Neutralistic | — | — |

Source: Kellert 1980b.
[a] All scores are approximate as estimated from graphs.

high on the moralistic scale. Despite some media portrayals and the opinions of some animal-rights activists this finding suggests that these people believe that the animals they study should be treated properly. Kellert found that having a high income and having an advanced education do not necessarily lead to the same perception of animals. Persons with high incomes ranked high on the dominionistic scale, though those with advanced educations ranked low even though both groups scored similarly on other scales. Those opposed to hunting ranked high on the negativistic scale, suggesting that they were more concerned with the ethical treatment of animals than with any genuine interest in animals.

Research findings on attitudes toward wildlife based on Kellert's (1980a, 1980b, 1987) studies can be summarized in a few main points: (1) the general public could not easily recognize or understand most philosophical, educational, economic, or ecological values of wildlife; (2) the general public responded more favorably toward mammals or other culturally important vertebrate species and toward those invertebrates, such as butterflies and bees, that were considered attractive or useful; and (3) data on changing attitudes toward wildlife from 1900 to 1975 indicated a decline in utilitarian and negativistic attitudes, although these views are still common among lower socioeconomic, elderly, rural, and natural resource–dependent groups.

Despite the results of the study Kellert warned that these attitudes refer only "to broadly integrated feelings, beliefs and values possessed

Table 5.4. Attitudes toward wildlife by animal activity group based on a 1978 survey.

| Attitude | Animal activity group Highest rank (score[a]) | Lowest rank (score[a]) |
|---|---|---|
| Naturalistic | Nature hunters (8.5) | General population (3.0) |
| Ecologistic | Environment protection organization member (7.7) | General population (3.0) |
| Humanistic | Humane Society member (6.0) | Livestock raisers (3.1) |
| Moralistic | Environment protection organization member (9.6) | Sport/recreational hunters (2.9) |
| Scientistic | Scientific study (2.7) | General population (0.9) |
| Aesthetic | — | — |
| Utilitarian | Livestock raisers (7.2) | Environment protection organization member (1.6) |
| Dominionistic | Sport/recreational hunters sportsmen organization member (4.1) | Humane Society member (0.9) |
| Negativistic | Livestock raisers (4.5) | Environment protection organization member (2.2) |
| Neutralistic | — | — |

Source: Kellert 1980b.
[a] All scores are approximate as estimated from graphs.

by individuals" (1980b:31). We should remember that since attitudes refer to feelings and beliefs, they are not necessarily consistent with an individual's behavior.

Several other studies on attitudes toward wildlife were published during the 1980s. In one, public attitudes toward urban wildlife in Guelph, Ontario, were surveyed by means of responses to twenty-four wildlife-related questions on an Urban Wildlife and Aquatic Resources questionnaire administered during personal interviews in 1977 (Gilbert 1982). Principal findings of the survey indicated that most people obtained their information about wildlife from television, few knew the federal or provincial agencies responsible for wildlife management, and almost half of those interviewed were willing to subsidize wildlife conservation in the city by means of a special municipal tax. Furthermore, few wildlife species (or their signs) could be identified by over half of those surveyed; most people considered amphibians, reptiles, and invertebrates to be wildlife; and most could not relate habitat conditions to resident wildlife. In conclusion, Gilbert (1982) suggested that wildlife appeared to have a wider definition in the public view than that used by many wildlife professionals. Consequently, a more

Figure 5.1. Human attitudes influence actions, including financial support of wildlife conservation. The cardinal (*Richmondena cardinalis*) has been used as a logo to encourage Illinois residents to donate part of their state income tax refund to nongame programs of the state's Department of Conservation. (From the proceedings of the conference "Priorities for the Nongame Wildlife Conservation Fund," Dec. 3, 1983, Sangamon State University, Springfield, Ill.)

holistic, rather than a species-oriented approach, might find a receptive public audience. In addition, since there was significant interest in supporting urban-oriented wildlife programs through municipal planning or taxation, wildlife professionals should address these issues more aggressively.

Another study examined public attitudes toward a small, newly established wolf population in Montana using hunter responses and resident responses to a forty-seven-item questionnaire (Tucker and Pletscher 1989). Attitudes toward the idea of wolf recovery were generally favorable, with 72 percent of the local residents and 58 percent of persons who hunt in the area hoping that wolves would continue to inhabit the vicinity of the Flathead River's North Fork and be allowed to expand their range. Most respondents did not consider wolves a threat to human safety, and many (52 percent of residents and 41 percent of hunters) did not consider them a threat to livestock, even for ranches in wolf-occupied areas. Most hunters who had an opinion thought that the Endangered Species Act is too inflexible to properly manage wolves and their prey, whereas residents were evenly split on this issue. In general, respondents were unwilling to subordinate other human commercial or recreational uses of the area to wolf recovery. Hunters and residents of occupied wolf range were considered to have the potential for greater impact on wolf recovery than the general public. The study suggested that providing current information about wolves through channels most likely to reach hunters and residents, especially magazine and newspaper articles, will contribute to wolf recovery in the Rocky Mountains.

One final example is worth considering because it compared the attitudes of natural resource managers with those of the public. Members of five groups in Virginia—professional foresters, professional wildlife managers (expanded to include other southeastern states), bird-watchers, environmentalists, and hunters—were mailed questionnaires requesting information related to their outdoor recreation experiences and wildlife-related opinions (Leuschner, Ritchie, and Stauffer 1989). Some groups were then combined, and comparisons were made among responses from "resource managers" (foresters and wildlife managers), "nonconsumptive users" (bird-watchers and environmentalists), and "hunters."

Responses to demographic questions indicated that resource managers and hunters were younger (an average of forty-one years old) than nonconsumptive users (who averaged fifty years of age); that more than 90 percent of resource managers and hunters were males, whereas only about 50 percent of nonconsumptive users were males; and that nonconsumptive users had the highest average yearly household incomes ($46,700), followed by resource managers ($40,200), and hunters ($25,700). The median educational level of hunters was a high school diploma, whereas the median forester and bird-watcher had a baccalaureate degree, and the median wildlife manager and environmentalist had a master's degree. Forty-three percent of hunters were rural residents, while only 25 percent of resource managers and nonconsumptive users lived in rural areas. Nearly 90 percent of resource managers held professional or administrative jobs, compared with 68 percent of nonconsumptive users and 23 percent of hunters.

Asked why wildlife is personally important, almost 40 percent of resource managers and nonconsumptive users selected "wildlife is part of the ecological balance," and another 20 percent of the nonconsumptive users chose "wildlife has a right to exist." All groups indicated that seeing wildlife while on a nonwildlife outdoor recreation trip strongly increased their enjoyment of the experience, and hunters considered that "seeing a large number of the game animal" or "seeing other game species" contributed more to the hunting experience than actually bagging game. Questions about management policies showed that all groups favored management of wildlife; that foresters disagreed that "timber harvesting is reducing populations of some wildlife species," whereas all other groups agreed; and that environmentalists did not favor timber harvesting as a wildlife management tool.

Several significant findings emerged from this study. When respondents were asked why wildlife was personally important to them, altruistic reasons received high rankings, whereas more personal reasons (of watching or hunting wildlife) were given relatively low rankings. This suggests that resource managers should look beyond purely personal motives of resource users when making management decisions. Responses to questions about valued experiences suggests that hunting experiences could be improved by trying to maximize the number of times game species are seen and that nonconsumptive wildlife experiences could be enhanced by management strategies that increase species diversity. Opportunities to observe rare and endangered species are important, but clearly not of primary importance in adding to the outdoor experience.

Although differences were not so pronounced in the Virginia survey, other studies have shown that natural resource professionals often have attitudes and values that differ from those of the general public and important wildlife user constituencies (see Peyton and Langenau 1985). This may lead to misconceptions about public needs, to the establishment of goals or priorities that are not reflective of public values, or to decisions reflecting professional preferences. Wildlife personnel are responsible for making management decisions that affect, and must be acceptable to, a broad spectrum of wildlife interest and user groups; hence, they must be aware of their own attitudes and values and those of the various publics they serve (Peyton and Langenau 1985).

## PREFERENCES FOR WILDLIFE

Monetary expenditures and rate of participation are often used to estimate the total demand for wildlife-related activities. "Yet, even within a given activity there may be substantial variation in demand—are all birds equally attractive to a birder or all the animals at the zoo equally popular? Undoubtedly not! In our rush to estimate total demand, we have largely ignored the species-specific aspects of demand. One approach that has been used to surmount this difficulty has been the wildlife preference survey" (More 1979a:12).

Among the earliest wildlife preference surveys were those reporting the preferences of urban residents of Waterloo, Ontario (Dagg 1970, 1974). In a 1969 survey, 1,421 property owners in Waterloo indicated strong preferences for having birds on their lots (Dagg 1970): at least 97 percent liked the flicker, cardinal, goldfinch, blue jay, woodpeckers, red-winged blackbird, hummingbird, Baltimore oriole, and chickadee. The percentage of owners who liked urban mammals on their lots ranged from 86 percent for chipmunks to only 10 percent for skunks. Gray and red squirrels (68 percent), cottontail rabbit (64 percent), groundhog (36 percent), muskrat (32 percent), and bats (18 percent) fell between the extremes. Among the reasons given for disliking various mammals included their eating crops and garbage, digging holes in the lawn, entering houses (squirrels and bats), and carrying rabies.

In a second survey (Dagg 1974), 195 Waterloo residents were asked whether they liked, disliked, or were neutral about the four most common bird species in the city and the cardinal, which was added to the list. The cardinal (93 percent) and robin (92 percent) were almost universally liked, whereas the starling (32 percent) was least "likable." Starlings were thought to be too messy, noisy, and numerous.

To summarize these Canadian studies, Dagg commented that most urban dwellers liked seeing birds in the city, with the exception of the starling and pigeon (both exotic species that have become pests). People generally liked chipmunks, squirrels, and cottontail rabbits, but other mammals were unpopular because of the damage they cause.

In addition to the animal attitudes typology, Kellert (1980a) also was able to estimate Americans' preferences for various kinds of animals from his nationwide study. Responses to a thirty-three-animal, seven-point like/dislike query provided the basis for appraising species preferences.

According to Kellert's analysis, the animals most preferred were two domestic species, the horse and dog, followed by two familiar birds and an insect—the robin, swan, and butterfly. The trout was the most preferred fish (ranking sixth overall), while the eagle (ranked seventh) was the best-liked predator, and the elephant (ranked eleventh) was the highest ranking wild mammal. On the negative side, three of the four least preferred animals were biting or stinging invertebrates: the cockroach, mosquito, and wasp. In addition, the animals ranked third, fifth, and sixth among those most disliked are often associated with human injury or disease—the rat, rattlesnake, and bat. Finally, views on the coyote, wolf, and crow were ambivalent, and the vulture, shark, skunk, and lizard elicited relatively negative views.

The thirty-three animals presented were grouped by generically related qualities. Those types most preferred were domestic, attractive, and game animals. Least preferred were biting and stinging invertebrates, animals considered unattractive, and those known to cause injury to humans. Intermediate between the extremes were predators and animals that cause property damage. Among vertebrate classes, birds and mammals were best liked, and invertebrates were preferred less than any vertebrate class (including amphibians and reptiles).

One part of a survey of municipal conservation commissioners in Massachusetts was designed to ascertain their preferences for wildlife species (Gray, Larson, and Braunhardt 1979). Species (or groups of species) native to the state were listed in a wildlife preference questionnaire, and each respondent's first five choices were awarded 5, 4, 3, 2, and 1 points, respectively. Mean preference scores for all respondents were then computed and species were ranked based on their scores.

Completed questionnaires were returned by 469 of 1,054 commission members polled (44.5 percent). Results indicated the preference among taxonomic classes of wildlife was only slightly higher for mammals (7.9) than for birds (7.8), whereas scores for reptiles (2.4) and amphibians (1.4) were very low. Preferences among all species produced high scores for deer and moose (2.28), raptorial birds (1.72), upland game birds (1.71), waterfowl (1.43), and songbirds (1.40). The beaver (0.71), whales and seals (0.63), other water and shore birds (0.62), the swift and hummingbird (0.45), and black bear (0.42) completed the top ten. Lowest scores were received by insectivores (the moles and shrews, 0.00), mice (including meadow, woodland, and jumping mice, 0.02), bats (0.02), tailed amphibians (including salamanders, newts, and the mudpuppy, 0.03), and the opossum (0.03).

In general, preference among wildlife species was highest for animals that are common, popular, visible, well publicized, better understood, and not dangerous. Nearly all avian groups received relatively high scores. This may be due to the ubiquity and visibility of birds and the influence of active and well-organized Audubon societies in Massachusetts. Marine mammals received surprisingly high scores, which may reflect their exposure on television and publicity directed toward endangered whales.

Overall, survey participants expressed a preference for seeing rare, threatened, or unusual members of most taxonomic classes. There was considerable interest in the group containing the southern bald eagle, a species considered threatened at the time of the study. However, several taxonomic groups containing species that were rare or threatened in Massachusetts when the survey was conducted received low rankings. These included the Indiana bat, beach vole, and bog turtle.

There are several possible explanations why respondents were unable to identify the rare and threatened species for which they professed concern: the lay perspective on which animals comprise this category may have been confused; lay persons in the seventies may not have understood the meaning of the term *rare and threatened wildlife* or there may even have been a public misconception that most wildlife species were rare and threatened. In another part of this survey, conservation commissioners did not specify wildlife or wildlife habitat as a prime factor in their land-acquisition programs; hence, there may also have been a lack of public recognition that rare and threatened wildlife—and, indeed, all wildlife—relies on its supporting habitat.

The significant findings of several other preference surveys were briefly summarized by More (1979a): Bart (1972) found that mammals were most preferred, especially horses and dogs; Henry (1976) reported that visitors to a national park in Kenya generally devoted most of their viewing time to lions and cheetahs, both large carnivores, whereas other species received little more than a passing glance; Fazio and Belli (1977) indicated that nonconsumptive users in Idaho expressed a preference for deer, followed by bears, eagles, elk, bass, and songbirds; Brown and Dawson (1978) stated that metropolitan residents of New York State preferred seeing butterflies, robins, cardinals, sparrows, bluejays, hummingbirds, and squirrels around their homes, but preferred viewing woodpeckers, blackbirds and starlings, chipmunks, ducks and geese, frogs and toads, rabbits, pheasants, and turtles when visiting nearby public parks or in the country; and Schweitzer et al. (1973) noted, in a Saskatchewan study restricted to birds, that residents who enjoyed observing birds rated songbirds highest, followed by upland game birds, geese, ducks, other water and shorebirds, and birds of prey, in descending order, although ratings for all species were highly positive.

Many factors undoubtedly affect human preferences for wildlife (More 1979a). Important socioeconomic and demographic influences probably exist that have yet to be identified. *Recreational interests and activities* certainly affect preferences; for example, consumptive users may rank species differently than nonconsumptive users (Fazio and Belli 1977). *Relative abundance* of a species may influence preferences: sightings of the rare Ross's gull in Massachusetts attracted more than one thousand people per day, some from throughout the United States (More 1979a). Preferences also vary with the *situation.* It is one thing to enjoy watching squirrels in a park and quite another to discover them in your birdfeeder. Finally, *physical characteristics* of animals—their form, size, color, vocalizations, etc.—may strongly affect preferences (More 1979a).

## KNOWLEDGE ABOUT WILDLIFE

The level of knowledge about wildlife may be another determinant in one's species preferences (More 1979a). More knowledge about a subject frequently promotes an appreciation of it and may lead to an increased demand for associated activities. This is probably no less true of wildlife and wildlife-related activities than other topics. Unfortunately, there have been few studies of people's knowledge about wildlife (More 1979a).

Those studies that have investigated public knowledge about wildlife have generally adopted a quiz format in which the number of correct responses is used as an index to a person's knowledge (More 1979a). In Kellert's (1980a) study of wildlife typologies he incorporated a section on public knowledge. He used thirty-three true-false and multiple choice questions, scored from 0 to 100, to construct a knowledge-of-animals scale. Questions covered all vertebrate classes, and six dealt with invertebrates. The distribution of scores was approximately normal, with a mean of 52.8.

The public as a whole displayed an extremely limited knowledge of animals. Only 57 percent responded correctly to the statement "Most insects have backbones." Just 26 percent were aware that the coyote is not an endangered species, only 26 percent knew that the manatee is not an insect, and a mere 13 percent realized that raptors are not small rodents.

The knowledge questions were grouped into several categories, which revealed that the public was most knowledgeable about animals that can cause injury to humans (mean score = 63.4), pets (55.6), basic animal characteristics (such as "all adult birds have feathers") (55.3), and domestic animals in general (53.4). The public was apparently least knowledgeable about predators (47.1), taxonomic relationships (for example, "koala bears are not really bears") (39.8), and invertebrates (36.6).

Demographic groups demonstrating the most knowledge about wildlife were the college-educated (especially persons with a graduate education), residents of Alaska and the Rocky Mountain states, professionals, and persons with high incomes. The least knowledgeable respondents were African-Americans, persons with less than a high school education, those older than seventy-five and younger than twenty-five, and residents of large cities. Members of all animal-related activity groups had scores above the mean—but the most knowledgeable, judging from their high scores, were bird-watchers, members of conservation organizations, nature hunters, and scientific study hobbyists.

## OPINIONS ON IMPORTANT WILDLIFE ISSUES

Respondents to Kellert's (1980a) survey were also questioned about their perceived familiarity with several prominent wildlife issues. Responses to endangered-species questions indicated a greater willingness to protect endangered wildlife among persons in the following demographic groups: college-educated persons, singles, those under thirty years old, large-city residents, and Alaskans. Lowest scores were found among persons over seventy-five years of age, those with less than an eighth-grade education, farmers, residents of very rural areas, and Southerners.

The issue of predator control focused on coyote predation on livestock. The general public was moderately, but significantly, opposed to indiscriminate coyote reductions by shooting or trapping as many as possible. Furthermore, over 90 percent were against the use of poisons, even though this control option was described as being least expensive. Almost 70 percent were in favor of controlling only individual coyotes known to be livestock killers. About two-thirds supported capture and relocation of problem coyotes, even though this was not offered as a practical alternative. A significant majority disapproved of compensating ranchers for livestock losses due to coyotes out of general tax revenues.

On the subject of wildlife habitat protection, survey respondents expressed a willingness to protect wildlife habitat in spite of substantial socioeconomic impacts. For example, an overwhelming 86 percent supported restrictions on off-road vehicles if their use harmed wild animals; 76 percent favored forest harvesting practices beneficial to wildlife, even if higher lumber prices resulted; 60 percent approved of restrictions on livestock grazing on public lands to save vegetation for wildlife, even if higher beef prices were the consequence; and 57 percent were opposed to building homes on wetlands needed by waterfowl.

Responses to hunting showed that 82 percent approved of traditional native subsistence hunting, and 85 percent agreed with hunting for meat. Recreational hunting was endorsed by 64 percent as long as the meat was used, but 80 percent of respondents were opposed to trophy hunting. The issue of trapping found 70 percent of the national sample objecting to the use of steel leg-hold traps.

Reactions to harvesting wildlife seemed ambiguous—57 percent opposed killing furbearers for clothing (even if the species was not endangered), and 70 percent were willing to pay more for tuna if fewer dolphins and porpoises were killed in fishing nets; however, 77 percent approved of killing whales for useful products as long as they were not threatened with extinction.

Possibilities for wildlife management funding showed that 82 percent of respondents supported an excise tax on clothing made from wild animal pelts; 71 percent favored a similar tax on off-road vehicles; 75 percent endorsed entrance fees to wildlife refuges and other public wildlife areas; 57 percent approved of excise taxes on backpacking and bird-watching supplies and equipment; and 57 percent felt that an increase of general tax revenue should go for wildlife management.

## STUDENT ORIENTATIONS TOWARD WILDLIFE: IMPLICATIONS FOR EDUCATION

A survey questionnaire comprised of three sections—attitudes about wildlife, perceptions of wildlife, and wildlife-related activities—was administered to two groups of students in Texas: 118 high school students who were taking, or had taken, a biology class, and 110 university undergraduates enrolled in wildlife and fisheries courses (Adams, Newgard, and Thomas 1986). The purpose of the study was to determine student orientations toward wildlife and to identify changes in educational programs that might enhance students' understanding and appreciation for wildlife.

The questionnaire contained illustrations of eight animal species (butterfly, cockroach, coyote, lobster, rabbit, rat, scorpion, and white-tailed deer) chosen because they represent both invertebrates and vertebrates, are all readily recognizable, and all tend to elicit strong like/dislike responses.

To identify student orientations toward wildlife, Adams, Newgard, and Thomas developed a conceptual model—based on Triandis's (1971) attitudinal theory—that human wildlife orientations are multidimensional and include three components: feelings, beliefs, and actions.

The questionnaire was divided into three parts paralleling the three model components. In the first section, "Attitudes about Wildlife," corresponding to the "feelings" component, students were asked to respond to a series of twelve attitudinal statements (for example, "I tend to avoid this animal") about each animal pictured. The statements were designed to isolate three attitudinal categories—positivistic, utilitarian, or negativistic (Kellert 1976)—representing the continuum of human orientations toward wildlife, while minimizing overlap between categories.

The second part, "Perceptions of Wildlife," corresponding to "beliefs," consisted of fifteen bipolar pairs of adjectives (for example, "good/bad") meant to measure each respondent's perceptions of the species illustrated. In addition, students evaluated each animal on a five-point semantic differentiation scale; for example, "pleasant" 5 4 3 2 1 "unpleasant" (Adams, Newgard, and Thomas 1986).

For the third model component, "Wildlife-Related Activities," corresponding to "actions," twenty-four wildlife-related activities were listed. Students were asked, for each activity, whether they have ever been involved, would like to be involved, or have no interest. The extent of participation was also used to classify respondents into one of four wildlife orientations (see Table 5.5) on the assumption that a higher level of involvement with wildlife represented a more positively oriented individual.

Scoring for the attitude component consisted of summing the response values (agree = 1, disagree = 0) for each of the six attitude statements and repeating the procedure for all eight species. Scoring for the perceptions component involved summing each respondent's scores on the 1-to-5-point semantic differentiation scale for the five pairs of adjectives and repeating the procedure for all eight animals. The activities component was scored by summing the response values (have done = 2, would like to do = 1, no interest in doing = 0) for the twenty-four activities listed.

To determine each student's wildlife orientation, it was first necessary to isolate the scores for each of the model components (attitudes, perceptions, and activities) into a continuum from high to low. Scores above the mean for each model component were considered high (H) for that component, whereas scores below the mean were considered low (L). Repeating this procedure for each model component resulted in eight combinations of possible responses. The eight response combinations were then collapsed to correspond to the four orientational categories (of Table 5.5), and the resulting action, satisfaction, frustration, and apathy typologies defined according to combinations of high and low scores on the three model components (see Table 5.6). Differences in the number of college and high school students in each category were statistically significant ($p = 0.0001$).

Findings showed the mean attitudinal score toward all eight animals in the survey was 35.39 (range = 22 to 48) for college students, com-

Table 5.5. The four human wildlife orientational typologies, derived from Adair's four dimensions of human social behavior.

| Orientational typology | Brief description of characteristics |
|---|---|
| Action | Individuals with high aspirations—inclined toward studying, learning, and acting |
| Satisfaction | Individuals with a high level of involvement but with low aspirations |
| Frustration | Individuals with high aspirations but a low level of involvement |
| Apathy | Individuals who are indifferent—with low aspirations and lacking involvement |

Source: Adams, Newgard, and Thomas 1986; LeHart and Tillis 1974.

pared to 24.29 (range = 9 to 42) for high school students. A more positive attitudinal orientation was reflected by a higher score. The mean perception (emotion) score for college students was 80.77 (range = 44 to 102) and 93.44 (range = 53 to 115) for high school students. For this component, a lower score showed a more positive orientation. Finally, the mean activity score for college students was 174.58 (range = 87 to 218), and 132.41 (range = 55 to 193) for high schoolers. Differences between mean scores for college and high school students were significant ($p = 0.0001$) for all three components.

Differences between the numbers of college and high school students in each category were not surprising. They had been predicted, based on the intentional selection of two survey groups that exhibited distinct differences in age, education, and vested interests in wildlife. In fact, selecting two such different groups was necessary so that the sensitivity of the procedures and conceptual model could be tested.

The investigators saw this study as significant because the identification of wildlife orientations based on a model having three components (attitudes, perceptions, and activities) resulted in mutually exclusive elements contributing to the specification of attitudinal types and because the model is inherently flexible, allowing for the emergence of variation in each of the model components, depending on the species selected and the demographic characteristics of the population being surveyed.

From an educational viewpoint, the strength of the model and procedures developed in this study is that their application to other survey

Table 5.6. Orientations toward wildlife of high school and college students in Texas.

| Orientational typology | High/Low rating for the three components[a] | High school students | College students |
|---|---|---|---|
| Action | HHH | 16%; $N = 19$ | 77%; $N = 85$ |
| Satisfaction | LLH, HLH, LHH | 26%; $N = 31$ | 10%; $N = 11$ |
| Frustration | HLL, LHL, HHL | 37%; $N = 43$ | 13%; $N = 14$ |
| Apathy | LLL | 21%; $N = 25$ | 0%; $N = 0$ |

Source: Adams et al. 1986.
[a] H = High, L = Low. The three components are attitudes, perceptions, and activities, respectively; therefore, LHL refers to respondents who rank below the mean (L) for attitudes, above the mean (H) for perceptions, and below the mean (L) for activities.

populations (including selected socioeconomic groups) allows for diverse responses to each component. Thus, educators can develop wildlife curricula, or other educational materials, designed for specified groups keeping their known attitudes, preferences, and activities in mind.

The studies cited in this chapter repeatedly document human preferences for animals that are common, well known, and not dangerous. Indeed, our propensity for popular species amounts to another example of the Matthew Principle. We celebrate creatures that are already famous and neglect or ignore those that are not well known.

In thinking about future research, specialists may want to consider Fred Gilbert's comment before embarking on new studies related to attitudes and preferences for wildlife. He wrote, "Attitudinal surveys really only have meaning if they are used to formulate policy or redesign or design programs to either alter the attitudes (if desirable) or meet the desires of the public" (1982).

## PERSPECTIVE

### Wildlife Attitudes and Familiar Animals

Research on the development of attitudes toward wildlife point to ages ten to thirteen as providing the greatest opportunity for educating young people about wildlife. At this stage their factual knowledge of animals is rapidly increasing, whereas by adolescence (thirteen-sixteen years) their wildlife interests have already become more conceptual (Kellert and Westervelt 1983). During earlier formative years, from seven to ten, children are less well informed about animals—but attitudes, particularly attitudes formed during youth, may have much less to do with knowledge than with *feelings*.

I wonder if a kind of "bonding" occurs even sooner, in early childhood. I suspect we carry with us into adult life a special affection for the familiar animals of childhood stories and stuffed toys—deer and rabbits, and especially bears with their large eyes and round, furry bodies.

Butterflies, albeit colorful and attractive, don't evoke deep feelings of kinship or attachment (Kellert 1987). Birds, though interesting and familiar, are not "cuddly." Animals such as shrews and bats, while acknowledged to be ecologically important, fare even worse in preference surveys (Gray, Larson, and Braunhardt 1979).

As the conservation organization undoubtedly having the most extensive educational programs, the National Wildlife Federation has periodicals for every age group, from *Your Big Backyard* (for preschool children, ages three-five) and *Ranger Rick* (six-twelve), to *National Wildlife* and *International Wildlife* directed at adolescents and adults. These publications reflect a strategy of attracting readers with spectacular photographs and articles featuring popular animals such as bears and elephants, then exposing them to a wide range of current topics. Just one issue of *National Wildlife* (October-November 1990) included material on anatomy and physiology ("The Nature of Muscles"), environmental problems ("Plastic Rapt"), wildlife management ("New Look at a Deer Old Game"), resource issues ("Who Runs America's Forests?"), wildlife art ("Mastering the Art of Birds"), and what would surely qualify as an unpopular species ("Secret Creatures of the Night," about American eels).

The federation's product marketing efforts are also beginning to embrace the promotion of less popular animals. There is still an adult tee-shirt for just "Lion Around," but there are also kids' tee-shirts featuring "The Unhuggables" (showing a skunk, spider, and slug) and "Bug World" (depicting a lady bug, daddy longlegs, monarch butterfly, and ants). Clearly, the National Wildlife Federation is on the right track. If Americans prefer popular animals, then we must promote the unpopular ones so they, too, achieve a measure of recognition.

Perhaps even wildlife professionals, with their own creature interests based on research or management responsibilities, feel a special stirring when exposed to real animals in the natural world that are reminiscent of their stuffed and storied childhood chums.

One wonders if the World Wildlife Fund would be as successful in raising funds and enlisting members if their logo were a shrew instead of the cuddly panda.

## SUGGESTED READING

Noyes, J. H., and D. R. Progulske (eds.) 1974. *Wildlife in an Urbanizing Environment.* Holdsworth Natural Resources Center, Planning and Resource Development Series No. 28, University of Massachusetts, Amherst. 182 pages. Though based on a technical symposium, this monograph is nevertheless quite readable, with the idea of "attitudes and preferences for wildlife" implicit in many of the articles.

# Economic Valuation: Assessing Demand for Wildlife 6

Wild species were "the first resource," the sole source of food, fiber, fuel, and medicines for the first 99 percent of human history (Prescott-Allen and Prescott-Allen 1986:1). For nearly 2 million years humans had no thought of the "economic value" of wildlife; the need was absolute and all encompassing. That condition gradually changed with the origin and development of agriculture, beginning about ten thousand years ago. In the last century the human economy has been so thoroughly altered by mechanized agriculture, fossil fuels, and industrial development that wild plants and animals have been relegated to decidedly lesser roles. Wild species have become "the forgotten resource" (Prescott-Allen and Prescott-Allen 1986:1).

Wildlife resources obviously have economic value, yet Berryman (1987) contended that wildlife researchers and managers have considered it repugnant to apply economic values and economic tools to uses of wildlife. He issued a challenge to wildlife professionals: if retaining fish and wildlife resources "as a part of the fabric of our total landscape and environment . . . is really our 'conservation ethic,' " then "we must bring economic principles to bear in the management of the nation's fish and wildlife resources or they [will] continue to be considered as marginal luxury products" (8).

## THE FUNDAMENTAL PROBLEM—AND MEASURING VALUE

The activities made possible by wildlife are available, because of law and tradition, on a basis that does not reveal what they are worth; that is, they are not priced in a market. In the absence of data from market transactions, traditional economic models cannot be directly applied to problems of wildlife valuation (Langford and Cocheba 1978). These basic problems underlying our attempts to measure wildlife values were first outlined by Crutchfield in 1962.

The satisfaction (or utility) that individuals derive from wildlife-related activities represents a primary benefit. Therefore, we need a "cardinal index of satisfaction" to serve as a measure of the value or satisfaction generated by these activities. According to the consumer's surplus concept, money can function as such a cardinal index of satisfaction or value (Langford and Cocheba 1978).

Although money is certainly not a perfect unit of measure, some of the persistent arguments against using it for this purpose are indefensible. For example, people may argue that monetary valuation of wildlife is not acceptable because of the aesthetic aspects of experiences associated with wildlife—yet individuals make monetary assessments of works of art that have aesthetic qualities. The aesthetic appeal of a commodity has little to do with whether money is an acceptable measure of its value to a consumer. It is a fact that money is the medium of exchange in our society, and only the naive believe that using money to measure value implies a materialistic ethic (Langford and Cocheba 1978).

## A TOTAL VALUATION SYSTEM FOR WILDLIFE

In an attempt to measure the monetary values held by all members of society, economists have sought to develop a total valuation system to cover the full range of possible values that might be generated by wildlife resources. These total values can be divided into use values and nonuse values (Bishop 1987).

Use values are "sensory perception activities" that affect the satisfaction people get from current uses of wildlife, including consumptive activities, such as hunting and trapping; nonconsumptive recreation, such as wildlife photography and observation; and indirect use values, personal enjoyment of wildlife without direct contact (for example, reading about wildlife and watching wildlife programs on television) (Langford and Cocheba 1978; Bishop 1987).

*Nonuse values* encompass categories that are relatively new: existence value, option value, bequest value, and quasi-option value (Langford and Cocheba 1978; Bishop 1987; Cocheba 1987). *Existence value* refers to the satisfaction individuals derive just from knowing that wildlife exists, apart from any sensory contact at the moment or in the future. This is a contemplative, rather than a sensory, wildlife activity.

*Option value* is the idea that wildlife may create benefits from continued availability for future use, as well as from present uses. It can be thought of as the willingness to purchase a kind of insurance policy to retain the opportunity for possible future use, even if no immediate use is contemplated (Steinhoff et al. 1987). The concept of option value is particularly relevant to wilderness preservation and the conservation of rare and endangered species. Some people derive satisfaction from knowing that a rare species exists, even if they have never seen it, and they are willing to incur a cost to ensure that the resource is preserved.

*Bequest value* is the willingness to pay in order to ensure that future generations—your grandchildren, perhaps—will have the chance to see or benefit from a species. *Quasi-option value* refers to the value of preserving our options, given the expectation of growth in knowledge (Arrow and Fisher 1974). The value of the genome of wild animals for future use or research, and the value of wildlife as a future source of useful chemical compounds, fall within this category.

When considering values several qualifications should be kept in mind. First, any member of society may hold several categories of values for a species simultaneously. For example, a person may be a current deer hunter, may enjoy viewing and photographing deer, may watch TV programs about deer, and may be willing to pay for options to hunt and photograph deer in the future. Second, for all categories within the valuation system there are two possible ways of measuring value—willingness to pay and compensation demanded. The appropriate measure in any particular situation depends on whether those affected are "gainers" or "losers." Third, most management decisions involve increasing or decreasing wildlife abundance rather than outright extinction. But future participation in a particular wildlife activity will require the continued existence of a species, so an effective option demand implies maintaining a species well above the level at which extinction may be threatened. Thus, option demand should not be ignored even when numbers are large enough to permit legal hunting (Langford and Cocheba 1978; Bishop 1987).

## BASIC CONCEPTS OF ECONOMIC VALUATION

Economics examines public policy issues from the viewpoint of society as a whole. In this context, monetary economic values are derived from welfare economics, a branch of economics having to do with the well-being of all members of society, not—as the name suggests—with welfare programs for the poor. Welfare economics involves a comparison of two or more situations or "states of the world." A welfare economist might ask, for example, if social welfare would be improved by increasing deer numbers in a region rather than maintaining them at the current level (Bishop 1987).

But how is the welfare of society defined? Economic theorists base the concept of social welfare on the well-being of individual members of society, with each individual as the sole judge of his or her well-being. Increasing the number of deer in a region would affect an individual's well-being only to the extent that one *believed* that he or she would be be better or worse off. The logical conclusion to this line of reasoning is the *Pareto criterion of social welfare* (named for nineteenth-century economist Vilfredo Pareto)—that, using the deer example, society would be better off if increasing deer numbers would make at least one member of society better off without adversely affecting any other (Bishop 1987).

In practice, virtually any action that society takes harms someone. Increasing deer numbers may improve hunter success while increasing damage to agricultural crops, so hunters are better off whereas farmers are harmed. The Pareto criterion is therefore impractical, because applying its standard to all public policy issues would result in social paralysis (Bishop 1987).

The economic solution to this dilemma is the *compensation test.* If "gainers" are all members of society who believe a proposed action would benefit them and "losers" are those who believe the same policy would harm them, then the compensation test dictates that a "proposal will increase social welfare if the gainers would be able to compensate the losers fully and still be better off" (Bishop 1987:26). Increasing deer numbers would enhance social welfare if hunters were better off even after they had fully compensated the farmers. In fact, there is no requirement that compensation actually be paid—only that it be possible for gainers to fully compensate the losers.

The compensation test provides a way of applying economic values to wildlife management. Economists suggest that society may want to reconsider actions when gainers could not fully compensate losers. The compensation test alone is not an adequate basis for public policy, but proposals that fail the compensation test certainly merit sober reconsideration. Although this explanation is somewhat simplistic, it is adequate to explain the basic concepts of monetary valuation (Bishop 1987).

"Economic value is determined by application of the compensation test. The compensation test in turn forms the theoretical foundation for cost-benefit analysis." In theory, *cost-benefit analysis* defines the benefits of a proposed action as "the maximum amount that gainers would be willing to pay in compensation to losers," whereas "costs are the minimum amount required to compensate all losers fully" (Bishop 1987:26).

There are two kinds of limitations that are particularly troubling when the compensation test is applied to wildlife issues. One relates to the distribution of costs and benefits. What people are willing to pay, and the amounts they demand in compensation, depend on their incomes and wealth. Thus, the compensation test may give an unfair advantage to those who are wealthy. Cost-benefit analyses should therefore include an examination of who bears the costs and who derives the benefits—the so-called distributional effects. However, wildlife policies that do not satisfy the compensation test may still be justified on the basis of fairness. An example of fairness is the principle of equitability of hunting opportunity for all Americans without regard to socioeconomic distinctions (Bishop 1987).

The other limitation involves endangered species. The benefits of species preservation are often apparent only in historic retrospect. Since the course of scientific progress, social change, and cultural evolution are difficult to predict, it is virtually impossible to identify those species that may be particularly valuable to humans in the future. Furthermore, cost-benefit analyses are not amenable to issues of intergenerational fairness. How do we economically justify decisions that may deprive our grandchildren of seeing or benefitting from a species (Bishop 1987)?

Attaching a monetary value to wildlife using measures other than "willingness to pay" and "compensation demanded" occurs most often when wildlife is valued by measuring recreational expenditures. Such expenditures represent gross willingness to pay, or the maximum amount that gainers would be willing to pay for an action. However, only net willingness to pay—that is, the willingness to pay of gainers over and above what they actually will pay—is relevant in determining whether benefits to gainers would be sufficient to cover costs to losers. In economic language, net willingness to pay is referred to as the *consumer surplus* (Bishop 1987).

## ECONOMIC BENEFITS OF WILDLIFE-RELATED RECREATION

The wildlife-related recreational experience can be thought of as having four component attributes: physical, biological, social, and managerial. These attributes also constitute management options and should be considered before conducting a benefit estimation because they define the scope of the analysis. Any changes in these options will likely alter the attributes of a recreational experience (Dwyer 1980).

Changes in these attributes might stem from constructing new roads into a wildlife management area (physical); clear-cutting forest patches to increase habitat diversity (biological); seasonal differences in public usage levels of a wildlife area (social); and new regulations affecting the harvest of certain wildlife species (managerial) (Dwyer 1980).

The value of a wildlife-related recreational experience is influenced by its location in relation to users, by the availability of substitute experiences, and by the four attributes just mentioned. Because changing one or more of these attributes will affect the quality of recreational opportunity in a particular locale, it is generally not appropriate to estimate average values over a large geographic area. Instead, the estimate should pertain to the particular area influenced by the management option being evaluated (Dwyer 1980).

In the absence of market prices for wildlife-related recreation, consumers' willingness to pay must be calculated in other ways. Typically, willingness to pay is estimated from user behavior (the *travel cost method*) or user responses to bidding-game questions (the *contingent valuation method*). A third means, the gross expenditures method, has been extensively used in the past but is no longer considered appropriate since it cannot measure net value (that is, the consumer surplus) (Dwyer 1980; Sorg and Loomis 1985).

The travel cost method (TCM), developed by Clawson (1959), is based on the view that travel cost can be used as a proxy for price in estimating outdoor recreation benefits. Benefit estimation models using the travel cost approach take into consideration such factors as the number of trips, travel costs, and the travel time from various origins to a recreational destination area; the population of the origin; the characteristics of individuals at the origin; the entry fee for the use of the area; quality characteristics of experiences available at the area; travel times from the origin to substitute areas, both closer and farther away; and quality characteristics of experiences available at substitute areas. Then, regression analysis can be used to develop an equation for estimating visitation rates at the recreational area based on travel costs and socioeconomic data on populations at various points of origin (Dwyer 1980; Sorg and Loomis 1985).

The contingent valuation method (CVM) uses a bidding-game scenario in which individuals are asked to respond to changes in the hypothetical price of a nonmarket good, such as wildlife-related recreation. The term *contingent valuation* is derived from how individuals indicate their behavior would change contingent on a different hypothetical situation; this also suggests the origin of the bidding-game description. Under the CVM, data collected reflect individuals estimating their own consumer surplus (Sorg and Loomis 1985). Because the CVM is based on a mail, personal, or telephone interview, this technique is sometimes called the survey method (Dwyer 1980). Respondents are presented with a series of situations for which they make bids. After each bid they are asked successively if they would pay incrementally higher amounts until they respond negatively. Their last positive response is considered a measure of maximum willingness to pay.

In applying either the TCM or the CVM it is essential that the variables representing quality of recreational experience receive special attention as the model is developed. A measure of quality could be based on some combination of several factors, such as numbers of the "target species" seen, numbers and variety of all wildlife seen, frequency of encounters between recreational users (as a measure of crowding), weather conditions, etc. (Dwyer 1980). In one study, the willingness of users to pay for a season of waterfowl hunting was expressed in terms of waterfowl bagged and shots missed (Cocheba and Langford 1978).

Where only average values of willingness to pay (per day, season, or year of use) are calculated—by simply dividing total willingness to pay by total use—the value of the analysis is considerably reduced. Such calculations tell us nothing about changes in value associated with changes in various attributes of the experience. Thus, all benefit estimations should present the model from which their valuations were derived (Dwyer 1980).

Cost-benefit analysis is just one kind of socioeconomic exercise. No cost-benefit analysis, including both the TCM and the CVM, provides any information about the psychological or sociological bases for the economic values it describes (Dwyer 1980). Those considerations are the province of other psychosocial decision criteria, including expressions of attitude and preference, which we examined in the previous chapter.

Other available options also provide possibilities for wildlife benefit valuation. One of these, the *household production function,* is a way of connecting public actions that affect wildlife stocks and wildlife habitat with household decision-making about wildlife recreation (Bockstael and McConnell 1981). Think of a causal chain in which public policy actions (or *exogenous variables;* that is, those imposed from outside) affect wildlife numbers, which in turn influence success per day (measured as animals sighted, shots taken, or game bagged) on which net benefits depend. This relationship may be complicated by the fact that users can also affect success per day by purchasing inputs such as guide services, binoculars, scopes, etc. (which are *endogenous variables;* that is, under individual or household control) (Bockstael and McConnell 1981).

Public actions that change wildlife abundance can affect benefits by making it cheaper for households to "produce" a higher quality recreational experience, where success is measured by wildlife encountered or bagged. Within this framework, the value of an "extra" deer can be meaningfully estimated only by relating it both to public policy and to an individual's decision framework. Individuals may increase encounters or game bagged by incurring increased costs and may simultaneously choose the quantity of recreational days and the quality of each day's experience. The problem of estimating benefits by means of the household production function is a consequence of the interdependence of quantity and quality choices related to wildlife recreation (Bockstael and McConnell 1981).

*Hedonic pricing,* a technique within the context of the household production function, takes its name from hedonism—the idea that pleasure is the chief good in life. As such, this approach focuses on the satisfaction derived from the attributes of goods, rather than the goods themselves. This view has intuitive appeal for evaluating changes in recreational quality attributes because such changes affect the degree of pleasure associated with recreational experiences (Dwyer 1980).

The methodology used in hedonic pricing is similar to that of the travel cost method, with characteristics related to recreational quality being incorporated into the model as explanatory variables. Although several studies have applied hedonic pricing to wildlife-related recreation, it remains to be seen whether this method will prove to be an important tool for valuing wildlife (Dwyer 1980).

## NET ECONOMIC VALUE OF UPLAND GAME HUNTING IN IDAHO: A CASE STUDY

The economics of hunting upland game in Idaho was studied cooperatively by state and federal agencies to promote a consensus among agencies on the monetary value of this activity. Knowing the economic value of wildlife was considered useful in coordinating federal plans affecting wildlife habitat with state plans for managing individual species (Young et al. 1987).

Upland game in Idaho includes the cottontail rabbit, pheasant, quail, grouse, wild turkey, and dove. This study used results from a statewide survey to estimate the consumer surplus (or net willingness to pay) for upland game hunting in Idaho. Two techniques, the travel cost method (TCM) and the contingent value method (CVM), were used. Both were considered appropriate procedures for empirically estimating users' net willingness to pay (Young et al. 1987).

A relatively simple regional travel cost model (RTCM) was developed in which the dependent variable (that is, the outcome to be predicted and "explained") was trips per capita. Independent variables included round-trip distance from county of residence "i" to hunting area "j"; quality of the recreational experience at area "j"; the cost and availability of substitute hunting areas to residents of county "i"; and income, a measure of the ability of households in county "i" to afford the costs for recreation. Thus, the model was expressed as:

$$\text{Trips}_{ij}/\text{Population}_i = b_0 - b_1\ \text{Distance}_{ij} + b_2\ \text{Quality}_j - b_3\ \text{Substitute}_i + b_4\ \text{Income}_i$$

where $b_0$ through $b_4$ are coefficients that had to be estimated (Young et al. 1987).

The equation specified the per capita demand curve for hunting areas in the region. By assigning a quality value to a particular hunting area, the demand curve generated by the model became the demand curve for that specific area. A second-stage demand curve was then calculated from the per capita demand curve. This second-stage demand curve plotted the total trips to a site as a function of hypothetical added distance. When the hypothetical added distance was converted to dollar travel costs, the area under the second stage demand curve represented net willingness to pay, the consumer surplus (Young et al. 1987).

The CVM measured net surplus by having telephone interviewers ask recreationists how much more, above actual expenditures, they would be willing to pay to participate in the upland hunting experience. Respondents were asked if they would pay successively higher amounts to experience an upland game hunting situation that was described. In this study, trip cost, which is familiar and emotionally neutral, was used as the "payment vehicle" rather than an entrance fee, license fee, or tax (Young et al. 1987).

Question design is vital to the CVM, which is a direct measure of value, because poor questions would render the results useless. Thus, a protest mechanism was built into the questionnaire, so legitimate bids related to upland game hunting could be differentiated from bids made in protest to the survey. The data were screened before analysis to exclude all but the legitimate bids (Young et al. 1987).

Several hunting area quality measures were examined during data compilation for the travel cost method (TCM). Shooting opportunities per hour, which had seemed like the most plausible measure of quality, proved to be statistically insignificant. Eventually, total opportunities to shoot, which was statistically significant, was selected to represent hunting quality. This was considered sensible from a management viewpoint as well, since the Idaho Department of Game and Fish can influence animal densities in specific areas through stocking programs, hunting regulations, and cooperative habitat management programs with federal agencies. Thus, total opportunities to shoot could be used to estimate the economic efficiency benefits (in a cost-benefit analysis) of any management actions that altered the animal densities of an area (Young et al. 1987).

Estimates of hunters' incomes were not collected for the survey, so the U.S. Department of Labor's estimate of a median wage of $8.00 an hour was used. Per mile transportation cost was estimated at $0.12 for all upland game combined and $.011 for pheasant hunting, which translated into total travel costs per mile of $0.19 and $0.18 for all upland game combined and pheasant hunting, respectively. These figures were based on the reported cost per mile, rather than standard cost per mile, and took into consideration the use of pickup trucks and campers and poorer gas mileage when driving on backroads (Young et al. 1987).

Data resulting from the upland game hunter survey are summarized in Table 6.1 for the TCM analysis. These data indicated that the estimated average net economic value of an upland game hunting trip in Idaho was $34.77, which means that the average hunter would pay approximately $35 more per trip to have the hunting sites maintained (Young et al. 1987).

The contingent value method (CVM) used in the study to elicit "simulated market bids" from hunters was considered to estimate the net economic value of the last trip taken during the 1982 hunting season. The CVM per trip value for all upland game hunting under prevailing conditions was $25.82, which converted to $69.62 per twelve-hour wildlife and fish user day (WFUD) (Young et al. 1987).

In this study, (1) both the travel cost method and the contingent value method provided acceptable results; (2) the construction of a regional (or zonal) TCM proved successful; (3) distance, substitute areas, and the hunting quality measure were all statistically significant variables; (4) the predicted number was within 10 percent of actual trips taken; and (5) the average CVM value of $25.82 for an upland game hunting trip for all species combined was bracketed by the TCM values for standard ($23.21) and reported ($34.77) cost per mile (Young et al. 1987).

Both the travel cost and contingent value methods had advantages and disadvantages in this study. The CVM was considered to have two advantages over the TCM. First, researchers could determine willingness to pay for hypothetical changes in hunting quality as well as

Table 6.1. Economic valuation of hunting in Idaho using the travel cost method.

| Parameter estimated | Valuation[a] | |
|---|---|---|
| | All upland game[b] | Pheasant only[c] |
| Net willingness to pay per trip (for current conditions) | $34.77 | $28.84 |
| Number of days hunting per trip | 1.22 | 1.18 |
| Number of hours hunting per day | 4.22 | 3.93 |
| Value per day[d] | 28.50 | 24.44 |
| Value per twelve-hour WFUD[e] | 81.04 | 74.63 |

Source: Young et al. 1987, tables 4 and 5.
[a] Valuation is based on the state average.
[b] Reported cost per mile was $0.28.
[c] Reported cost per mile was $0.26.
[d] Value per day was computed as (Net willingness to pay per trip) ÷ (Number of days hunting per trip) = $34.77 ÷ 1.22.
[e] WFUD stands for Wildlife and Fish User Day, which was computed as Value per day × (12 hrs. per WFUD) ÷ (No. of hrs. hunting per day) = $28.50 × (12) ÷ (4.22).

willingness to pay for hunting under current conditions. And second, the CVM made it possible to estimate the value per day for hunting on multipurpose or multidestination trips, whereas the TCM permitted accurate estimates of value only for trips having hunting as the primary purpose and destination. The primary advantages of the TCM related to its reliance on actual behavior, rather than simulated market bids, and its applicability to all upland game hunting trips taken during the season rather than just the final one (Young et al. 1987).

Since time and effort are nearly always considerations, it is worthwhile noting that a CVM study can be completed more quickly than the TCM if a survey must be conducted to collect data for valuation. However, if origin-destination data already exist in the form of permits or license plate numbers recorded, the TCM would be a more cost-effective way of valuing recreational activities (Young et al. 1987).

## AN ALTERNATIVE METHOD OF ESTIMATING DEMAND

We can think of economic valuations of wildlife as ways we use money to measure the relative degree to which we demand services from the wildlife resource. Believing that economic valuation might be inappropriate in some circumstances, Gray and Larson (1982) proposed an alternative technique for estimating demand based on direct human actions.

Their method utilized a *demand intensity score* (DIS), derived from the extent of an individual's involvement in outdoor recreation and conservation activities, as a weighting device to adjust the importance of that individual's preference rankings for wildlife uses and species relative to other members of a survey population. In this study the investigators assumed that (1) the activities comprising the DIS represented personal preferences translated into actions; (2) that a total of the relevant actions for a specific wildlife resource can be called the "relative demand" for that resource; and (3) that each person's opportunity costs in time and money are implicitly embodied in the activities subsumed under the DIS.

In the example used to illustrate this methodology, a wildlife preference and demand questionnaire was developed, evaluated, pretested, and revised. The first section of the questionnaire elicited responses to ten questions about the frequency and extent of involvement in outdoor recreation and conservation activities to produce a demand intensity score (DIS) for each individual. For all questions, higher frequencies or levels of participation were awarded more points, with a maximum possible DIS of 100 for each respondent (Gray and Larson 1982).

The second section of the questionnaire sought responses reflecting attitudes toward, and preferences for, nonconsumptive wildlife uses as well as various species and taxonomic groups of wildlife. For example, a series of three questions required respondents to choose which of the following they would rather see on a walk or drive: (1) a common frog, toad, or salamander; a common turtle; a common snake; a common bird; or a common mammal; (2) which one of these groups they would prefer to see if all representatives were unusual; and (3) which one of these groups they would prefer to see if all representatives were rare or threatened species. Five additional questions asked respondents to check whether they would prefer to see a common, unusual, rare or threatened, or no representative at all from among the five groups previously mentioned (for example, a common bird, unusual bird, rare or threatened bird, or no bird at all).

These kinds of questions were used as the basis for a matrix comparison of preferences for different types of wildlife under different levels of expected occurrence, resulting in a series of preference scores for all respondents. Each respondent's DIS was then multiplied by each of his or her preference scores yielding "relative demand levels" (RDLs) for nonconsumptive wildlife uses and for species. The RDLs of each individual were considered to reflect an estimate of demand for the wildlife-related activities and species listed, relative to other persons in the survey. Mean RDLs were then computed and ranked for the entire sample.

The technique described was used to estimate relative demand among nonconsumptive wildlife-related activities and groups of wildlife species in a 1974 survey of municipal conservation commissioners in Massachusetts. Questionnaires were mailed to a 50 percent sample of commission members in the state, with the number of commission members from each wildlife management district sampled proportional to the population density of each district. Usable questionnaires were returned by 469 commission members. The mean DIS was 41.9 on a scale of 0 to 100, with a range of 0 to 87.5, which indicates that the DIS scores did not differ significantly from a normal distribution.

One finding from the survey illustrates the use of demand intensity scores (DIS's) to arrive at relative demand levels (RDLs) for wildlife-related activities and species. Poisonous snakes were ranked third in preference among five groups of reptiles by the survey respondents (Table 6.2). However, multiplying each respondent's preference scores by his or her DIS weighting factor resulted in the relative demand level for poisonous snakes being last among the five groups (Table 6.3).

The technique described seems reasonable because it invests the preferences of individuals who exhibit higher levels of involvement in relevant endeavors with a greater degree of importance and does so in proportion to their levels of activity. Persons who exhibit high levels of involvement in conservation and wildlife-related outdoor recreation are likely to be among the most knowledgeable and committed proponents of such activities and the underlying wildlife and habitat resources that make these activities possible. Their opinions should therefore be weighted more heavily than the views of the general public in making wildlife resource decisions.

It is important for resource managers and land-use planners to be in touch with the demands and perceptions of the publics they serve; however, it may not always be possible, or desirable, to estimate demand for wildlife using traditional economic means. By presenting an alternative, Gray and Larson (1982) hoped to stimulate a consideration of other techniques for estimating demand. A more complete knowledge of public demand for and among wildlife-related activities and wildlife species should help identify problem areas, suggest educational needs, and reduce conflicts.

A conceptual framework derived from the outdoor recreation research of Bryan (1980) may have applicability to wildlife value determination using extraeconomic methodologies such as the one just described. The central thesis of Bryan's scheme is that leisure behavior of outdoor recreationists can be arranged along a continuum of experience and specialization from generalists and novices to specialists

Table 6.2. Mean preference scores for groups of reptiles by 469 municipal conservation commissioners in Massachusetts in 1974.

| Preference rank | Reptilian group | Mean preference score |
|---|---|---|
| 1 | Freshwater and land turtles | 3.8 |
| 2 | Sea turtles | 3.6 |
| 3 | Poisonous snakes | 2.7 |
| 4 | Snapping turtles | 2.6 |
| 5 | Harmless snakes | 2.5 |

Source: Reprinted from "Estimating Relative Demand for Wildlife: Conservation Activity Indicators" by Gary G. Gray and Joseph S. Larson, *Environmental Management* 6 (Sept. 1982): 373–76. © 1982 by Springer-Verlag. Used with the permission of the publisher.

and experts. An individual's position on this continuum is reflected in the equipment used, the skills required, and the outdoor settings chosen for recreational experiences (Bryan 1980).

The satisfactions and benefits that persons are likely to seek from their outdoor experiences can also be predicted from their position on the continuum. Experienced sportsmen want to be able to sufficiently control their environment so that they can distinguish between luck and their own skill. Thus experienced outdoor recreationists having very specialized skills—whether hunter, birder, or wildlife photographer—are highly resource dependent.

Such high levels of resource dependency by skilled and experienced outdoor recreationists has implications for the notion of "fairness" in wildlife resource allocation. Consider several "fair" ways of allocating resources: (1) based on *equality,* in which all persons receive an equal share or have an equal chance to participate; (2) based on *equity,* which takes into account the ratios of "inputs" to "outcomes" so that some persons may be more deserving than others; (3) based on *need,* which considers whether or not a person's requirements can be met in another way; and (4) based on *social efficiency,* which involves putting a resource to its most highly valued use (see Bryan 1980). In Bryan's view, "fairness" according to three of these four criteria would dictate preferential consideration for experienced outdoor recreationists having specialized needs in the pursuit of their wildlife-related activities.

Although developed independently, Bryan's (1980) idea seems to furnish a conceptual rationale for using the demand intensity score (DIS). The DIS, on the other hand, provides a means for actually estimating the relative position of wildlife users along Bryan's continuum of experience and specialization.

Table 6.3. Mean relative demand level for groups of repitles by 469 municipal conservation commissioners in Massachusetts in 1974.

| Relative demand rank | Reptilian group | Mean relative demand level[a] |
|---|---|---|
| 1 | Freshwater and land turtles | 156.1 |
| 2 | Sea turtles | 148.4 |
| 3 | Harmless snakes | 108.2 |
| 4 | Snapping turtles | 105.5 |
| 5 | Poisonous snakes | 95.6 |

Source: Reprinted from "Estimating Relative Demand for Wildlife: Conservation Activity Indicators" by Gary G. Gray and Joseph S. Larson, *Environmental Management* 6 (Sept. 1982): 373–76. 
[a] The relative demand level (RDL) for each group was calculated by multiplying the demand intensity score for every respondent by each individual preference score. Mean RDLs for each group were then computed and ranked.

## INTEGRATING ECONOMICS INTO WILDLIFE MANAGEMENT

It was wildlife biologists rather than economists who first expressed an interest in the economic aspects of wildlife (Davis and Lim 1987). In the early thirties Aldo Leopold (1933:391–405) included a chapter on economics and aesthetics of game animals in his classic book *Game Management.* After World War II a number of studies were conducted on the economic value of wildlife within various states. These typically estimated total private expenditures that could be attributed to wildlife and the gross values of raw furs or other wildlife commodities, based on surveys of hunters and fishermen. In 1955 the first nationwide survey of hunters and fishermen was conducted by the U.S. Fish and Wildlife Service, a project that has been repeated every five years since. In view of this record we cannot claim any dearth of wildlife economic research. As Stoddard (1951) contended, however, it may be that wildlife economics is a neglected management tool.

Maybe a strong predilection of wildlife professionals toward the resource they hold so dear makes them reluctant to submit wildlife to economic scrutiny. "The astute wildlife professional realizes that to embrace economics wholeheartedly would require deemphasizing a deeply held personal commitment" (Bishop 1987). Wildlife professionals may, however, be more successful in securing advantages for "their resource" if they would use economics for its benefit. This might be done by employing their specialized knowledge and expertise to discover and enumerate all of the uses and benefits of wildlife relevant to a proposed project and working with sympathetic economists to estimate the *true* economic value of wildlife. Perhaps in a fuller accounting the wildlife resource can withstand economic evaluation more successfully than we have generally thought possible.

PERSPECTIVE

## Picasso and Pachyderms: Markets for Art and Wildlife

What is a Picasso masterpiece worth? A Picasso self-portrait, *Yo Picasso* (painted in 1901 when the artist was twenty years old), brought $5.3 million in 1981. When sold again in 1989, this work went for an astronomical $47,850,000, a record price for a Picasso and the second-highest price ever paid for a single artwork at auction. Vincent van Gogh's *Irises* commanded the largest price at $53.9 million in November 1987.

Does anyone really believe that auctioning off a work of art detracts from its aesthetic qualities? In fact, probably not one person in a hundred has the expertise to appreciate fully a given work of art. For the plebeian population, hearing quotations of astronomical prices may in fact give an art work some meaning where it previously lacked any at all. Those who do not esteem art at least understand that uniqueness confers value, and figures in the millions of dollars certainly indicate handsome values.

What Picasso and van Gogh paintings share in common with wildlife is a perception by sizable publics that consider art and wild animals to have aesthetic properties. On the other hand, art and wildlife differ in many respects, but one is germane to our discussion: there is an acceptable market for works of art, whereas, tragically, much wildlife is valued and traded on black markets.

One wildlife commodity—ivory—has gotten widespread coverage by the news media because the demand for this product is jeopardizing the very existence of elephants in Africa. Poachers, often armed with semi-automatic weapons, are ravaging elephant populations. In 1979, there were approximately 1,300,000 elephants in Africa. Today, optimistic estimates suggest that less than 750,000 remain. Poaching is the major cause of this decline (Brian 1988).

It is easy to understand the temptation. Poachers are usually poor Africans who can earn more from a pair of large tusks than they could from a year's honest labor. Most of the revenue, however, goes to ivory smugglers, go-betweens, and traders. Ultimately, beyond money, there is sadness—for slaughtered elephants, the very symbol of African wildlife, and for the human casualties, especially wildlife rangers who have died in gun battles with poachers (Schindler 1988).

A market is inevitably created whenever there is a demand, and there is certainly a demand for ivory. Americans who purchase ivory products are implicit accomplices in the killing. Once ivory has been carved, it is impossible to determine the legality of its source. And experts estimate that nearly 80 percent of all ivory being sold in world markets came from elephants that were poached (Brian 1988).

This problem can be attacked by a combination of two actions. First, through negative incentives—by eliminating the market for ivory. A campaign several years ago curtailed the trade in spotted cats, so that one rarely sees a leopard coat worn anymore. The African Wildlife Foundation is pressing for a similar ban on ivory (Brian 1988; Schindler 1988).

The second action involves education and positive incentives. The greatest value of elephants is as a tourist attraction. In Kenya, a living elephant generates approximately $14,375 each year in tourist revenues. Ivory from the same animal yields a one-time dividend of about $1,880 (Morell 1990). This comparison should be widely publicized in Africa—to government officials and villagers alike. Then, a share of the tourist revenue must be passed down to the local level. The results of an experimental project in Zambia are relevant here. They showed poaching was greatly reduced, local economies benefited, and village attitudes toward wildlife conservation improved when residents were trained and employed in various activities related to protecting and managing wildlife resources (Lewis, Kaweche, and Mwenya 1990).

PERSPECTIVE

## An Economic Approach to Ecological Studies

From a human perspective, wild animals are economic goods. They provide at least some members of society with satisfaction, and they are too limited in abundance to meet all human wants and needs at no cost (McDivitt 1987). But animals can be thought of as economic beings as well as economic goods. They require—demand, we might say—resources (food, water, space, shelter, etc.) to live and reproduce, and these resources are likewise limited in supply. Some ecologists are now employing an economic approach to certain ecological problems—considering what an animal can afford to do under certain conditions in order to minimize its costs and maximize its benefits. Energy is the currency of exchange for "economic interactions" of wildlife with its environment. In particular, an economic approach is being used to study energetic constraints on survival and maintenance behaviors, and reproductive behaviors, of individual social vertebrates under group conditions (see Gosling and Petrie 1981).

One type of behavior that falls under the general heading of survival and maintenance behaviors is avoiding predation. Some social behaviors thought to be important in reducing predation include using other animals as cover, using other animals as an information system to detect predators, group defenses (including mobbing), and intraspecific avoidance (that is, increased distances between members of the same species). One can ask, "What are the energetic costs and benefits of these behaviors?" as part of what Gosling and Petrie (1981) called the central question: "How does social behavior affect the ergonomic efficiency of the individual and how far is ergonomic efficiency a corollary of inclusive fitness [in evolutionary terms]?"

Looking briefly at just one aspect of applying economics to predator avoidance, we might consider the antipredator significance, to an individual animal, of joining a group. An animal is less likely to be killed by a predator in open habitats when in a group than alone. But as group size increases there are costs associated with group membership; for example, the amount of food available per individual is correspondingly smaller when groups are comprised of many members (see Gosling and Petrie 1981).

Other costs of group membership include interference and competition, which reduce the time available for feeding as well as involving energy expenditures. And since animals will occasionally make mistakes in predator identification, the number of false alarms might increase with group size (see Gosling and Petrie 1981).

In a study of territorial marking by the gerenuk, a medium-sized African antelope, Gosling (1981) used an economic approach. He was interested in testing a model "that assumed both increasing advantage to the male in occupying a larger area and increasing cost in marking it." Findings of the study indicated that the area male gerenuks mark, using antorbital gland secretions, forms an irregular oval shape with occasional radiating arms. Conspicuous twigs, and plant species frequently eaten by gerenuks, were most often marked, and plants were marked at a height that allowed the secretion to be easily detected. These results were consistent with the model's main prediction "that the male should place its limited supply of marks [due to a finite supply of secretion and limited time available] only where they were most likely to be found and to avoid marking where detection was less likely" (Gosling 1981).

Energy, rather than money, has also been proposed by Howard Odum as a currency of exchange for dealing with human problems in such diverse fields as economics, politics, and religion. He remarked that "when systems are considered in energy terms, some of the bewildering complexity of our world disappears." Diagramming human systems using energy flows "helps us consider the great problems of power, pollution, population, food, and war free from our fetters of indoctrination" (1971:vii).

---

## SUGGESTED READING

Decker, D. J. and G. R. Goff (eds.). 1987. *Valuing Wildlife: Economic and Social Perspectives*. Boulder: Westview Press. 424 pages. Based on a symposium sponsored by the New York Chapter of the Wildlife Society, this readable book successfully achieves its intent "to serve as a state-of-the-art guide to the methods of determining the economic and social values of wildlife, the applications for environmental impact assessment and mitigation concepts in wildlife valuation, and strategies in wildlife planning and policy."

# Wildlife Law, Policy, and Administration 7

In every wildlife conservation problem there is some aspect of what Garrett Hardin (1968) called "the tragedy of the commons." Self-interest dictates that individuals confronted with a wildlife exploitation decision should "take what they can get." The result, with wildlife as with other goods that society holds in common, is "immediate benefit to a few at the expense of long-term cost to the many." The solution to the problem lies in some form of deterrence—the imposition of legal and political authority to control exploitation (Brokaw 1978).

## WILDLIFE LAW

Just as wildlife cannot exist independent of its natural environment, wildlife law cannot be separated from its legal context. Wildlife law comprises an enormous collection of statutes, judicial decisions, and legal doctrines, even when the term is used in a narrow sense to refer "only to laws expressly designed to regulate wildlife and our use of it or to benefit wildlife in some substantial way" (Bean 1978).

### *Historical Background*

Wildlife occupied a unique legal status in Western civilization extending as far back as the Roman Empire. In their natural state, wild animals were "commons"—they were the property of no one, yet they became the property of whomever captured or killed them. Roman landowners had an exclusive right to the wild animals on their properties, but this restriction seems to have been related more to the rights of land ownership than to limitations on the use of wildlife (Bean 1983).

Wild animals themselves apparently had no rights or legal protection under Roman law. They inspired works of art and were a source of entertainment, but were never held in reverence as they had been in the cultures of ancient Egypt and Greece. Paradoxically, the Romans—who recognized and appreciated the grace and beauty of wildlife—treated animals with utter cruelty. Large numbers of exotic animals were often put to an agonizing death after they had been exhibited. The biblical commandment that gave humans dominion over animals was carried to a perverse extreme in the exercise of the Roman tenet that animals existed for the use and pleasure of humankind (Favre 1983).

The Jewish culture in existence before and during the Roman period manifested a much different attitude. Cruelty to animals was prohibited, and killing animals for sport was considered improper (Favre 1983).

There are no references to the welfare of wild animals in the New Testament of the Bible, and the Catholic Church likewise expressed no concern for animals as its power and authority grew during the Dark and Middle Ages. In the *Summa Contra Gentiles,* St. Thomas Aquinas expressed the Catholic doctrine that animals were provided by divine providence for human use, so that it is not wrong to kill them or to make use of them in any other way (Favre 1983).

It is instructive to see how different historical attitudes toward wild animals in the Jewish and Catholic religions also represent the dichotomy of views toward wild animals in modern society (Favre 1983).

## *Early English Law*

According to Sir William Blackstone, the eminent eighteenth-century legal scholar, the origins of the feudal system and early European regulations on taking wild game were one and the same. To retain their conquests, the nobles of feudal Europe sought to prevent those whom they had conquered from keeping weapons. This could be done most effectively through a prohibition on hunting; thus the use of nets and snares was proscribed and commoners were forbidden to carry arms (Bean 1983).

Restrictions on hunting in England date to shortly after the Saxon invasion, about A.D. 450. Parcels of land were given to nobles, and the tracts not distributed were known as "royal forests" and reserved for the sole use and pleasure of the ruling monarch. The royal forests were enlarged considerably after the Norman Conquest in 1066, which was accompanied by an expansion of the legal and political system necessary to administer them (Bean 1983).

William the Conqueror enlarged his exclusive authority to hunt beyond the mere boundaries of royal forests and soon claimed the sole right to hunt throughout the kingdom. Hunting prerogatives were often bestowed on the favored nobility, however. These privileges included franchises of "park," the right to pursue such "superior" beasts as deer and fox across one's own land; "chase," the right to pursue "superior" creatures across the lands of others; and "free-warren," which allowed the holder to kill "inferior" beasts such as fowl and hares so long as the noble prevented others from doing likewise (Bean 1983). Obviously, hunting became a means for the nobility to preserve their status and served to distinguish them from the peasants, who simply thought of wildlife as food and materials (Favre 1983).

One of the earliest English laws actually intended to protect wild animals was passed in 1581, in response to declining numbers of pheasants and partridges. The statute regulated the time and manner of hunting these game birds—night kills and "hawking of birds in corn fields" both being prohibited—but it was aimed at protecting a food source and a sport rather than recognizing the rights of these species to exist (Favre 1983).

### *Early American Wildlife Law*

The ultimate source of wildlife law in the United States was English common law up to 1776. Two features were central to English wildlife law of this period: first, "qualification statutes," which restricted hunting privileges to the prominent or propertied elite who were trusted friends of the crown; and second, the "forest jurisdiction," an extensive area reserved for hunting by the monarch, which had its own courts and doctrines for wildlife protection and was administered as a jurisdiction separate from the common law (Bean 1978).

These two features of English wildlife law had different fates in the United States. The fundamental idea of sovereign authority over wildlife was established early in the history of the American republic, but whether that sovereign authority was vested in the federal government or resided with the states was a matter of long and acrimonious dispute. The other notion—that laws governing the use of wildlife should favor one group or class over another—never took root in American soil (Bean 1978).

There were few federal wildlife laws in the eighteenth and nineteenth centuries. Those that did exist regulated hunting in federal territories and banned hunting in Yellowstone National Park. As a consequence, states successfully moved into this regulatory void, and state authority over wildlife was upheld every time it was challenged during the 1800s. The rationale was that the states had inherited the legal powers of the English crown, including the right to regulate wildlife (Matthews 1986).

## *Wildlife Litigation in the Supreme Court*

The first Supreme Court case involving public rights to wildlife—*Martin v. Waddell*—may have been the most important. The plaintiff in that 1842 case, an owner of land adjoining the Raritan River in New Jersey, asked the court to affirm his exclusive right to take oysters from the river. He claimed ownership of the river bottom, as well as its banks, based on his title that traced to a 1664 grant from King Charles II to the Duke of York (Bean 1978, 1983).

The opinion written by Chief Justice Roger Taney reasoned that the original grant, insofar as the river and its bottom were concerned, was not simply a conveyance of ordinary property rights; it involved a "public trust." Accordingly, the right of the public to fish superseded the landowner's property claim. Taney's opinion established the "public trust" doctrine, which was unique in English as well as American legal thought of the time, but is now well established in American jurisprudence (Bean 1978, 1983).

An 1896 Supreme Court case, *Geer v. Connecticut,* gave rise to the "state ownership" doctrine. Edgar Geer was convicted of possessing game birds with the intent to ship them to another state. The birds had been lawfully killed in Connecticut, but Geer's intent to ship them out of state was unlawful because he was not a Connecticut resident. "Thus, the narrow legal question was whether the state law improperly interfered with the power conferred on Congress to regulate interstate commerce" (Bean 1978). The decision upheld Geer's conviction and affirmed the authority of states to regulate their wildlife, but interjected continuing controversy by referring to the states' authority over wildlife as "ownership." During the eighty-three years this decision stood it was the primary justification for exclusive wildlife management by the states (Matthews 1986).

Later, the federal government's first step into wildlife regulation, with the Lacey Act of 1900, was a cautious one. Its provisions placed limits on importing foreign animals and prohibited interstate transportation of wildlife killed in violation of state laws. Because market hunting was illegal in many states, this statute had an impact on the activity. Thus, the power of the federal government was enlisted in enforcing state game laws (Bean 1978; Matthews 1986).

The Migratory Bird Act, passed in 1913, was found unconstitutional in two federal district court cases. While on appeal to the Supreme Court, the Department of Agriculture sought a constitutional basis for the legislation by urging negotiation of a treaty with Great Britain on behalf of Canada. Such a treaty was signed in 1916, followed by passage of the Migratory Bird Treaty Act in 1918, which implemented the treaty, so the appeal of the 1913 act was dismissed without its constitutionality ever having been decided. The treaty and act completely prohibited hunting of migratory insectivorous birds and regulated the hunting of certain migratory game birds (Bean 1978).

The validity of the treaty and act was upheld by the Supreme Court in the case of *Missouri v. Holland,* which was prompted by the arrest of Missouri's attorney general (who had violated the act) by federal game warden Ray Holland. Justice Oliver Wendell Holmes reasoned, in effect, that Missouri based its claim of exclusive authority to regulate migratory birds on an assertion of title, that ownership is required for title, that possession is the beginning of ownership, and that wild birds are not in the possession of anyone. Furthermore, without the federal protection afforded by the treaty and its associated statute there might be no more migratory birds to regulate, and nothing in the Constitution compelled the federal government to stand idle as the resource was being destroyed (Bean 1978).

The next major development in the state ownership controversy involved the question of whether the federal government had authority to regulate wildlife on federal lands. The secretary of agriculture had ordered the well-known deer reduction in the Kaibab National Forest because overbrowsing by deer was destroying their habitat. In *Hunt v. United States* the high court ruled that the federal government's authority to "protect its lands and property does not admit of doubt" and therefore takes precedence over state game laws or other state statutes. This action referred to the property clause of the U.S. Constitution (Article 4, section 3) (Bean 1978; Matthews 1986).

More recently, a 1976 Supreme Court ruling on the federal lands issue involved the constitutionality of the Free-Roaming Horses and Burros Act. In *Kleppe v. New Mexico* state authorities, responding to the request of a rancher holding a federal grazing permit, had captured some protected burros and sold them at auction. The Bureau of Land Management demanded that the burros be returned, whereupon the state filed suit to have the act declared unconstitutional. The Supreme Court's decision in the case affirmed the "complete power" of Congress over federal lands, including its authority to regulate the wildlife present there (Bean 1978; Matthews 1986).

## *Federal Land Management Laws and Wildlife*

Several significant pieces of federal legislation related to land management and policy are crucial to wildlife. The Multiple-Use Sustained-Yield Act passed in 1960 provided for outdoor recreation, range, timber, watershed, wildlife, and fish uses of national forests and authorized the U.S. Forest Service to establish wilderness areas. According to this legislation, multiple use may be achieved in several ways: by alternating the use of resources in an area over time, by the concurrent use of several resources in an area, by geographical separation of uses within a larger area, or by combinations of these.

The 1964 Wilderness Act established a National Wilderness Preservation System. Some language in this act recalls exhortations of wilderness philosophers, as in the definition of wilderness as "an area where the earth and its community of life are untrammeled by man, where man himself is a visitor who does not remain." In order to qualify, federal land must be undeveloped, "retaining its primeval character and influence, without permanent improvement or human habitation," and must appear "to have been affected primarily by the forces of nature with the imprint of man's work substantially unnoticeable"; have "outstanding opportunities for solitude or a primitive and unconfined type of recreation"; be five thousand acres or more in area; and, optionally, contain features of ecological, geological, scientific, scenic, or historical value.

In essence the National Forest Management Act of 1976 replaced the 1897 legislation that had established the U.S. Forest Service. Its provisions, in large part, are broad, addressing the contemporary challenge of using an interdisciplinary approach to manage Forest Service lands for their watershed, fish and wildlife, rangeland, and outdoor recreation values as well as for timber resources. Continuing accusations and legal writs directed at the Forest Service by several conservation organizations attest to strong views that the agency does not carry out timber harvests with sufficient consideration for the wildlife, recreation, and aesthetic resources of forest lands.

The Federal Land Policy and Management Act, another 1976 piece of legislation, constituted an organic act for the U.S. Bureau of Land Management (BLM). It provided for the multiple-use, sustained-yield management of most BLM lands, so wildlife interests received some consideration along with rangeland allocations for livestock production and mineral extraction.

Two well-known statutes—one long established, the other more recent—mandate a consideration of wildlife values in planning for development of land and water resources. One of the first "consultation" statutes, the Fish and Wildlife Coordination Act of 1934, was forward-looking in philosophy and intent—by calling for studying pollution effects on wildlife and development of a program to maintain wildlife on federal lands. Unfortunately, it proved weak and almost worthless in practice (Bean 1978).

In 1946, Congress amended the act to require joint consultation of any federal agency (or private party with a federal permit) planning a project that would impound, divert, or control any body of water with the U.S. Fish and Wildlife Service and the affected state wildlife agency. The intent was to give wildlife conservation adequate consideration consistent with the other aspects of a project. This legislation, too, fell short of the desired results. Thus, Congress enacted sweeping amendments in 1958 that required that wildlife conservation be given equal consideration with the other aspects of water resource development (Bean 1978).

The role of the Coordination Act was largely conscripted by the National Environmental Policy Act (NEPA) of 1969. This legislation requires that major federal actions thought to have potentially significant environmental impacts be preceded by an environmental impact statement (EIS) fully disclosing those effects. Gradually, as the implications of the NEPA process have become clear, this act has assumed the protective role envisioned for the Coordination Act.

## *Other Important Federal Wildlife Laws*

A few other federal laws have particular significance for wildlife. The Endangered Species Act of 1969 and subsequent reauthorizations of this legislation provide for protection of selected species of threatened and endangered wildlife. Protection includes prohibitions against harvesting, importation, and possession and designations of "critical habitat" to prevent habitat deterioration or destruction.

Passage of the Marine Mammal Protection Act in 1972 brought a moratorium on taking or importing marine mammals and their products, though there are exemptions for scientific research and for subsistence hunting by Native Americans.

The Federal Aid in Wildlife Restoration Act of 1937, often called the Pittman-Robertson (P-R) Act after its congressional sponsors, levied an excise tax (now set at 11 percent) on sales of sporting arms and ammunition. Revenues realized from this tax are collected by the federal government and apportioned to the states according to their land areas and numbers of licensed hunters. The actual distribution of P-R monies requires that states furnish one dollar for every three dollars of P-R funding they receive. Furthermore, any state that diverts revenues derived from hunting license sales to activities unrelated to wildlife is not eligible for P-R funds. This provision was instrumental in ensuring that wildlife funding is actually used for wildlife projects. State legislatures can no longer tamper with state wildlife funding, or hold wildlife budgets hostage, so wildlife management at the state level is assured of financial stability.

The Pittman-Robertson Act has been amended several times in the years since its passage. Presently, P-R monies can be used to maintain projects already completed and to manage state wildlife areas, as well as to fund new P-R projects. In addition, funding can be requested for comprehensive five-year plans, as well as for individual federal-aid projects.

The Federal Aid in Fish Restoration Act was passed in 1950, largely because of the success of the P-R legislation. The D-J (for Dingell-Johnson, its congressional sponsors) Act also provides for funding based on a 3:1 federal-to-state dollar ratio, with the federal share derived from a 10 percent tax on selected fishing tackle. As with the P-R Act, D-J monies are allocated on the basis of numbers of each state's licensed anglers and the extent of water within each state.

## *Native American Treaty Rights to Wildlife*

Treaties between the United States and Native American tribes are similar to treaties with foreign nations in that they impose obligations on the federal government. Because such treaties also supersede any conflicting state laws, they may restrict certain regulatory or management prerogatives of state wildlife agencies (Bean 1983).

The 1896 *Ward v. Race Horse* case was one of the first in which the Supreme Court considered the conflicting claims of a state's authority to regulate wildlife and the treaty hunting rights reserved to Native Americans. This case involved a Bannock named Race Horse who had been convicted of killing elk in violation of Wyoming law. Race Horse contended that his conviction violated an 1869 treaty that gave the Bannock "rights to hunt on the unoccupied land of the United States, so long as game may be found thereon." The conflict arose because, soon after Wyoming was admitted to the Union in 1890, the state enacted game laws it claimed were applicable even on federal lands within the state. The offense for which Race Horse had been convicted was committed on just such federal lands. In writing the court's majority opinion, Justice Edward White reasoned that the federal government lacked authority to regulate wildlife on federal lands within a state, an assumption not finally rejected until the 1976 *Kleppe v. New Mexico* decision mentioned earlier (Bean 1983).

Justice White's interpretation of treaties in *Race Horse* was abandoned by the Supreme Court a few years later. In *United States v. Winans* (1905), the court held that the Yakima had "the right of taking fish at all usual and accustomed places, in common with the citizens of the

Territory." Thus, they were even entitled to use privately owned lands if their usual fishing places occurred there.

These two cases concern state wildlife regulation, as do many adjudicated since. There has, however, been some litigation of federal wildlife regulations as well. Congress has the right to alter or nullify existing treaty rights, but the courts have generally been unwilling to infer such a right in the absence of an explicit directive from the legislative body. In *United States v. Cutler,* for example, the Migratory Bird Treaty Act was considered to be inapplicable to hunting by Shoshone on a reservation. Treaty rights have led to exemptions for Native Americans in recent federal wildlife legislation (Bean 1983).

## *Historic Goals of Wildlife Law*

Historically, wildlife law has had four major goals. First, laws can be used to facilitate periodic harvests of populations managed to produce sustained yields. In this respect, wildlife management was, and still is, little more than a glorified livestock operation. Early English lawmakers did not impose elaborate restrictions on harvest levels of game animals because weapons were primitive and numbers of hunters were very limited. They were quick to act, however, if stocks of desirable species were thought to be in danger (Lund 1980).

Second, wildlife statutes can be written so as to regulate human behavior. Hunting provides one of the few justifications for the use of weapons; therefore, laws purportedly intended to regulate hunting can be designed to restrict or encourage the use of arms (Lund 1980).

Third, wildlife laws can be written so as to favor one socioeconomic group over another. Discrimination on the basis of class was openly embraced until the midnineteenth century, and access to wildlife was treated as a unique form of wealth or privilege (Lund 1980).

Fourth, wildlife laws can aim to vindicate the supposed rights and desires of wild animals. Several hundred years ago, the view that animals might have rights was not considered so preposterous as it often is today. It was only necessary that someone champion their interests—and that person was the ruling monarch. Although one might argue that this monarch was interested solely in fostering sporting opportunity for the nobility, the sixteenth-century judge and scholar John Manwood asserted that the ruler also found "delight and pleasure" from the animals that "rest and abide" in the forest, content in the noble's "safe protection" (Lund 1980).

In reviewing these historic goals of wildlife law, it is instructive to realize how fully they have been preserved. Laws still ensure that most harvested wildlife populations will continue to produce sustained yields by controlling the manner, amount, and timing of harvests. Laws still regulate human behavior by licensing hunters, specifying the animals that can be hunted, defining the areas open to hunting, setting the dates of open seasons, limiting access to control hunting pressure, stipulating the daily bag and possession limits, and indicating which arms are permissible. Furthermore, laws such as the Endangered Species Act and the National Environmental Policy Act accord certain rights to wildlife. Only the third goal, that laws can be written to favor a particular socioeconomic group, does not seem pertinent to the contemporary North American situation, although it may still apply elsewhere.

## WILDLIFE POLICY

A policy is a particular course of action chosen from among several alternatives as a guide to determining present and future decisions. By its very nature, policy is a product of the political process.

### *Wildlife Policy, Administration, and Liberal Education*

"Policy is a reflection of the culture in which it is formulated and operates" (Henning 1974:18). In American society, pragmatic and pluralistic characteristics tend to dominate. As a consequence, there is often no comprehensive policy where natural resource issues are involved. Instead, there may be a collection of fragmented short-term policies "focusing on problems and performance rather than principles, upon action rather than upon ideas" (Wengert 1962).

One reason for some of these shortcomings is that wildlife and other natural resource agencies are often staffed, particularly at the local level, by administrators who have been educated as technical specialists (Henning 1974). Yet "a merely technical education, however excellent, does not prepare one sufficiently for the task of developing long-range policies" (as quoted in Henning 1974).

Business and corporate leaders have found that a liberal education is the best undergraduate preparation for a policy-making career. Former International Harvester president John L. McCaffrey put it this way: "The world of the specialist is a narrow one and it tends to produce narrow human beings. The specialist usually does not see over-all effects . . . and so he tends to judge good and evil, right and wrong, by the sole standard of his own specialty" (Pamp 1955).

How, then, are the humanities pertinent to persons making policy decisions about wildlife resources? First, there is evidence that one's language ability is an important factor in administrative success. "Language is not only a tool; it is the person himself" (Pamp 1955). Second, the study of literature adds breadth and depth to the personality. Third, "the most valuable commodity in management is ideas," and the humanities provide the most experience in exploring ideas.

In dealing with human problems in wildlife, the successful wildlife administrator must do pretty much what a literary critic does: perceive the "theme" of a situation, produce several different perspectives on the problem "combining the ingredients of people and data," develop insights that are subjective yet analytic, and fashion a creative solution. "The creative element in management, as in the humanities, is developed by the disciplined imagination of a mind working in the widest range of dimensions possible" (Pamp 1955).

It is probably unrealistic to expect that wildlife biologists—with educational needs ranging through several scientific disciplines to statistics, communications, and economics—will also have time to acquire a full-blown liberal education. Still, as Peek observed, "We would do well to ensure that the undergraduate [wildlife] education remains as diverse as possible in recognition that the field itself is diverse, with room for a variety of people with a variety of interests and skills" (1989). Likewise, in an era when environmental problems and natural resource conflicts are increasingly prominent, it is no less desirable that students of the liberal arts round out their educations with course offerings such as introductory wildlife ecology and natural resources conservation.

In a role-reversal experience, fourteen professors of science or engineering at Cornell University participated in a week-long intensive course in which they studied the poetry of Chaucer and Wordsworth (Peterson 1990; Tobias and Abel 1990). The experiment was prompted, in part, by the hypothesis that scientists are just as uncomfortable studying humanities as humanists are studying science. In one outcome, most of the participants thought that taking some humanities courses might help students in the sciences to develop the kind of intellectual flexibility that is useful in scientific research, especially the ability to see patterns and trends and to make decisions about which data are important. Thus, exposure to the humanities may have worthwhile research rewards for wildlife scientists as well as broadening their frame of reference for policy-making roles.

The Aspen Institute programs immerse business leaders in the humanities for short stints during summer sessions. A similar program with a natural resources flair might well be a useful adjunct to the personal and professional lives of wildlife administrators. This would be one way of expanding the horizons of midcareer wildlife professionals occupying administrative positions.

## *Historic Wildlife Policy Statements*

The first comprehensive American wildlife policy was presented at the American Game Conference held in 1930. As chair of the committee that drafted the statement, Aldo Leopold urged its adoption, which he believed would help settle conflicting opinions by experimentation: "The only really new thing which this game policy suggests is that we quit arguing over abstract ideas, and instead go out and try them." In Leopold's view, the necessity of this approach was grounded in the observation that game conservation was "in a particularly difficult stage," and that game stocks, habitat, and even species were being lost (Leopold 1930).

Seth Gordon (1930) advocated passage of the policy in words that sounded almost desperate, saying "that we *will get nowhere unless we try something.*" He further commented that there seemed to be two points of common agreement: first, that hunters must find a way to pay for their shooting or there will be none in the future; and second, that landowners must be treated equitably lest they prohibit hunting and ignore the game crop.

The policy statement itself noted that game animals can be safely hunted only where they are protected against excessive harvesting and furnished with cover, food, and protection from their natural enemies. These provisions constitute game management (Leopold et al. 1930). The report went on to recommend seven fundamental actions:

> 1. *Extend public ownership and management* of game lands just as far and as fast as land prices and available funds permit. Such extensions must often be for forestry, watershed, and recreation, as well as for game purposes.
>
> 2. *Recognize the landowner as the custodian of public game on all other land,* protect him from the irresponsible shooter, and compensate him for putting his land in productive condition. . . .
>
> 3. *Experiment* to determine in each state the merits and demerits of various ways of bringing the three parties [landholder, hunter, and public] into productive relationship with each other. . . .
>
> 4. *Train men* for skillful game administration, management, and fact-finding. Make game a profession like forestry, agriculture, and other forms of applied biology.
>
> 5. *Find facts* on what to do on the land to make game abundant.
>
> 6. *Recognize the non-shooting protectionist and the scientist* as sharing with sportsmen and landowners the responsibility for conservation of

wild life as a whole. Insist on a joint conservation program, *jointly formulated and jointly financed.*

7. *Provide funds.* Insist on public funds from general taxation for all betterments serving wild life as a whole. Let the sportsmen pay for all betterments serving game alone.

The 1930 policy statement was remarkable for its time: it recommended development of a wilderness system when wilderness preservation was just a dream of a few conservationists; it called for the training of wildlife professionals when the wildlife managers in North America consisted primarily of a few gamekeepers imported from Great Britain; it advocated expansion of the national wildlife refuge system and cooperation between the United States and Canada in the management of migratory waterfowl; and it called for emphasis on the natural production of wildlife through habitat development and for a more understanding and sympathetic attitude toward predators, in an age when game farms and predator control were common practice (Leonard 1973).

Reading this 1930 policy statement is worthwhile as a reminder that we continue to confront some of the same issues today. Furthermore, even in this early policy statement there was a recognition that wildlife values should extend beyond hunted species: "The public is (and the sportsman ought to be) just as much interested in conserving non-game species, forests, fish and other wild life as in conserving game" (Leopold et al. 1930).

Forty-three years later, in 1973, Durward Allen presented to the North American Wildlife and Natural Resources Conference a new North American wildlife policy formulated by a multidisciplinary committee he chaired (Allen et al. 1973). The report of this committee addressed the entire range of wildlife issues, so it is virtually impossible to provide a brief, yet adequate, summary of its statements and recommendations. Nevertheless, it seems desirable to attempt to impart the tenor of its message, since much of it remains relevant today.

The introductory "Principles and Premises" section reminds us that all living things have an essential role in self-maintaining ecosystems, and that human dependence on living things is a reality of human survival. Since soils, waters, vegetation, and animal life are inevitably human resources, their optimal use is achieved when they yield "the most significant benefits to generations of the present while improving productivity for the future."

Wildlife uses and values are among the satisfactions of life that are largely taken for granted and therefore poorly appraised. Nevertheless, wildlife is an important part of a living standard that Americans should strive to preserve. Although wildlife is valued for nonconsumptive recreation, aesthetic amenity, sport and subsistence hunting, and commercial harvesting, clearly its most important role is biological—as part of the intricate and interrelated biotic scheme that supports us all. As human numbers continue to increase, the very survival of many species is threatened; therefore, the plight of endangered species must be a priority for utilitarian as well as ethical reasons.

Looking at wildlife in land and water use, the welfare of wildlife is determined by the fate of wildlife habitats. Farmland wildlife is adversely affected by many "big-business" agricultural practices, including large expanses of crop monocultures, which are in turn ecologically vulnerable to animal pests and disease organisms. Challenges in farmland wildlife management include trespass control, compensation to farmers for habitat improvements, professional wildlife input into planning by soil conservation and watershed districts, and assistance—technical as well as financial—to farmers for crops damaged by wildlife.

Forest and rangeland wildlife are greatly affected by silvicultural practices and timber harvest cycles on forest lands and by stocking rates (that is, per hectare livestock numbers) and rotation periods of domestic animals on rangelands. Commercial timber and livestock interests commonly have undue influence on forest and range management policy and practices to the detriment of wildlife. Forest management practices that benefit wildlife include limiting clearcuts to small areas, maintaining a mixture of tree species and age classes, retaining fruit- and mast-bearing trees and shrubs, letting good hollow trees stand, keeping undisturbed borders of trees along waterways, and leaving piled cuttings unburned. Rangelands on which brush control treatments are performed should have critical areas reserved to maintain cover for wildlife and to ensure the interspersion of vegetation types. New plantings on improved rangelands benefit wildlife most when a variety of plant species are used.

Three problems stand out from among many threatening waters and wetlands: pollution; dredging, channeling, and other "artificializing" of rivers and floodplains; and wetland conservation. The destruction of wetland habitats, in particular, has reached a crisis stage. We can begin to remedy this situation by ending subsidies that degrade or destroy aquatic habitats, compensating farmers for maintaining and restoring wetland habitats, creating and restoring wetlands along highway rights of way, and adding wetland units to wildlife refuge systems at all levels of government.

Wilderness preservation provides a variety of environmental and social values, including scientific study of biotic communities and ecological relationships, preservation of species, and opportunities for primitive recreation. Pervasive human influences have rendered authentic primordial ecosystems rare. Designated wilderness can be maintained or upgraded, however, by timely acquisition of privately held lands, enforcing quotas on recreational use of wilderness areas, phasing out incompatible uses, such as grazing and mining, and continual review of candidate areas for wilderness status.

Several problems and controversies related to the biology and sociology of hunting remain unresolved despite the passage of years. Antihunting sentiment has grown as people are further removed from their rural roots. Public outrage over wanton killing of nongame wildlife imperils the interests of all who engage in shooting sports. Loss of habitat to urban sprawl deprives hunters of places and things to shoot, causes dissatisfaction with the quality of the outdoor experience, provokes antagonism leading to posting of land and trespass violations, and creates political and social pressure for artificial stocking. Hunting opportunities can be increased by such means as forming landowner-hunter cooperatives to manage hunting, granting access to commercial lands as a corporate public-relations gesture, paid shooting preserves, private gun clubs, sale of hunting privileges on farms and ranches managed for wildlife, and expanded government acquisition of lands for outdoor recreation including hunting.

Briefly, in other issues addressed by the 1973 policy statement: it was deemed desirable that hunting conditions be kept natural (with any "put-and-take" hunting to be fully supported by participant fees); indiscriminate predator control was considered to be unwarranted (with funded research to improve acceptable control measures and instances of necessary control to be discriminate and minimal); it was urged that the principle of "fair chase" have legal standing (with prohibitions on the pursuit, spotting, or killing of game from any motorized conveyance); landowners permitting trespass access for hunting or other recreational purposes should have statutory liability protection; the police powers of conservation officers should be broadened in consideration of the risk associated with their duties; natural resource policies were recognized as being indispensable to legislators and administrators who may be subjected to pressures, with policies being most useful when formulated in anticipation of their need; and government wildlife and natural resource agencies were urged to seek opportunities for cooperation rather than simply guarding their prerogatives.

Finally, the wildlife policy committee recognized that the "most neglected and crucial [wildlife] research needs are those concerning human social behavior," that the public relations and education functions of wildlife agencies "have a vital part in making and carrying out natural resource policies," and that environmental education should be promoted at all levels so "that the environmental crisis of today and tomorrow [will] be met in the minds of children." "Mankind emerged from the natural order; we must continue to live as part of it. We have but one earth, our home, our keep, our borrowed estate. We must accept the charge, at whatever cost, to maintain its abundance and guard its quality."

## *Wildlife in the Policy Arena*

Statistics from the chapter on economic valuation indicate that wildlife enjoys a high level of public demand for a variety of commodity and noncommodity purposes. Therefore, we might reasonably assume that wildlife resources are highly valued in social and economic terms. However, Labisky, Stansbury, and Smith (1986) contended that it is often impossible for wildlife professionals to meet their "stewardship commitment" to the resource because of insufficient funding.

This funding plight has been attributed "to the fact that fish and wildlife is a neglected if not forgotten resource in national policy." The underlying problem is that wildlife professionals have been inept at demonstrating the value of wildlife programs to public policymakers. As an adjunct to this problem, wildlife professionals have also failed to effectively communicate their own professional worth—even to users of the wildlife resource. Since public demand stimulates political action, the absence of such demand from wildlife users has largely relegated wildlife to a position of "bureaucratic lip service and welfare handouts" relative to competing interests.

An assessment of wildlife in the nation's political agenda suggests that wildlife issues directly associated with hunting have a fairly high degree of political visibility. Wildlife research has very little political visibility, however, even though it is the foundation for resource decision making. Unfortunately, limited political visibility translates into limited funding support (Labisky, Stansbury, and Smith 1986). Furthermore, land-grant universities—where much wildlife research is conducted (via graduate student programs and cooperative fish and wildlife research units)—are beset with almost chronic funding problems. Another complication is that wildlife management programs of state and federal resource agencies often conflict with economically motivated land-use practices on agricultural lands, forestlands, and rangelands.

A plausible short-term solution to the problem is to "piggyback" wildlife issues onto politically popular issues. Wildlife concerns are very much a part of such high visibility problems as clean water, acid rain, toxic waste, soil erosion, and reforestation. Hence, it is logical to make wildlife "an issue within an issue" with these highly publicized problems. In the longer term, it is important that wildlife interests forge cooperative coalitions with agricultural, forestry, range, and water interests to ensure that wildlife issues receive a fair hearing (Labisky, Stansbury, and Smith 1986).

## *Wildlife and Agricultural Policy*

The first European settlements on the East Coast survived only because they adopted Native American agricultural practices and plant resources. This was the foundation of American agriculture. Today the economically important plants domesticated by the Native Americans—maize (corn), cotton, peanuts, pumpkins, squashes, beans, potatoes, sweet potatoes, tobacco, and tomatoes—still comprise a high proportion of the value of American agricultural production (Edwards 1940).

An upward trend in farm production began in the late thirties and early forties as the economy recovered from the Great Depression and geared up for World War II (Giles, Leedy, and Pinnell 1970). This trend has continued unabated for half a century. Agricultural development has been accompanied by land-use policies that favor intensified use and large cropping units (Hervey, Hill, and Leedy 1970).

Changes in social and economic patterns were accompanied by major changes in landscape patterns. Smaller, less efficient "patch farms" had provided excellent habitat for farmland wildlife: fields were small, bounded by fencerows; crops were diversified; crop residues were left standing through the winter; and vegetated streambanks were common (Karr 1981). The conversion of these small farms into large agricultural management units characterized by monoculture and mechanization caused a drastic deterioration in wildlife habitat (Giles, Leedy, and Pinnell 1970).

While there has been some yearly fluctuation in the amount of harvested cropland over the past two decades, the total harvested cropland has remained relatively constant—with 115.8 million hectares harvested in 1970, and 114.9 million hectares in 1987. There is, however, a significant upward trend in foreign consumption of American agricultural produce. In 1970, 72 million acres were harvested for export compared with 107 million acres in 1987 (Batie and Taylor 1990). In 1980, the produce from one out of every three U.S. cropland acres was exported: nearly two-thirds of our wheat, 30 percent of our feed grains, and 55 percent of our soybeans went to foreign markets (McCorkle

1981). This trend is expected to continue as American foreign trade policy increasingly calls upon the agricultural sector to help reduce the balance-of-payments deficit.

Another complicating factor is cropland conversion. From 1958 to 1967, cropland was removed from agricultural use and converted to urban-suburban development (including transportation routes) at the rate of 461,500 hectares per year. But from 1967 to 1975 this rate had increased to 842,100 hectares per year (Batie and Taylor 1990). Although wildlife habitats in agricultural environments can be enhanced or degraded depending upon the management practices employed, croplands converted to large-scale residential or commercial uses are permanently lost to farmland wildlife.

Fragmentation is an associated problem since development often leapfrogs over adjacent agricultural lands rather than expanding continuously. Some intervening farmland habitats thus become "isolates," ecological islands in a sea of suburban sprawl. The principles of island biogeography (insular ecology) suggest that these areas will support fewer species of wildlife, which are also more vulnerable to localized extirpation, than areas of comparable size that are part of a continuous agricultural landscape (Wilcox 1980).

The Food Securities Act (FSA) of 1985 was the core of national agricultural policy from 1985 to 1990. One significant feature of this legislation was its revival of the Conservation Reserve Program (CRP) originally created by the Agriculture Act of 1956. The updated version of the CRP authorized the U.S. Department of Agriculture (USDA) to enter into ten-year contracts with farmers, making annual rental payments in exchange for removing highly erodible croplands from cultivation. It was the intent of Congress to retire approximately 16–18 million hectares of land from commodity crop production (Robinson 1988; Sampson 1988; Isaacs and Howell 1988). If this goal is eventually realized, then over 10 percent of the nation's cropland will be available for farmland wildlife habitat (Langner 1989).

The CRP had two primary purposes: first, reducing soil erosion; and second, reducing the surplus of agricultural commodities. Significant secondary goals included improving environmental quality (Robinson 1988; Sampson 1988; Isaacs and Howell 1988). Through the late eighties the CRP had little impact on total wildlife habitat availability, although some of the benefits will probably occur over a longer time frame (Langner 1989). From a practical standpoint, many CRP participants do not make a special effort to seek information on wildlife habitat; therefore, aggressive "marketing" by wildlife and extension agencies can motivate some farmers to enhance their CRP land for wildlife. As one farmer put it, "Wildlife practices are not fully appreciated by the ASCS-SCS; they have a full plate with farm plan compliance. Somebody with a wildlife mission needs to get the word out" (Miller and Bromley 1989).

Companion provisions of the Food Securities Act (FSA) of 1985 included sodbuster, swampbuster, and conservation easements. The sodbuster provision withholds program benefits from farmers who produced agricultural commodities on fields newly converted to cropland if those fields contained a large proportion of highly erodible land (HEL). Exemptions were granted to farmers already having an approved conservation system, a provision that applied to most farmers since over three-quarters of them have usually participated in USDA commodity support programs. Sodbuster was not expected to create additional wildlife habitat, but rather to help maintain existing habitat, including much that was developed through the Conservation Reserve Program (Brady 1988).

The wetland conservation provisions of the Food Security Act have been dubbed "swampbuster," a major intent of which was to reduce the conversion of wetlands to agriculture by denying federal farm benefits to farmers who drain and cultivate these areas. If strictly enforced, swampbuster regulations could have made wetland conversion more costly, thus discouraging drainage and conversion of wetlands. Over two million hectares of wetlands in the United States are vulnerable to cropland conversion and could have benefited from swampbuster requirements. Unfortunately, swampbuster provisions still had not been implemented two years following passage of the Food Security Act (Goldman-Carter 1988).

Conservation easements under the 1985 Food Security Act promised a way of contributing to wildlife conservation while strengthening the farm economy. These easements were to be acquired in lieu of repaying part of the indebtedness when farm loans were restructured. Again, the U.S. Department of Agriculture has not implemented this part of the Food Security Act (Evans, Tieger, and Graham 1988).

Several factors have posed implementation problems for the 1985 Food Securities Act. First, interagency coordination was necessary since responsibilities were fragmented among the Soil Conservation Service (SCS), Agricultural Stabilization and Conservation Service (ASCS, including its state and county committees), and Farmers Home Administration (FmHA). Second, the regulatory role of SCS had not previously been so extensive. Historically, SCS field technicians have been well accepted by rural people because they were perceived as helpful advisers rather than "enforcers." Third and perhaps most important, ASCS and its state and county committees had much of the final authority to approve or deny benefits under the act, yet over the years this agency has been much more supportive of production-oriented practices than conservation programs (Robinson 1988; Sampson 1988).

Annual set-asides, the portion of the commodity program intended to control crop production by removing farmlands from active cultivation, typically have such high funding levels as to attract more farmland than the Conservation Reserve Program and other conservation programs. And the set-aside program has a host of deficiencies with negative impacts on wildlife. Lenient rules for managing set-aside farmlands often leave these areas exposed to wind and water erosion and are detrimental to wildlife. Many times, ASCS committees have been so concerned with issues such as weed control that they have neglected the conservation aspects of their mandate. There is no professional natural resource representation on ASCS committees and no obligation to use natural resource information in states where the ASCS is required to "consult" with resource professionals. Farmers who plant fencerow to fencerow have a larger base area from which to calculate commodity program benefits, so farmers who leave windbreaks are penalized. In general, the set-aside program has had a limited effect on crop production, which is its main purpose, but has tended to work against soil and wildlife conservation and often penalizes farmers for using sound conservation techniques (Robinson 1988).

Most wildlife habitat management on privately owned farmlands has been voluntary and therefore virtually inconsequential (Deknatel 1979). Shelterbelt plantings, streamside vegetation, food and cover plots in odd-shaped field corners, planted field borders, greenbelts, and late mowing of roadsides all benefit farmland wildlife, yet these practices are rarely seen in present-day agricultural landscapes (Karr 1981).

Of the government programs directed to wildlife management on agricultural lands, some have been effective in terms of numbers of cooperators enlisted or areal extent treated. However, there is no evidence of continuing widespread success from a wildlife perspective (Madsen 1981). Piecemeal individual efforts are rarely worthwhile. "Most farmland wildlife species do not respond to a 'bit here and a tad there'—they need county-wide efforts, or better yet, state-wide or region-wide efforts" (Burger, Wagner, and Harris 1986).

### *Wildlife and Forest Policy*

The primeval American woodlands comprised a tremendous variety of forest types, and forest wildlife was correspondingly diverse. Opening the frontier was devastating to all virgin forests and their wildlife.

Forests were carelessly logged or simply slashed and burned; much of the woodland wildlife was decimated (A. S. Leopold 1978). Nevertheless, four hundred years after settlement, forests are still a prominent part of the American landscape: nearly one-third of the United States is forested (Hagenstein 1990).

Forest land is commonly defined as an area of one acre or more that is at least 10 percent stocked by forest trees of any size. This includes land that formerly had such tree cover and will be naturally or artificially regenerated. Strips of timber—as in roadsides, streamsides, or shelterbelts—must have a crown width of at least 120 feet to qualify as forest land. *Forest land* is a general term that encompasses *timberland* (forest land that produces, or is capable of producing, more than twenty cubic feet per acre per year of industrial wood in natural stands), *reserved timberland* (forest land that meets the definition of timberland except that it has been withdrawn from timber utilization through statute or regulation), and *other forest land* (forest land not capable of producing twenty cubic feet per acre per year of industrial wood because of arid climate, high elevation, poor drainage, rockiness, steepness, or sterile soils and urban forest land that is unavailable for sustained harvesting due to its location) (Hagenstein 1990).

Several measures are used in assessing trends in the condition of forest lands. One measure is timber inventories and growth statistics, which provide a view of the status of forest products as well as a general indication of the condition of forest land. Although there are regional variations, overall timber inventories on U.S. timberlands have been increasing steadily since 1952. The volume of softwood growing stock (trees with a diameter greater than five inches) increased 5 percent from 1952 to 1987, while the total increase in hardwood volume over this period was 69 percent. Considering the decline in timberland area—from 206 million hectares to 195.6 million hectares during the 1952–87 period—the average per acre volume increases are particularly notable (Hagenstein 1990).

Other measures used in assessing trends in the condition of forest lands include timber removals, up 27 percent from 1970 to 1986; net growth of stock timber, which increased 0.8 percent per year during this period; and timber prices, which have exhibited a long-term upward trend beginning at least as long ago as 1920. Although the statistics mentioned show consistent increases, other measures of forest condition are less encouraging. These suggest that forest conditions, by some interpretations, have deteriorated (Hagenstein 1990).

Among the indications of impaired forest conditions are increased public demands for greater regulation of forest practices, concerns about the effects of air pollution on timber growth rates and mortality, and heated disputes over the management of national forests, especially with respect to clear-cutting and the harvest of old-growth timber stands. Such indications of declining forest conditions are qualitative, but they suggest the need for definitions of forest quality that embrace a broader spectrum of forest uses (Hagenstein 1990).

The National Forest System in the United States includes 77.3 million hectares of forest land, or more than one-quarter of the national total. However, national forests contain almost half of standing saw timber stocks because past timber production tended to utilize accessible, higher quality stands owned by private industry. Much of the standing sawtimber in national forests is mature old-growth timber, or timber growing on low-productivity sites (Repetto 1988).

The potential for controversy over forest management policies is obvious when we realize that national forests also attract more than 225 million visitor days of recreational use each year. Recreation and conservation interests have long contended that the Forest Service conducts timber harvesting and associated road building in areas that are unsuitable for commercial timber production. Many of these areas have recreational value or are roadless tracts potentially eligible for wilderness designation (Repetto 1988).

When the Forest Service was created in 1905, the goal of federal policies was to facilitate development of the West. Thus, although the Forest Service is supposed to take economic efficiency into consideration in its operations, it has never been required to cover its own costs of growing and marketing timber (Repetto 1988). Rather, appraised timber values on Forest Service lands are based on estimates of the buyer's costs of cutting, transporting, processing, and selling the wood, plus a reasonable profit (Beuter 1985). Despite congressional urging, the Forest Service still does not have an adequate accounting system for assessing its supply costs, an omission that has complicated the debate over timber valuation in national forests (Repetto 1988).

One early piece of legislation offering policy guidance to the Forest Service was the 1930 Knutson-Vanderberg Act. This legislation set aside deposit monies from timber purchasers to be used for reforestation and brush disposal and was later expanded to include conservation and wildlife provisions. Other statutes of that period financed forest road building and directed a percentage of timber receipts to local governments, thus linking these actions to timber sales. These linkages, and the interests of timber purchasers, fostered incentives for routinely harvesting even marginal sites where timber has a negative stumpage value (Repetto 1988). In one view, the simplest remedy for this situation is to impose "minimum acceptable bid prices high enough to recover the government's full separable costs of growing and marketing timber" (Gillis and Repetto 1988).

The Multiple-Use Sustained-Yield Act of 1960 codified the policy of managing national forests for sustained yields of the resources they produce. However, the legislative guidelines for multiple-use management were so general they did not materially affect Forest Service actions; the emphasis on wood production remained (Repetto 1988).

The Wilderness Act of 1964 confirmed wilderness status for federal lands previously designated as such by administrative action, including large tracts of national forest land. This bill thus emphasized the importance of forest lands for uses other than timber production. The legislation also mandated the first public hearings in the American public-land policy process. With it, Forest Service autonomy in managing its public lands came to an end. The Forest Service had often boasted of establishing the first administrative wilderness areas, but it opposed the Wilderness Act and resisted virtually every newly proposed wilderness area (or supported only areas of minimum size for protection) (Shanks 1984).

Passage of the National Environmental Policy Act (NEPA) of 1969 had a profound impact on all natural resource policy, especially through its requirement of Environmental Impact Statements (EIS's) for government actions having potentially significant impacts on the environment. The EIS provision facilitated public challenges of such ecologically questionable Forest Service timber harvest practices as extensive clear-cutting.

NEPA also provided impetus for congressional action that resulted in the Forest and Rangeland Renewable Resources Planning Act (RPA) of 1974 and the National Forest Management Act of 1976 (Repetto 1988). The RPA was a comprehensive plan for the use of the national forests and grazing lands, which included timber production goals. The National Forest Management Act revised the Forest Service mandate by requiring that social, cultural, and environmental—as well as economic—aspects of renewable resource management be incorporated into multiple-use planning. The language of this legislation also meant to assure perpetual timber supplies, rather than allowing harvest practices that are so damaging they amount to a one-time "mining" of timber (Shanks 1984). Almost in anticipation of present concerns over biodiversity, the National Forest Management Act also provided for maintaining the diversity of biotic communities, within the limitations of land capability, as part of multiple-use of forest lands. However, Forest Service practices rarely suggest support for this directive.

During the seventies the Forest Service administered two major wilderness reviews, the Roadless Area Review and Evaluation (RARE) I and II programs. Both were so biased that federal courts determined them to be essentially useless. The RARE programs served to heighten the controversy over timber harvesting versus wilderness preservation. Forest Service defenders contended that conservationists used invalid economic arguments to support restrictive forest usage for their favored purposes, while critics accused the Forest Service of conducting below-cost timber sales to justify road construction in roadless areas, thereby forestalling future wilderness designation (Shanks 1984; Repetto 1988). These arguments have not changed much in the years since.

Forest landscape ecologist Larry Harris identified four major forest-land research and management issues (Burger, Wagner, and Harris 1986), all of which are the consequence of public policies. Each one, in turn, also has significant implications for future policy. One is the reduction of total forest area on a global scale, which Harris called "one of the most important ecological and socio-economic problems of our time." This encompasses destruction of tropical forests, the crisis in fuelwood supplies in almost all developing countries, and the loss of forested wetlands in North America.

The second problem is the fragmentation of remaining forests into patches too small to sustain their original biotic communities. With this comes altered microclimates, loss of forest "interior" species, and negative impacts on the original forest biota by aggressive forest "edge" species (through predation, nest parasitism, and competition).

The third problem is the widespread forestry practice of converting original hardwood (or mixed hardwood-conifer) stands to fast-growing conifer plantations. These conifer plantations are not "real" forests any more than a cornfield is tallgrass prairie, and they have little value for wildlife.

Harris referred to the fourth problem as "the internal degradation of existing stands"—that is, the "liquidation" of old-growth forests and their replacement with single-species plantations; and "timber stand improvement" (TSI), which amounts to eliminating anything that interferes with "fiber production," including the removal of such important components of wildlife habitat as "snags" (standing dead or dying trees) and "dead and down wood."

Wildlife species that depend upon mature forests are vulnerable to the policies of production forestry that view climax forests as decadent. The passenger pigeon's extinction in the early 1900s, though due largely to commercial exploitation, was hastened by the elimination of large virgin stands of mast-bearing beech and oak trees in the Midwest. More recently, the demise of the ivory-billed woodpecker was linked to widespread reduction of mature southern hardwood forests (A. S. Leopold 1978). The red-cockaded woodpecker is currently presenting management problems in the Southeast, as it needs old-growth living pines at least seventy-five to ninety-five years old for nesting, whereas commercial timber harvest rotations are generally under fifty years for southern pines (Seagle et al. 1987). The controversy surrounding the status of the spotted owl in old-growth forests of the Pacific Northwest has reached crisis proportions and will almost certainly be repeated in years to come with other wildlife that require mature-forest habitats. Society's wants, expressed through resource policy, will determine whether those habitats will be preserved.

### *Wildlife and Rangeland Policy*

The term *rangeland* is uniquely American, and refers not so much to a place or a land use as to a kind of land. "Rangelands are those areas of the world which are, by reason of physical limitations, unsuited to cultivation or intensive forestry" (Box 1990). They may be too hot, cold, wet, dry, high, or rocky for growing crops or they may be unsuitable for other reasons—shallow soils, rough topography, poor drainage, or low soil fertility. Whatever their limitations, rangelands produce forage for wildlife and free-ranging livestock and are often valued for outdoor recreation and other uses. Although rangelands encompass the deserts of North Africa, steppes of China, tundra of Russia, and swamps of Florida, the common American image is of cowboys on horseback working cattle in the plains and mountains of the West (Box 1990).

Western rangeland wildlife and habitats are diverse, encompassing waterfowl on playa lakes, cougar and bobcat in canyons and rough breaks, pheasant, quail, prairie chickens, prairie dogs, and jackrabbits. However, the idea of rangeland wildlife often conjures a vision of big-game mammals. It is these animals—bighorn sheep, deer, elk, pronghorn (and, in bygone days, bison)—that stir the greatest public interest and that most often are the source of conflicts with the range livestock industry (Wagner 1978).

Throughout the first half of the nineteenth century stockraisers expanded their herds on western rangelands, so that by the 1880s cattle or sheep occupied nearly all the grazing lands in the West. Native grasses were grazed to oblivion on ranges overstocked with cattle. Then record-breaking storms hit the northern Great Plains and Rockies in the winter of 1886–87. Cattle froze to death where they stood or were driven by the winter gales to seek shelter in gullies and arroyos where their carcasses piled up in crusted mounds. By spring, tens of thousands of cattle had perished and many ranchers were bankrupt (Biggers 1901; Shanks 1984).

The next stage of the western livestock industry saw herds of sheep brought in to graze the range plants and rough country not suited to cattle. As forage in these areas was depleted, sheep were moved to ranges where they competed with cattle. The bitter range wars that followed cost many cattle ranchers and sheepherders their lives. Public lands were considered by stockraisers as private property, and first-comers to ranges were not timid about defending their tenure (Shanks 1984).

Stockraisers had already perverted Abraham Lincoln's 1862 Homestead Act, which was clearly intended for settlers. Often, hired hands were forced to file homestead claims on public lands adjoining a ranch, then sign them over to the ranch owner as a condition of their employment. Another loophole was the act's "commutation clause," which enabled settlers to purchase land for $1.25 per acre after a residence of only six months. As a consequence, many tracts were resold soon after the six-month period elapsed. The Homestead Act was thus used as a means to enlarge many western ranches (Stoddart, Smith, and Box 1975; Shanks 1984).

The Desert Land Act of 1887 was also used for ranch enlargement. Settlers, who were permitted to purchase up to 640 acres of land, could configure their parcel boundaries to abut or include stream bottoms. This created claims that were linear and highly irregular in shape—snaking for miles along stream beds—but claims that were nevertheless very valuable, since whoever controlled the water also controlled thousands of hectares of surrounding dry rangeland (Shanks 1984).

In an attempt to increase food production during World War I, federal authorities gave permission in 1918 for an additional million grazing animals on forest ranges despite already severe grazing pressure. By 1932 the serious deterioration of rangelands, which had long been evident, finally prompted Congress to ask the U.S. Forest Service to survey range conditions. The survey indicated that overgrazing had reduced rangeland productivity by 50 percent and had exposed 80 percent of the range to some degree of erosion (Owen 1975).

Congressional response to the Forest Service report led to the passage of the Taylor Grazing Control Act in 1934. This legislation had three major objectives: stopping range deterioration, initiating projects designed to maintain and improve range condition, and stabilizing the rangeland economy. Following World War II, the Grazing Service and General Land Office were merged, and management of most of the federally owned rangelands was entrusted to the newly created Bureau of Land Management (Owen 1975).

The Bureau of Land Management (BLM) lacked the good fortune of the other federal natural resource agencies, which were blessed with charismatic leadership in their early years. The BLM staff has generally been considered inferior to those of the Forest Service and National Park Service, and BLM has always lacked the esprit de corps of the other agencies. When Secretary of the Interior Stewart Udall named Charles Stoddard as its head in the early sixties, the agency finally had a dynamic leader. Stoddard reorganized the bureau, raised its level of professionalism, and projected the vision of a multiple-use agency dedicated to serving the general public. However, his efforts were sabotaged by provincial staff members tied to the agency's tradition of promoting livestock and mining interests, and Stoddard was fired. Because of its industry orientation, BLM is sometimes said to stand for the "Bureau of Livestock and Mining" (Shanks 1984).

Some abundance of wildlife is compatible with some kinds of livestock grazing on some western rangelands. Pronghorn, for example, are numerous on the plains of Wyoming and Trans-Pecos Texas where ranges are stocked with cattle. In general, however, livestock compete with wildlife for forage. Furthermore, livestock grazing gradually changes vegetation composition on rangelands to the detriment of most wildlife species. Nearly all rangelands in the western United States have been grazed by domestic animals for more than a century. As a consequence, "livestock grazing probably has been the most pervasive influence for ecological change in the West" (Burger, Wagner, and Harris 1986).

Aside from competition for forage, other effects of livestock on wildlife are primarily a consequence of actions that people take on behalf of domestic animals. Some of these effects are due to decisions consciously intended to have an impact on wildlife, others are indirect or inadvertent (Wagner 1978). Nevertheless, all are the result of range management policies, whether stated or implied.

Techniques that improve range condition for livestock may be detrimental to wildlife. Removal of woody species of range plants can be accomplished by mechanical means, by fire, or by applications of herbicides. Treated areas may then be left to natural invasion by grasses or seeded artificially where desirable species are too sparse for rapid regeneration. However, some wildlife biologists think that such range improvement practices, especially those involving removal of pinyon-juniper woodlands and control of sagebrush, may reduce mule deer abundance. Concern has also been expressed over the impact of sagebrush control on pronghorn antelope and sage grouse (Wagner 1978).

Widespread predator control has affected wildlife. Personnel of the Division of Wildlife Services (in the U.S. Fish and Wildlife Service) and ranchers who use the division's services have maintained that its predator control program benefits wildlife as well as livestock in the West. The discussion partly revolves around the question of whether, or under what conditions, predators can limit ungulate populations (thus preventing habitat damage from their overgrazing). The companion questions require a realistic appraisal of predator impacts to livestock and the responsibilities of stockraisers for husbandry of their herds, particularly during the calving and lambing season. Whether or not predator control has been "effective," it has been responsible for killing many thousands of coyotes, for virtual extirpation of wolves from the West, and for drastic reductions in bear and mountain lion numbers. Persons who value these species are not likely to regard their wholesale reduction as desirable (Wagner 1978).

Range livestock industry efforts to limit wild ungulate numbers exerts additional pressure on wildlife. Livestock grazing has been the dominant land use since the West was settled. Stockraisers, related business interests, and agencies that manage rangelands are an integral part of the western economy and social fabric. Thus, the values embraced by livestock interests have permeated the region's politics and influenced the policies of government agencies. In some cases the range livestock industry has been tolerant of wild ungulates. Ranchers in the Great Plains, for example, generally have not objected to high numbers of pronghorn, which are small and do not compete directly with range cattle for forage. Wildlife species, such as elk, that pose problems are not viewed so sympathetically, however. Elk numbers may intentionally be maintained at relatively low levels for two reasons: first, as a large, aggressive species capable of causing considerable damage, yet virtually impossible to fence in or out, elk are widely regarded as a regal nuisance; second, elk compete directly with range cattle for forage plants. A tacit policy of suppressing elk numbers reduces their economic impact on the range livestock industry while simultaneously reducing problems for agency personnel responsible for elk management (Wagner 1978).

The most basic of all rangeland resources is soil. In the time span of human lives, soil loss amounts to irreversible change. Therefore, no rangeland policy decisions should be made that would seriously impair range soils (Wagner 1978).

Against this backdrop of historic conflict and policy by fiat, only a handful of legislative actions provide explicit policy direction for the utilization of rangeland resources. One of these is the General Mining Law of 1872, still in effect today, which encouraged prospecting on public lands by allowing title to be conveyed not just to underground mineral rights but to surface areas as well. As a consequence, some of the most desirable public lands were claimed first and thereby removed from public ownership (Council on Environmental Quality 1981).

The Multiple-Use Sustained-Yield Act of 1960 established the policy that rangelands, as well as forest lands, within the National Forest System were to be managed for the multiple use of their natural resources. In the seventies the Forest and Rangeland Renewable Resources Planning Act of 1974 (RPA), amended by the National Forest Management Act of 1976 (NFMA), the Federal Land Policy and Management Act of 1976 (FLMPA, also called the BLM Organic Act), and the Public Rangelands Improvement Act of 1978 all reemphasized the multiple-use, sustained-yield policy. "These statutes established the principle that the management of federally managed forests and rangelands would be based on detailed inventories of the resources, careful planning, and public participation, with the goal of achieving a balance among competing uses" (Council on Environmental Quality 1981:297).

North American rangelands are increasingly viewed from the same land-use perspective as other lands—as "resource system[s] with the potential for producing an array of goods and services" (Wagner 1978). Within this framework, the use or production of one resource often competes with others. Thus, choices must be weighed and decisions made about the type of use, or the mix of goods and services, to be sought from particular range sites (Wagner 1978).

Despite multiple-use directives, many rangelands are in fact devoted to "dominant uses" of timber production, livestock grazing, or mineral extraction. In the absence of effective policy implementation that ensures protection for wildlife, as well as other interests, we can expect continuing losses of range wildlife. These losses will be due to more intensive use of rangelands for livestock, conversion of rangelands to cropland and pasture, destruction of wildlife habitat by mining operations, disturbance of wildlife by petroleum exploration and extraction, and fence building that interferes with big-game movements (Committee 1982). Rapidly growing human numbers in the West, with their outdoor recreational demands and requirements for water, will put additional pressures on arid and fragile rangelands, and on range wildlife resources (Burger, Wagner, and Harris 1986).

## *Wildlife and Wetland Policy*

Wetlands are lands where water is the dominant factor in determining the nature of the soil and the types of biotic communities that can live in the soil and on its surface. The feature most wetlands share is soil saturation, or water actually covering the land, on a periodic if not a persistent basis (Cowardin et al. 1979; Larson 1982).

Wetlands perform vital services that still are neither well understood nor widely appreciated by the general public. They filter pollutants from water, trap and neutralize pesticides and toxic substances, regulate and absorb floodwaters, assimilate organic matter and dissolved nutrients (thereby slowing eutrophication of associated waters), recharge underground aquifers, serve as coastal spawning and nursery areas for many species of marine fish and shellfish, are sources of peat and timber, constitute living educational laboratories, provide visual contrast and diversity to the landscape, and furnish critical habitat for a tremendous variety of plant and animal life (Larson 1982).

Wetland areas in primeval North America were so extensive that beavers ranged throughout the continent except for the coastal region of the Southeast and the deserts of the Southwest. The destruction of wetlands by draining and filling, and actions like killing off the beaver and deforestation, greatly modified wildlife habitats. This has been called "one of the most significant changes affecting wildlife since the discovery of America" (Allen 1970).

As early as colonial times, American wetlands were widely regarded as wastelands harboring pests and a threat to public health. One of the nation's earliest corporations was the Dismal Swamp Canal Company, which completed a canal in 1794 to drain the Dismal Swamp in North Carolina and Virginia for agricultural purposes. Backers of this venture included such prominent citizens as George Washington and Thomas Jefferson (Brande 1980).

Although it is impossible to determine the actual extent of wetlands at the time of European settlement, approximately 87 million hectares seems to be a common estimate (Roe and Ayres 1954; Barton 1986; Goldstein 1988). By the midseventies only 40 million wetland hectares (46 percent) remained. Between 1955 and 1975 about 3.6 million hectares of wetlands were lost (Goldstein 1988). An estimated 300,000 hectares of bottomland hardwoods were destroyed in the eight-year period ending in 1982. Bottomland hardwood forests in the lower Mississippi alluvial plain are of special importance for wintering waterfowl (Teels 1990). In all, agricultural development has accounted for fully 87 percent of recent wetland conversions (Tiner 1984).

Wetland policy is contained in federal statutes, as well as numerous state laws and local ordinances. Section 404 of the Clean Water Act, administered by the U.S. Army Corps of Engineers, contains language establishing controls on the discharge of dredged or fill material into aquatic or wetland habitats. It includes a statement that filling operations in wetlands are considered to be among the most severe environmental impacts covered by the guidelines. In effect, the Section 404 regulations constitute an aquatic and wetlands protection program, though they are deficient in several important respects. For example, this law does not regulate such activities as draining, clearing, and chemical pollution, all of which can destroy wetlands (Griffin 1989, Teels 1990).

Some states have implemented their own programs to remedy the defects of Section 404 protection. State wetland regulatory programs often cover a broader range of activities than does Section 404 and are most effective when administered jointly with federal wetland protection efforts. Coastal states have effectively used their authority under Section 307 of the Coastal Zone Management Act (which determines whether a proposed wetland alteration is consistent with that state's coastal zone management plan) to protect wetlands for a number of years. At the local level, the zoning authority of city, county, and township governments is one of their most useful vehicles for wetland protection (Teels 1990).

As previously indicated, wetland conversions for agricultural production have been responsible for the loss of well over 80 percent of the nation's wetlands. Incentives provided by the U.S. Department of Agriculture (USDA), through its commodity programs, brought more land into crop production, greatly contributing to wetland losses. Ironically, the increased production of agricultural commodities also led to surpluses that depressed the prices paid to farmers (Teels 1990).

The Wetland Conservation (or so-called "swampbuster") section of the 1985 Food Security Act was designed to reduce wetland losses due to agricultural conversions. Swampbuster provisions deny specified USDA program benefits to anyone planting an annual crop after the date the Food Security Act was passed. Furthermore, wetlands created or restored on eligible lands can be entered in the Conservation Reserve Program. Existing wetlands are not eligible, however, unless they are highly erodible or are part of a highly erodible field. Finally, sections 1314 and 1318 of the Food Security Act give the Farmers Home Administration (FmHA) authority to put conservation easements on FmHA property prior to resale as farmland and to place conservation easements on certain FmHA borrower properties in exchange for debt forgiveness (Teels 1990).

The North American Waterfowl Management Plan, an international agreement for waterfowl and wetlands conservation, was finally signed in 1986 after years of planning. It listed numerical goals for increased abundance of 37 species of ducks, geese, and swans; set a target for ducks of 62 million breeders and a fall flight of 100 million (a level common in the seventies); and called for the conservation and management of the most important waterfowl breeding, staging, and wintering areas in the United States and Canada. The intent is to protect or enhance more than 2.4 million hectares of prime waterfowl habitat between the two countries. A six-point strategy is being used in an effort to meet these waterfowl population and habitat acreage goals: (1) financial incentives to farmers for waterfowl habitat protection; (2) encouragement to local governments and public land management agencies to regulate land use to prevent destruction of wetlands; (3) acquisition of a few key areas that support large numbers of waterfowl or populations in severe decline; (4) intensified management on public lands to increase their productivity for waterfowl; (5) public works projects to mitigate or prevent further waterfowl habitat loss; and (6) educational campaigns to raise public awareness about soil and water conservation and other wetland issues (Macaulay 1989; Madsen 1989; Teels 1990).

In addition to Section 404 of the Clean Water Act, the Food Security Act, and the North American Waterfowl Management Plan, four other federal laws enacted in the mideighties also contribute to wetland conservation. The Tax Reform Act of 1985 eliminated deductions for most drainage expenses and did away with the capital gains benefit on appreciation of the value of converted wetlands. The Water Resources Development Act of 1986, authorizing new Corps of Engineers flood control and navigation projects, emphasized the mitigation of wetland losses to a greater degree than any previous water law. The Emergency Wetlands Resources Act of 1986 refined several wetland protection programs, notably by increasing the funding for wetland acquisition by the Fish and Wildlife Service. Finally, the Water Quality Act of 1987 authorized financial grants to state and local governments for control of nonpoint water pollution, including a consideration of the capability of wetlands to improve water quality (Teels 1990).

Beyond their own unique policy problems and conflicts, wetlands sometimes become entangled in even broader issues of water policy. Several natural characteristics and uses of water contribute much to the complexity of water policy planning, including (1) the pervasive and evasive character of water—it can be present in, under, and over lands—making it subject to a multitude of governmental and private claims; (2) the fact that political jurisdictions almost never include entire watersheds or drainage basins, which are the natural units of water management; (3) the reality that water is where it is, so water problems and uses are ordinarily localized, with governmental responses likewise tending to occur at local or regional levels; and (4) the variability of water—in quality (from pure to contaminated by a variety of pollutants), in quantity over time (from trickle to flood, and including seasonal flows), in location, and in use—is often the cause of problems or conflicts (Henning 1974).

National Wetland Inventory Data suggest that the highest rates of wetland loss in the twentieth century occurred during the sixties and seventies, when the average annual rate of loss was 194,000 hectares. By 1984 the wetland conversion rate was down to approximately 122,000 hectares per year (Teels 1990). Whether the rate of loss has been further reduced by the expanded wetland protection programs of the eighties is a matter of considerable concern. Recent data are limited, so the current situation is not clear. However, the general consensus at a symposium on the protection of wetlands from agricultural impacts (Stuber 1988) was that wetland drainage for agricultural purposes has not been significantly reduced, and, in fact, that there had been recent increases in wetland conversion, particularly in the prairie pothole region. This suggests that recent wetland policy initiatives, such as swampbuster, may not be effective. On the other hand, policy implementation and effectiveness lags behind policy pronouncement, so there is yet hope that these legislative actions will prove fruitful. The larger question is "Can we expect adequate wetland protection without federal authorities designed specifically for that purpose?" There will always be incentives to drain wetlands: many of them yield excellent cropland, pastureland, and urban/suburban land. The critical challenge is to find effective ways of protecting these vital resources (Teels 1990).

Some resource managers view policy as abstract pronouncement having little relevance to their workaday activities. In fact, policies determine how natural resources will be managed, designate who will manage them, set standards that guide managers in fulfilling their responsibilities, and often dictate acceptable options for management (Lyons and Franklin 1987). Students exposed to resource policy may be "turned off" because courses sometimes require learning the names and enactment dates of a multitude of natural resource laws, or because of "the complex array of factors that affect policy development." Yet, it is important to see how public concerns, political pressure, and historical trends intersect to influence resource policy. Budding resource managers are still sometimes taught that they will be the "trained experts who dispassionately and rationally apply scientific truths to achieve public goals" (Lyons and Franklin 1987). However, natural resource management decisions are often made for social or economic rather than for biological reasons. Wildlife biologists need to understand and involve themselves in policy processes to achieve objectives that will not be decided solely on ecological evidence.

## WILDLIFE ADMINISTRATION

Environmental administration is conducted in an atmosphere of responsibility and challenge amidst a concern for the quality of life and with ecological complexities, environmental problems, and political interests all impinging on the process (Henning 1974). Wildlife administration involves all of these considerations with the added complication of heightened emotions. People readily identify with wild animals and often respond quickly to what they perceive as threats to wildlife, whereas issues related to air pollution or soil erosion seem more abstract until they reach crisis proportions.

Administration is the implementation of determinations directed by law or policy, as distinguished from the legislative or policy-making processes that produce those decisions. The mandate of environmental administration should be a management style attuned to ecosystems (Henning 1974). This approach seems particularly appropriate to wildlife administration at a time when the emphasis is moving from single-species management to a community and ecosystem orientation.

Adapting a definition of environmental administration (Edmunds and Lety 1973) to our particular interests, we might say that wildlife administration seeks to maintain compatible relations between human activities and the natural communities that include and sustain wild animal populations. Put another way, wildlife administration is concerned with managing human affairs so as to maintain wildlife populations, promote biotic diversity, and preserve ecological relationships.

### *The Social Science Role in Wildlife Administration*

Most of the problems confronted by wildlife administrators involve people and values and belong more to the realm of the social sciences than to any scientific discipline. Given an ecological orientation, the social sciences can contribute much to wildlife administration (Henning 1974).

Each social science discipline has a particular focus, with the possibility of furnishing a unique perspective. For example, anthropology studies culture, which encompasses values, myths, and attitudes pertaining to human-wildlife relationships. One contribution of anthropology would be to describe the people and institutions of our culture in terms of their wildlife values (Henning 1974).

Economics, like ecology, is concerned with supply and demand—

with the production, movement, and consumption of goods and services—but in human rather than natural environments. In a word, we might characterize economics as studying scarcity. The "environment" of economic interactions that humans have constructed is part of the total environment of nature, so a truly modern economics must integrate fiscal with environmental considerations (Henning 1974). In this context, wildlife must be accorded its real worth rather than being assigned mere incidental values.

Geography refers to place. All wildlife has its characteristic place in the environment, and zoogeography is concerned with this from a biological viewpoint. However, location also establishes patterns of wildlife use and may introduce complications based on state or national political boundaries (Henning 1974). There is also another concept of place with a uniquely personal significance: the "sense of place" that fosters human attachments to "home" and other locations having special meaning. Wildlife gives every location a special flavor as part of our feelings about places.

As geography refers to place, history refers to time. The concept of time gives us a context for viewing past environmental patterns, values, and myths. As circumstances change, outdated assumptions and values may be detrimental to wildlife and an impediment to wildlife administration. The Bureau of Land Management, for example, continues to emphasize grazing management in an age that demands a strong commitment to a broad range of environmental values. Also, a historical analysis might show that dying lumber and mill towns in the Pacific Northwest were really subsidized as public welfare entities while old-growth forests were being recklessly overharvested, and cities regarded as "underdeveloped" now were really overdeveloped in the past (Henning 1974).

Political science is a study of the uses of power, and power is a central issue in wildlife decision-making processes. Ultimately, all significant decisions affecting wildlife are political and involve resolving conflicts between competing interests and values. As important as scientific factors or ecological considerations are, they rarely take precedence over human interests (Henning 1974).

Finally, two social sciences, psychology and sociology, deal even more pointedly with people. Sociology recognizes the group as a focal point for understanding human interactions related to wildlife. Wildlife agencies are groups, as are the organizations that seek to influence wildlife policy. An understanding of group dynamics is often essential to successfully promoting a wildlife policy. Psychology recognizes the importance of the individual personality. Key persons often manipulate groups and wield power in ways that have significant impacts on wildlife. Understanding the motivations of key individuals, perhaps through in-depth interviews, may help to elucidate the values and forces propelling group actions in wildlife controversies (Henning 1974).

### *Land Ownership Policy and the Decision Structure*

Settlers who struggled to free themselves from the oppressive feudal land system in Europe embraced the other extreme in trying to prevent a landed aristocracy in the United States. Under the American system, land is owned in fee simple absolute, just as any other commodity. It can therefore be easily sold and freely mortgaged (Edmunds and Lety 1973).

In many other societies, the idea of selling or trading land as a commodity is almost inconceivable. Native Americans consider land to be a "common" and the root of their being. East Indian custom promotes cross-cousin marriage as a way of keeping land in a family. British law restricts land claims to the eldest offspring as a way of maintaining tracts of land intact (Edmunds and Lety 1973).

Land-use restrictions throughout Europe are quite stringent compared with those in the United States. European owners may be limited in their use of land by what officials deem to be in the public interest. By contrast, American zoning laws are less confining, and zoning variances are granted almost routinely (Edmunds and Lety 1973).

From an ecological viewpoint, the idea of treating land as a commodity also seems incomprehensible. In effect, this shows that we are willing to barter with the life-giving functions of the earth itself—the foundations of the photosynthetic energy-trapping processes and biogeochemical cycles. The land-use patterns resulting from this bargain are ecologically disastrous because natural ecosystems are becoming so fragmented that their ability to function is being impaired (Edmunds and Lety 1973).

With respect to land-use policy, the framework within which wildlife administrators must operate assumes that: (1) land is a commodity, owned in fee simple absolute, and can be bought, sold, used, or subdivided for the sole benefit of the owner; (2) residence or direct dependence on the land is not a condition of ownership, so the owner may be an absentee with a speculative interest in its market value but no subsistence or ecological interest; (3) land may be bartered in any parcel size, so the desires of the owner are satisfied without any regard for ecological effects; (4) land is usually subdivided along rectangular lines, with no regard for landforms, drainage patterns, or ecological characteristics; (5) land may be used or left dormant through time, and leased or transferred to others, without regard for social or ecological needs; and (6) land is normally used for its locational value without recognizing its role as parent material for organisms that maintain ecosystem functions (Edmunds and Lety 1973).

Americans alive today are paying for the development incentives and land-use policies of past generations. Land was divided into convenient parcels with no relation to landscapes—and with no thought for the integrity of ecological processes. Human bonds to the land were broken as landscapes were fragmented, a probable contributing factor to our alienation from the land (Edmunds and Lety 1973).

From the standpoint of wildlife administration, the fragmentation of landscapes has had several undesirable effects: it has left fewer ecosystems intact that can be managed as whole entities; it has complicated the management of many wildlife populations that are no longer part of complete ecosystems; and it has reduced the range of options for preserving threatened and endangered species.

## *Wildlife Administration by Federal Agencies*

Wildlife administration by the federal government probably originated with a grant from the Division of Entomology (in the U.S. Department of Agriculture) to the American Ornithologists' Union in 1885 to determine the status of bird distributions and migrations in the United States. The project was shifted to the Division of Economic Ornithology and Mammalogy the following year. This division was renamed the Bureau of Biological Survey in 1896.

The Bureau of Biological Survey was simultaneously transferred to the Department of the Interior, and its name changed to the U.S. Fish and Wildlife Service in 1940. Later, the organization was designated as the U.S. Bureau of Sport Fisheries and Wildlife for a time, but the name reverted back to the U.S. Fish and Wildlife Service in the seventies (Robinson and Bolen 1984).

The first federally sponsored wildlife research resulted in W. B. Barrow's monograph "The English Sparrow (*Passer domesticus*) in North America, Especially in Relation to Agriculture." This 1889 publication was designated as Bulletin 1 of the U.S. Department of Agriculture's Division of Economic Ornithology and Mammalogy (Robinson and Bolen 1984).

The first federal efforts to protect wildlife habitat came in 1903 when Pelican Island, off Florida's east coast, became a sanctuary for wading birds (especially herons and egrets, which were hunted for their plumes) by the executive order of President Theodore Roosevelt. Wildlife preserves were soon created on public lands throughout the country (Greenwalt 1978).

The first federal wildlife management activities can be traced to 1915 when the Bureau of Biological Survey became involved in direct control of predators, especially coyotes and wolves, on public rangelands in the West (Cain 1978). Management with a view to enhancing wildlife followed the Migratory Bird Treaty of 1916 and its companion act of 1918, which combined to bring many species of birds under federal protection.

From these beginnings, federal administration of wildlife has grown to encompass several agencies in three cabinet-level departments. These agencies and their principal wildlife responsibilities are summarized in Table 7.1.

In this administrative structure, heads of cabinet-level federal departments—including the secretaries of agriculture, commerce, and interior—are presidential appointees ratified by the Senate, as are their top staff. Traditionally, the secretary of the interior has been a prominent politician from a western state, often a former governor, senator, or member of Congress. Chiefs of bureaus and their deputies may either be career civil servants or political appointees, with or without professional wildlife credentials. The mix of civil service and political appointees depends upon the administration in office (Gottschalk 1978).

### *Wildlife Administration by State Agencies*

The first state fish and wildlife administration was established by the Commonwealth of Massachusetts in 1865. By 1880, all states had laws protecting wildlife and most had game protectors (Gottschalk 1978). Only since 1910, however, has there been a wildlife agency in every state (Giles 1978).

In the early years, state wildlife agencies functioned largely as an employer for game wardens and as quasi-commercial producers of fish and pheasants. Jobs were usually dispensed in return for political support, and patronage was controlled by the governor. With the election of a new governor, virtually all personnel in the agency might be replaced. Of this system C. R. Gutermuth said, "In those cases where it did work, the incumbent commissioner usually was a man of exceptional ability with the political influence or good fortune to stay in his post long enough to learn his job" (1971).

The *single commissioner system* was the dominant organizational structure for state wildlife agencies through the thirties. Dictators may be efficient, but they can also be ineffective. Thus, although commissioners had considerable authority and administrative discretion, they

Table 7.1. Principal federal agencies responsible for wildlife programs.

| Department | Agency | Principal wildlife responsibilities |
|---|---|---|
| Interior | Fish and Wildlife Service | Migratory birds, some mammals; national wildlife refuges; endangered species coordination; federal aid projects; international agreements |
| | National Park Service | Wildlife in national parks, monuments |
| | Bureau of Land Management | Wildlife on public-domain lands; multiple-use management |
| | Bureau of Indian Affairs | Wildlife on tribal lands |
| | Bureau of Reclamation | Wildlife in western water developments |
| Agriculture | Forest Service | Wildlife on national forests and grasslands; multiple-use management |
| | Soil Conservation Service | Wildlife habitat on private lands, primarily in soil and water districts |
| Commerce | National Marine Fisheries Service | Marine mammals |

Source: Adapted from Robinson and Bolen 1984, table 20-1.

were also subject to pressure and vulnerable to enticements. Furthermore, program stability was constantly in jeopardy, for commissioners might die, retire, or be summarily removed by the governor (Giles 1978).

In 1934 the Model State Game and Fish Administrative Law was adopted at the annual convention of the International Association of Game, Fish, and Conservation Commissioners (Robinson and Bolen 1984). This was the basis for fundamental reforms in the administrative structure of state wildlife agencies throughout the country. The basic provision of this system was replacement of the single commissioner by a commission comprised of several people.

The *commission system* is now used in most states. Commissioners are appointed by the governor and have staggered terms. This ensures a measure of continuity and prevents a governor from making wholesale changes in the commission (Giles 1978). Commissions vary in size from three to fifteen members, and those with fewer than six usually function more efficiently (Gutermuth 1971). Members may represent the state at large or designated regions, depending upon informal tradition or formal agreement.

In a sense, state wildlife commissions are small legislatures with a responsibility to citizens for the well-being of the wildlife resource. As with representatives at other levels in a democracy, the commissioners' responsibilities often outweigh the desires of the public they represent. There are conflicts inherent to the simultaneous role of public representative and policymaker, and commissioners who cannot effectively be both will not endure. A conscientious commission will keep the public informed of the rationale for decisions that may not always be popular. A successful commission will be able to convince a skeptical public that decisions made were really in the public interest (Towell 1979).

In practice, a commission usually acts like a corporate board of directors—setting policy, establishing wildlife regulations, and entering into legal agreements. It typically leaves the agency's day-to-day operations to a professional staff supervised by a director. Most state wildlife agencies are organized by sections; for example, Game Management, Nongame Management, Fisheries, Research, Information and Education, Law Enforcement, Lands and Properties, and Fiscal Affairs (Giles 1978).

The *departmental system* is an organizational structure used in some states. Under this arrangement there is a single Department of Natural Resources or Environmental Conservation, with Divisions of Wildlife, Forestry, Freshwater Fisheries, Parks and Recreation, and the like. Each division has its own director with a professional staff organized into bureaus or sections. Often, the wildlife division is arranged, within the department structure, along the lines of a commission system. One potential advantage of this system is that there may be Divisions of Planning, Lands and Properties, Administration and Finance, etc., that are shared by all the resource divisions, resulting in the coordination of resource policy and management activities, and often in fiscal savings as well (Giles 1978).

Whatever the particulars of organizational structure, virtually all state wildlife agencies now operate under guidelines set by policy-making boards or commissions. It is the role of these commissions to be a buffer between a nonpartisan wildlife agency staff and the politically oriented executive and legislative branches of state government (Towell 1979).

## *Planning in Wildlife Administration*

*Planning* is an integrated system of management that includes all activities leading to the development and implementation of goals, program objectives, operational strategies, and progress evaluation" (Crowe

1983). The planning system is dynamic and cyclical—it involves the continuous evaluation of objectives and monitoring of progress. A generalized planning cycle is made up of four components: inventory, strategic planning, operational planning, and evaluation. These are not separate and independent elements, but intergrade to form a continuous process (Crowe 1983). The meaning and relationship of each element is evident from Figure 7.1.

*Step-down planning* is one example of operational planning, which is also referred to as tactical planning. It can be a practical tool since it promotes identification of all the constituent parts necessary to solve a problem. Its intent is to use deductive reasoning to break a complex problem down, by successive steps, into a series of simpler elements. The step-down process is really an action plan, a "travel itinerary," for wildlife research or management that identifies the ingredients necessary to attain an objective. Inductive reasoning is employed to develop alternative hypotheses at each stage in the process, whereas deductive reasoning is used to show the logical relation between levels or echelons. Plan development is from the top down, from the complex to the simple. Plan execution is from the bottom up, from terminal levels back to the primary objective. Just as a trip itinerary allows travelers to gauge their progress and helps ensure they reach their destination by a specified time, a project itinerary—that is, a tactical plan—specifies a project objective and identifies the steps needed to reach the objective (Phenicie and Lyons 1973). In wildlife research or management, as in travel, if you don't specify where you are going and how you propose to get there, you are liable to end up somewhere else instead (Mager 1962).

*Goal planning* is a tactical planning process that is often used as a decision tool in business. It has also found frequent applications in agricultural economics and farm management, but is not widely used in wildlife planning. One important advantage of goal programming over linear programming, another useful device that has occasionally been used in wildlife studies, is that goal programming allows multiple conflicting goals to be modeled. Rather than optimizing goals directly, the goal programming procedure minimizes deviations from goals. This allows satisfactory goal levels to be achieved even when optimal levels are not feasible. Goal programming may be especially well suited to decision processes in wildlife habitat planning, which are often characterized by multiple conflicting goals (Ludwin and Chamberlain 1989).

The Missouri experience provides a practical example of tactical planning. There, the state's Department of Conservation adopted the Wildlife and Fish Habitat Relationships (WFHR) system developed pri-

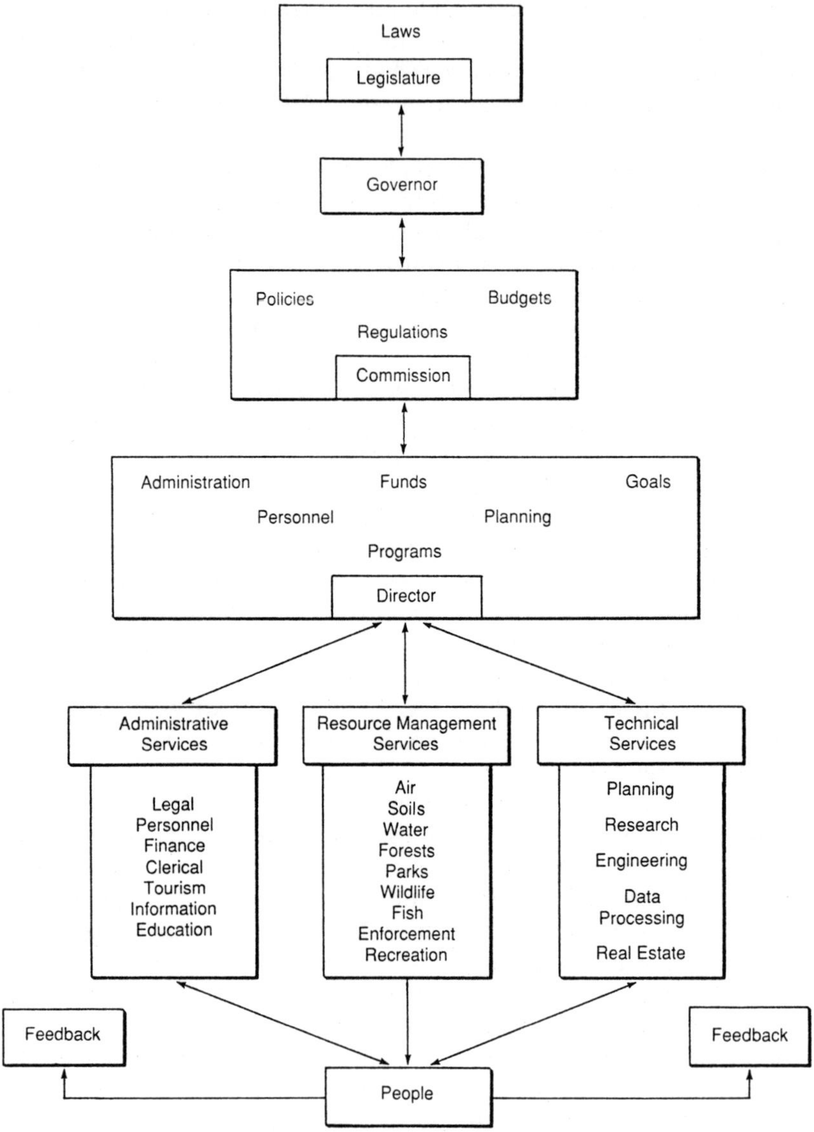


Figure 7.1. A generalized organizational structure for state natural resource management. (Reprinted from *Organization, Authority and Programs of State Fish and Wildlife Agencies* by the Wildlife Management Institute, Washington, D.C., 1977. Used with permission of the Wildlife Management Institute.)

marily by the U.S. Forest Service (Nelson and Salwasser 1982). The Missouri version was produced by the Department of Conservation in conjunction with five other state natural resource agencies as a comprehensive procedure for organizing, applying, and integrating information on fish, forest, and wildlife resources. Working from remote computer terminals, biologists are able to retrieve and sort data on the life history, distribution, and management of Missouri's 728 vertebrates and six aquatic molluscs. Fifty-five management emphasis species (MES) were selected, however, to reduce the number of species considered in planning to a manageable level. Fourteen indicator species were chosen from among the management emphasis species to address several resource management issues: game management and associated consumptive recreation, habitat fragmentation, wildlife-wood products conflicts, and optimum forest silvicultural management. The habitat categories selected represent seven major land-use groups (such as cropland, grassland, and upland hardwoods). Management guidelines, divided into three sections (habitat guidelines, regional guidelines, and species guidelines), were developed to provide accessible information for addressing the resource issues and for integrating multiple-use objectives. Computerized species-habitat relationship models for indicator species are used to assess the wildlife capabilities of Missouri's wildlife management areas (WMAs) and predict species responses to various management actions. This is significant because the state has an active program of land acquisition, so management planning for new wildlife management areas is a priority. Management objectives were proposed to ensure a high diversity of species in each region of the state, but the choice of emphasizing a featured species or managing for species diversity on individual wildlife management areas is left to resource managers and interdisciplinary planning teams (Urich, Graham, and Kelley 1986).

Don Minnich (1978) made a telling point when he defined planning as "administration without authority." Planners engage in the same kind of thinking as executives, but they lack the authority to make final decisions. The primary products of an effective planning section within an agency are good decisions—made by someone else. The wildlife planner should strive to ensure that the agency's chief executive does not have to say, "Something is wrong, and I don't know why or what to do about it." Top-level wildlife administration is always fraught with risks and uncertainties. Wildlife planners cannot reduce all executive decisions to absolute certitude, but they can maximize the probability that top administrators will make good decisions (Minnich 1978).

In times of rapid social change, the best administrators are futurists—able to describe alternatives for the future, to assist the rest of us in formulating a vision of a desirable future, and to guide us toward securing that vision (Edmunds and Lety 1973). Wildlife administrators have a special opportunity and obligation to help assure that healthy ecosystems with viable wildlife populations are a part of our vision of the future and that we are successful in translating that vision into reality.

We take pride that our nation is ruled by law, rather than by people, but the conduct of government is not immune from political pollution. The deplorable actions and assertions of Secretary of the Interior James Watt and EPA Administrator Ann Gorshuch Burford during the Reagan presidency showed again that enforcement of laws can be lax, policy can be perverted, and administration can go awry. The only safeguard for our wildlife resources, as for our freedom, is a concerned citizenry that is constantly vigilant.

---

## SUGGESTED READING

Bean, M. J. 1983. *The Evolution of National Wildlife Law.* Revised and expanded ed. New York: Praeger. 448 pages. Widely considered to be the definitive book on this complex subject.

Crowe, D. M. 1983. *Comprehensive Planning for Wildlife Resources.* Cheyenne: Wyoming Game and Fish Department. 143 pages. An excellent overview of wildlife planning.

# Selected Topics Related to Human Dimensions of Wildlife 8

## WILDLIFE LAW ENFORCEMENT

The first laws pertaining to wildlife were game laws enforced by local peace officers. Later, special officers known as wardens were assigned the job of enforcing game laws. Among the earliest of these were the deer wardens of Massachusetts (1739) and New Hampshire (1741). The first salaried state game wardens were appointed in Michigan, Minnesota, and Wisconsin during 1887 (Bavin 1978).

Early in the nation's history, enforcement of game laws was ineffective and often nonexistent, but the same was true of law enforcement in general (Bavin 1978). Developments in wildlife law enforcement have generally lagged behind those in other police agencies; however, new techniques are increasingly being applied to problems in wildlife law enforcement, and the field is gradually developing toward a full-fledged and respected profession (Morse 1987).

### *The Role of Wildlife Law Enforcement*

Under ideal circumstances there would be total public understanding and support of laws, and compliance would be voluntary. The central lesson of the Prohibition era, however, was that it is difficult, if not impossible, to enforce a law that does not have public support. Historically, the primary problem in wildlife law enforcement has been the lack of public support for strict enforcement of conservation laws (Bavin 1978).

The general public, and even some wildlife professionals, tend to think of wildlife law enforcement solely in terms of the officers themselves. Thus, it is necessary to put the role of wildlife law enforcement in its proper context: game wardens and conservation officers are just one part of the criminal justice system that includes other state and federal enforcement agencies and the federal, state, and local judiciaries.

Each of these has its complement of judges, prosecutors, defense attorneys, parole and probation officers, and corrections personnel staffing prisons and jails (Bavin 1978).

It is also common—and erroneous—to equate enforcement of game laws with the regulation of game species harvest; the former pertains to law enforcement, the latter is a management technique. The misunderstanding of this distinction often leads to confusion about the role of conservation officers in wildlife management (Bavin 1978).

Effective wildlife statutes and regulations require more than vigorous law enforcement efforts. The laws and regulations themselves must be sensible and enforceable, and sufficient funding must be available to ensure that enforcement is implemented. Therefore, it should be the aim of wildlife professionals to propose sensible, useful, and enforceable laws; of legislative bodies to draft these laws in understandable language and to stand behind them with adequate fiscal appropriations; and of conservation officers to enforce legal mandates equitably and professionally (Bavin 1978). The ultimate goal of law observance, whether by voluntary compliance or compelled enforcement, can never be achieved unless sensible wildlife laws and regulations command public respect by logically relating to the needs of the wildlife resource (Stevens 1944).

### *Wildlife Law Enforcement Activities*

It is more desirable to prevent violations than to apprehend violators, so wildlife law enforcement activities should emphasize the observance of conservation laws. Thus, one important function of conservation officers is to create a favorable climate—by their presence and visibility and through their relations with the public—that tends to promote voluntary compliance and prevent violations of wildlife laws (Kenney 1975). Another means of preventing violations is to create a deterrent; that is, to make it clear that conservation officers are willing and able to discover violations and that offenders will be punished for noncompliance (Zimring and Hawkins 1973).

Patrol—whether afoot, by wheeled vehicle, boat, or aircraft—is central to law enforcement. It is this process that helps to create a positive law enforcement atmosphere and tends to create a deterrent. Observations and conversations that take place while on patrol may yield information on illegal wildlife activities. Furthermore, officers on patrol help to reinforce the belief that they may be anywhere, so violators should expect to be apprehended (Kenney 1975).

Under ordinary law enforcement circumstances, there is often a victim who complains to authorities about a crime against person or property. Wildlife, however, cannot complain, and witnesses to violations of conservation laws rarely come forward. In most situations, then, wildlife officers depend upon an investigation to identify the violator and to collect enough admissible evidence to sustain a conviction. Investigative techniques include searches of the crime scene, interviews and interrogations, laboratory analyses, audits of records, surveillance, and undercover work (Bavin 1978).

In many jurisdictions, the activities of wildlife law enforcement officers have been expanded beyond their original role as enforcer of the game laws. Over half the states now invest conservation officers with peace officer status, so they are trained and authorized to enforce the entire state penal code (Bavin 1978).

Wildlife law enforcement on federal lands is the responsibility of the administering agency—the National Park Service, Forest Service, Bureau of Land Management, or Fish and Wildlife Service. The Customs Service also has responsibility for enforcement of laws pertaining to importation of wildlife or wild animal products. In addition, there are federal wildlife law enforcement officers, with the title of special agent, whose duties are concentrated on investigating large-scale or commercial violations and on wildlife law enforcement activities outside the scope and authority of state and local authorities (Bavin 1978).

These special agents of the U.S. Fish and Wildlife Service are especially valuable in combating the complex problems posed by black markets in wildlife and wild animal parts and by highly mobile violators. Some hunters are willing to pay large amounts to kill a record animal illegally in another part of the country, or even another continent, then return home quickly by air. The illegal trophy is surreptitiously shipped to the violator through interstate commerce or smuggled into the country at a later time. Coping with such enforcement challenges demands the use of new approaches, including undercover operations (Bavin 1978, 1987).

### *Wildlife Law Enforcement Problems*

The basic problems confronting conservation officers today are the same ones that have plagued wildlife law enforcement since its inception—"that is, public indifference toward wildlife in general and toward wildlife law enforcement in particular" (Bavin 1978).

Public apathy often allows special interest groups—whether seeking complete protection or excessive exploitation—to exert undue influence. The outcome, in the absence of scrutiny by a concerned public, may be laws that are unreasonable and almost unenforceable. This places a difficult and frustrating burden on conservation officers (Bavin 1978).

Furthermore, public apathy, or even opposition to strong wildlife laws, leads to poor laws and noncompliance and eventually to limited budgets for state and federal wildlife agencies as well. This means that conservation enforcement positions are often understaffed and existing personnel are overworked or spread too thin for optimum effectiveness. All these problems come at a time when the human population continues to increase and people are spending more of their leisure time outdoors (Bavin 1978).

Ultimately, the absence among so many hunters of an ethic—the lack of sportsmanship—perpetuates noncompliance with wildlife laws. A person who would never consider hunting out of season may, nevertheless, shoot more than the legal limit during the season. Selective violation of wildlife laws may be condoned or ignored by hunters, but it undermines the spirit of compliance and sets a poor example for persons less knowledgeable and experienced (Bavin 1978).

### *Discretion in Wildlife Law Enforcement*

Discretion has a significant function in the enforcement of wildlife laws, as it has in the administration of criminal justice generally. However, there are few guidelines for exercising discretion, so conservation officers often rely on their own judgment in applying wildlife laws (Bavin 1978).

Those guidelines that do exist are generally informal and unwritten. Some wildlife agencies use a "tolerance limits" concept similar to that employed by traffic officers in enforcing speed limits. Where agencies have not established "tolerance limits," the behavior of individual officers may reflect their own idea of fairness (Bavin 1978).

There are several reasons for exercising discretion in the enforcement of wildlife statutes: (1) a legislative body may not desire total enforcement; for example, a legislature may define some action as criminal to satisfy prevailing social attitudes, but without regard for the enforceability of the law; (2) most state and federal wildlife statutes are overly general, but they impose strict limits on public actions; therefore, a person may be unaware of a violation or a violation may occur without criminal intent; and (3) a trivial offense or technical violation in which there was no intent to harm the wildlife resource and actual damage was slight (Bavin 1978).

### *Wildlife Law Enforcement Research: A Case Study*

An investigation of discretion in enforcement by Beattie (1981) provides an example of research in wildlife law enforcement. Questionnaires returned by 1,245 Virginia firearm hunters were the basis of a study to determine whether attitudes toward game laws, game law enforcement, and game wardens differed between hunters who were issued citations for violations and those who received only warnings. The hypothesis was that hunters receiving warnings for violations would have more favorable attitudes than hunters receiving citations for violations. In fact, the converse occurred for two of the three attitudes. Of those who received one or more warnings between 1973 and 1978, 73 percent had very favorable attitudes toward game laws compared with 92 percent of those who were issued citations. Likewise, 72 percent of hunters receiving a warning had very favorable attitudes toward game law enforcement, whereas 87 percent of hunters who were given a citation expressed very favorable attitudes. Percentage differences in attitudes toward game wardens were not significantly different between the two groups.

Initially, Beattie had thought that a warning, which carries no penalty, would result in more favorable hunter attitudes than a citation, which imposes a fine. Violators may reason differently, however. Persons given a warning may be relieved that they do not have to pay a fine, but may also feel that warnings do not act as a deterrent against future violations. Their logic may lead to the conclusion that wildlife would be better protected by the strict issuance of citations in all cases, so that less vigorous enforcement leads to less favorable attitudes toward laws and their enforcement. Another possible explanation is based on the notion that violators who received a citation may have a sense of relief because they have "paid" for their violation. Although the findings of this study were considered tentative due to data limitations, the conclusion that warnings do not necessarily improve game law–related attitudes certainly warrants consideration and further research.

### *Academic Training for Wildlife Law Enforcement*

Wildlife and conservation agencies have increased the eligibility standards and training requirements for conservation officers as the law enforcement responsibilities of these agencies have been expanded. Many agencies that formerly hired high school graduates now require some pertinent college coursework, or even a college degree, of applicants for enforcement positions.

A study by Giovengo (1988) indicated that diversity and flexibility of training should be the major objective of students interested in pursuing a university degree leading to a career in conservation law enforcement. Conservation officers obviously bring their entire educational and experiential background to their enforcement duties, but some academic fields contribute more to their preparation than others.

The chiefs of state and federal conservation law enforcement agencies who responded to Giovengo's survey ranked a list of thirty-two academic courses according to their perceived value to conservation officers. In general, courses in law enforcement, wildlife, and communications were judged to be most useful. The course ranked first in importance, however, was from the communications category—Public Speaking. The other communications course considered especially valuable was Technical Report Writing (ranked fourth). Important law enforcement courses included Behavioral Aspects of Investigation (second), Criminal Law (third), Enforcement Discretion (fifth), and Introduction to Criminal Justice (sixth).

Wildlife courses judged most worthwhile were Waterfowl (ranked seventh), Wildlife Biology (eighth), and Upland Game Birds (ninth). The general biology course Conservation of Natural Resources ranked tenth.

Some other courses that might seem especially valuable were ranked much lower. These included Human Relations and Criminal Justice (fifteenth), Introduction to Criminal Behavior (seventeenth), Emergency Medical Technician (EMT) (eighteenth), Sociology (twenty-second), Martial Arts (twenty-fifth), Recreation in Wildlands Environment (twenty-sixth), and Chemistry (thirty-second).

Students anticipating a career in conservation law enforcement should expect to attend a law enforcement academy at some stage in their training. In addition, the chiefs of state and federal conservation law enforcement agencies responding to Giovengo's questionnaire suggested coursework or training in subjects not covered by the conservative law enforcement program. These were often practical or vocational in nature, and included forensics, firearms training, driving, practical boat and trailer handling, advanced investigation, and public relations.

## WILDLIFE PUBLIC RELATIONS

Many people over the years have chosen a professional career in wildlife because of their love of the outdoors, their enjoyment of hunting and fishing, and their interest in wild animals. More recently, individuals have also been attracted to the wildlife profession by an interest in conservation or a concern for endangered species. They soon find, however, that their time is largely devoted to working with people rather than with wildlife. Most of their days are spent in offices and conference rooms rather than tramping the fields and forests (Kimball 1975).

All wildlife professionals eventually realize that technical knowledge matters little "if their publics do not understand their conclusions nor accept their recommendations." In fact, no wildlife agency can successfully exercise its authority or fulfill its responsibility without public support (Kimball 1975).

### *What is Public Relations?*

The varied definitions of public relations can be distilled into a simple idea: public relations is effective two-way communication (Gilbert 1975). Wildlife agencies must advertise their plans and publicize their achievements. They must also solicit responses from members of their publics—via telephone surveys, mailed questionnaires, public gatherings, and meetings with representatives of various interest groups. Then, they may also have to explain and persuade—to describe why a particular course of action was required and to convince the relevant publics that the action was justified.

Wildlife agencies do not sell goods—and they certainly cannot sell wildlife, which is already owned by the people. If anything, agencies "sell" ideas, services, and recreational opportunities. Positive public relations fosters the civic support that is essential to the success of their conservation and management missions (Gilbert 1975).

Public relations, whether good or bad, are continuous and always present. Like good health, good public relations are often taken for granted. Poor public relations are usually the result of neglect (Gilbert 1975). It is most important that good public relations be based on honesty—on the undistorted facts of a situation. That said, it is also true that public relations involves a conscious effort to influence, and even to change, public opinion (Gilbert 1975).

### *The Publics in Public Relations*

A public is two or more persons with a common interest. A public is similar to a group, except that a public does not have to be in a single location. Each public is different, with different characteristics, interests, and intentions. Therefore, one should know as much as possible about a public in order to tailor information to its specific needs. Furthermore, each public's state of receptivity to a particular idea is different, depending upon the personal, social, and cultural factors of its members (Gilbert 1975).

There are two basic kinds of publics: *internal publics,* those within an organization, and *external publics,* which are not part of the organization. Each of these may, in turn, contain several subpublics. The internal publics of a state wildlife agency, for example, might include administrators, research biologists, management biologists, conservation enforcement officers, maintenance personnel, and office workers. The management biologists might be further divided into subpublics of big-game biologists, upland-game biologists, waterfowl biologists, etc. (Gilbert 1978).

We should not minimize the importance of internal publics: they may be even more important than the external publics. The acceptance of an idea or plan of action within an agency is necessary before there can be any hope of successful implementation. Dissension within an agency is readily detected by those outside, who may well ask, "If this plan is so good, why can't employees of the agency agree on it?" Many ideas have been rejected by outside publics due to disagreements among agency personnel themselves (Gilbert 1975).

External publics are highly diverse: hunters, outdoor enthusiasts, business and professional people, blue-collar workers, retired persons, urban apartment dwellers, suburban homeowners, rural landowners, school and youth group members, personnel of other natural resource agencies, animal welfare organization members, newspaper and TV reporters, and many more. Obviously, each of us is simultaneously a member of several publics; one person, for example, might be an elk hunter, backpacker, electrical contractor, suburban homeowner, Scout leader, and Ducks Unlimited member. Whatever the public, a wildlife agency should make it aware of the agency's concern for "the public interest" and its commitment to wise natural resource conservation and management (Gilbert 1975).

### *Basic Public Relations Techniques*

The cardinal rule of wildlife public relations is that the internal publics must be convinced first. If the internal publics cannot agree, it may be impossible to convince external publics. Therefore, once a plan has been accepted as agency policy, internal publics (and personnel) not in agreement should avoid public statements of criticism (Gilbert 1978).

One of the most important public relations strategies for internal or external publics is *empathy*. Empathy, or sympathetic understanding, is trying to view an issue from your adversary's viewpoint. By trying to put yourself in other people's situations, you may come to a greater appreciation of their problems. From this effort, it may be possible to arrive at a mutual understanding. In any case, the fact that you made an effort may well result in future cooperation or even an ally (Gilbert 1978).

Act, don't react. Wildlife agencies often wait until they are besieged by complaints about a plan, then find it necessary to defend their proposal. By explaining a proposal during the planning stages, an agency can offset the need to defend an action later. Concomitantly, it will also cultivate the image of an organization that takes the initiative, rather than being seen as always scrambling to make tardy explanations (Gilbert 1978).

"Top down" communication saves time and effort. Identifying and working with the leaders of a public tends to be more efficient and effective than trying to work with an entire public. Proposals can be carefully explained to a few key people in an informal setting, thereby improving the chances they will understand the plan. If it is possible to secure their cooperation, their approval will influence other members toward acceptance (Gilbert 1978).

Wildlife managers should keep in mind that considering an idea is a sequential process. Acceptance or rejection of a plan rarely occurs the first time a person is exposed to it. Any idea with important consequences is usually considered over a period of time, and persons pass through a series of stages in their thinking before the idea is accepted or rejected. We can represent these stages as: awareness → interest → forming an attitude → having an opinion → developing a belief. As persons pass through this sequence there is an increasing firmness and constancy in their position, so it is much easier to influence their thinking at an early stage in the process. This illustrates why it is critical that wildlife agencies publicize proposals strongly and effectively while they are still in the planning stages, particularly if they are potentially controversial. It will be much more difficult to win public support for an idea after there has been negative publicity from other publics and interest groups (Gilbert 1978).

Lay persons often make decisions and argue points on the basis of emotions. Persons inclined toward a professional career in wildlife may be more likely to take positions on the basis of evidence. This tendency is reinforced by their scientific education and job experience in natural resources. When scientific methodology is so much a part of one's everyday thinking, it is easy to forget that most people look at the world in a very different way. Thus, you should not expect lay publics to be as impressed by logic as you are. In fact, you may find that your professional judgments can be communicated most effectively to some publics using emotional expressions—so long as they remain factually correct (Gilbert 1978).

### *Common Public Relations Problems*

Wildlife agencies often decry the lack of public involvement and presume that it can be increased by holding more public meetings. Many agency personnel have had traumatic experiences at public meetings and shudder at the thought of even more public involvement. When additional public involvement seems desirable, it may be possible to set up a semiofficial adviser group (not to be confused with the official state wildlife commission or board) made up of representatives of the publics directly concerned (Gilbert 1978).

Recalling our definition of public relations, it is obvious that a lack of communication would cause problems. A basic requisite of communication is interest. If either party lacks interest, communication is impossible. Communication can be promoted by immediate interaction—asking and answering questions face to face. From the standpoint of time and effort, personal meetings are not as efficient as the mass media or large-group approach. They may be necessary or desirable in certain circumstances, however, and a personal meeting with a key representative of an important public may be well worthwhile (Gilbert 1978). Failure to communicate effectively with the general public seems to be a congenital problem with wildlife personnel at all levels, from technicians to administrators (see Lautenschlager and Bowyer 1985). Yet the success of many wildlife agency initiatives absolutely depends on the ability of wildlife professionals to successfully communicate with their specialized publics and with the citizenry at large.

Special publics may vary from one agency to another, but four special publics always deserve extra attention: legislators, members of official commissions or boards, members of semiofficial advisory groups, and representatives of the electronic and print media. Cordial and productive relations with members of these groups are essential to a wildlife agency's success (Gilbert 1978).

Antihunting sentiment has been discussed previously in another context, but it is virtually certain to be an important public relations problem in the future. In some cases, antihunting sentiment may be a pragmatic problem related to hunter behavior. Where real philosophical differences exist, wildlife professionals should be careful not to antagonize the antihunting public by name-calling. Persons and groups opposed to hunting have a strong interest in wildlife and a sincere conviction that hunting is wrong. They, too, are working for wildlife conservation. In reality, the disagreement may be focused on "legitimate uses" of wildlife, but pro- and antihunting factions alike need to be concerned with such critical issues as loss of wildlife habitat. "Empathy and understanding resulting from good communication and education can reduce controversy and its adverse impact on wildlife management efforts" (Gilbert 1978).

## WOULD LEGAL MARKETS IN WILDLIFE MEAT AND PARTS HARM WILDLIFE CONSERVATION?

There has been renewed discussion over whether legal markets in wildlife meat and parts should be allowed. In North America this question was first answered—in the negative—by policies jointly adopted by the United States and Canada in the early 1900s (Geist 1988). These policies have gradually been eroded over the years. Recently, Valerius Geist (1985, 1988) has been outspoken in calling attention to how he believes markets in wildlife meat and parts, and the sale of hunting privileges, jeopardizes the system of wildlife conservation in North America.

Meanwhile, Gordon Grigg (1989) has argued that the situation with respect to the kangaroo in Australia is very different. He contends that "farming" kangaroos and selling kangaroo products might actually contribute to solving Australia's two major rural problems: land degradation and the kangaroo dilemma. The arguments of these two scientists are summarized here by way of an introduction to this controversial topic.

### *A North American Perspective*

In a brief historical review, Geist (1988) observed that wildlife conservation in North America is based on three primary policies that underlie the laws, regulations, attitudes, and beliefs that pertain to wildlife conservation. These policies disallow markets in wildlife meat and parts; allocate the material benefits of wildlife by law, not by market or socioeconomic factors; and prohibit the frivolous killing of wildlife.

These policies were "the work of North America's intellectual, social and political elite," instituted by Americans such as President Theodore Roosevelt and Chief Forester Gifford Pinchot and Canadians such as Prime Minister Sir Wilfrid Laurier and Conservation Commission Chairman Clifford Sifton. The policies "were not established for reasons of sentiment, but in hardheaded recognition of the potential economic worth of wildlife."

As a consequence of the first policy, only activities of living wildlife can be sold; dead wildlife has no economic value. The second policy makes every citizen of the United States and Canada a "shareholder" in wildlife. The third prohibits the waste of wildlife that has been killed and permits the destruction of noxious wildlife, but is ambiguous on the subject of sport and trophy hunting. There are, however, exceptions to these policies, most notably in the retention of markets in wild fur.

An effect of these policies has been to ensure that the killing of wildlife is an economic liability rather than a reward. To hunt requires an unrecoverable investment in time, effort, and equipment, so it is costly to kill an animal legally, and the dead animal cannot be abandoned under penalty of law.

Most people are unaware of the achievements of conservation in North America, yet these three policies have (1) fostered the recovery of many species that had been decimated; (2) led to a large service and manufacturing industry based on living wildlife, which actually increased economic returns compared to the old market-hunting system; (3) nurtured a model wildlife conservation and management system at the state, provincial, and federal levels and created teaching and research positions for training biologists to staff it; (4) encouraged the formation of citizen conservation organizations; (5) provided for financing of wildlife programs through hunting license sales, taxes on sporting equipment, and general tax revenues; (6) created an extensive system of national parks, wildlife refuges, and reserves; (7) encouraged the formation of private organizations such as the Nature Conservancy and Habitat Canada; (8) promoted the negotiation of international treaties to protect wildlife; (9) advanced the preservation of large predators, such as wolves and bears, which have been extirpated in much of the rest of the world; and (10) gave incentive for an inexpensive and fairly effective system of wildlife protection.

With the passage of time, all three policies have been eroded. In effect, the first policy would be abolished if current efforts to sell meat and parts of dead wildlife are successful. The second policy has already been compromised by hunting leases, shooting reserves, and private trophy and trespass fees, all of which allocate wildlife to those who can afford the price. The third policy has been weakened by "the notion that hunting is killing for 'sport' or 'fun,' and that wildlife is consequently a 'recreational' resource. Current public views do not support killing wildlife for sport, but they do support such killing for food."

Attempts are underway to shift wildlife from public to private control. Efforts by private interests to gain control over wildlife take several forms. In Canada, private parties are involved in game ranching and commercial caribou and musk ox harvesting. In the United States, efforts are primarily directed toward ranching native big game for hunting. "All hope to profit from luxury markets, selling wildlife as 'medicine,' as a delicacy, or for entertainment. These thrusts are quietly and effectively supported by agricultural interests in government and universities."

A policy that gives market value to living wildlife generates much more income than one giving economic value to dead wildlife. In Alberta alone, living wildlife stimulates over $1 billion yearly in business income, two-thirds from nonconsumptive uses. By comparison, the yearly value of the world venison trade is only about $200 million. Thus, from a purely monetary viewpoint, the goal should be economically *inefficient* exploitation of wildlife. Using an analogy from angling, to fish inefficiently is to use a dry fly; to fish efficiently is to use dynamite.

A policy that allocates the material benefits of wildlife by law, not by market or socioeconomic factors, permits access to wildlife by the greatest number of persons. The 1925 change in Texas trespass laws gave de facto control over wildlife to private landowners and permitted the development of game ranching. This has substantially reduced public access to wildlife. Texas has three times the human population of Wisconsin, and almost five times as many deer. Yet, there are twice as many Wisconsin deer hunters.

A policy that promotes sport hunting also undermines conservation. To the public, sport hunting may mean killing for pleasure. The public accepts subsistence and meat hunting, but not hunting for "fun." Promoting the idea of sport hunting is doubly harmful: it offends the prevailing ethic, and it erodes the old American idea of hunting for food. As Geist asserts, "Understanding the historical roots of American wildlife management is vital to nature conservation. Making all citizens de facto as well as de jure shareholders in wildlife deserves broad attention" (Geist 1988).

### *The Australian Situation*

Australia has two major rural land problems: land degradation and the kangaroo dilemma. Since 1987, Gordon Grigg has advocated "a marketing drive to increase the selling price of meat from Australia's three large species of kangaroos" (1989). His argument is that this would revitalize Australia's overgrazed semi-arid lands, reduce illegal killing of kangaroos by "inexpert shooters," and improve the long-range conservation of kangaroos by conserving their prime habitat. Thus, the kangaroo harvesting proposal might help solve both problems.

Land degradation is regarded as the more serious of the two problems. More than one-quarter of the Australian continent has been degraded by overgrazing by domestic livestock, particularly sheep. Fully one-quarter of the degraded area is at risk of becoming permanent desert. Most of the large kangaroos live in these degraded grazing lands.

The kangaroo problem arises out of a conflict between the public perception of kangaroos as being the very symbol of Australia and one of the world's most beloved animals and, simultaneously, a serious agricultural pest. Recent estimates indicate that every kangaroo costs the landholder as much as twenty dollars per year in lost revenue. Consequently, various levels of government license an annual killing of about 3 million red, eastern gray, and western gray kangaroos for pest control. This is done by a restricted industry that harvests the animals up to an annual quota, based on population surveys, and markets the hides and meat. In addition to animals harvested by the industry, landholders kill kangaroos outside the commercial zones on "destruction permits" to reduce the pest problem. Since these animals are prohibited from entering the trade, they are usually left to rot. Many more are killed without permits, often for "sport," which poses an animal welfare problem.

Critics of the kangaroo industry are mainly opposed to its activities on ethical grounds. They contend that kangaroos may not be as serious a pest as claimed, that there is widespread cruelty to kangaroos, that an industry based on native wildlife is morally wrong, and that the industry does not effectively control the animals because it concentrates on larger males. There are even claims that kangaroos are being threatened with extinction, despite considerable evidence to the contrary.

The so-called "sheep rangelands" of Australia occupy about 20 percent of the continent, supporting about 15 percent (20 million) of the sheep and over half (at least 10 million) of the kangaroos. These shrublands clearly show the enormous impact "of hard-footed, hard-feeding sheep." Now, since sheep grazing has become only marginally profitable in many areas, there is increasing interest in goat farming. If intensive goat farming becomes established, much of the barren and overgrazed sheep rangelands will become desert.

The solution Grigg proposes is the significant reduction or removal of sheep from the rangelands, which "would lead to an increase in kangaroos, improvement in the vegetation, and a reduction in soil erosion." Kangaroos have evolved in Australia, are soft-footed (unlike sheep and goats), and do not crop grass as closely when they feed. "Further, most seeds pass undamaged through kangaroos, whereas sheep grind seeds and so destroy the seed 'bank.' "

An increase in the market value of kangaroo products would provide an incentive for graziers to reduce or eliminate sheep and promote the harvesting of kangaroos. Two assumptions underlie this proposal: that kangaroo populations can sustain regular and substantial cropping and that the meat and leather are good enough products to support a sizable increase in price. Both assumptions appear to be supported by abundant evidence. More than one hundred years of data show "that direct killing by man has had little overall effect on the numbers and distribution of the large kangaroos." Kangaroo leather has always been in great demand because of its strength and suppleness; and the meat, which is flavorful and has less than 2 percent fat, is gaining favor as "the red meat you *can* eat."

How can a conservation biologist argue for an industry based on the killing of wildlife? First, the maintenance of habitat is mandatory if abundant and widespread kangaroo populations are to be conserved. Second, there would be no cruelty: the animals would live free and wild, and those harvested would be shot in the head at night and "not even hear the bullet that kills them." Third, the animal welfare and pest problems would be eliminated: casual illegal shooting, illegal drives and roundups, and poisoning of water holes would cease because kangaroos would be too valuable for such activities to be tolerated. In Grigg's opinion, "the manifold conservation and animal welfare merits of the case for a careful, controlled harvest of free-ranging kangaroos warrant thoughtful consideration by conservationists, graziers, agricultural economists, land managers, and the community in general" (1989).

## THE DEEP ECOLOGY MOVEMENT

The publication of Rachel Carson's book *Silent Spring* in 1962 ushered in what some have called the "age of ecology" and with it a questioning of the religious and philosophical roots of Western culture. Out of this questioning has come a "deep ecology" movement that seeks to reawaken in humans a sense of spiritual reciprocity with the rest of nature and to restructure contemporary societies so that they are ecologically harmonious (Sessions 1987).

This ecological consciousness has its historical roots in the ecocentric religions of primal peoples throughout the world, in the Romantic movement, and in Taoism, Zen Buddhism, and the teachings of St. Francis. In more recent times it has been expressed by Thoreau, John Muir, D. H. Lawrence, Robinson Jeffers, Aldous Huxley, Aldo Leopold, Rachel Carson, Paul Shepard, Gary Snyder, and Edward Abbey (Sessions 1987). It is also present in the philosophical works of Spinoza, Heidegger, and Whitehead (Meeker 1986).

In a 1973 article the Norwegian philosopher Arne Naess consolidated the insights that emerged from the ecological awakening of the sixties. He also contended that "insofar as ecology movements deserve our attention, they are ecophilosophical rather than ecological. Ecology is a limited science which makes use of scientific methods. Philosophy is the most general forum of debate on fundamentals." By asserting the primacy of philosophy, Naess apparently hoped to "close the positivist gap between the factual and valuational, and to raise the ecological/environmental debate to the level of ecological wisdom," or what he called "ecosophy" (Sessions 1987).

Although Naess continued to develop his ideas on deep ecology during the seventies, his distinction between "shallow" and "deep" approaches to ecology attracted little attention until it was promoted by two California academics—the sociologist Bill Devall and the philosopher George Sessions (Fox 1990). Their writings culminated in the book *Deep Ecology: Living as If Nature Mattered* (Devall and Sessions 1985). As a consequence, deep ecology is now at the center of ecophilosophical discussion and is occasionally even mentioned by "real ecologists" (for example, see the introduction to Ehrlich 1986).

Without going into great detail, the basic philosophical tenets of the deep ecology movement include (1) a rejection of the human-in-environment image in favor of the relational total-field image; (2) embracing an ecological egalitarianism; (3) supporting the principles of diversity and symbiosis; (4) an anticlass viewpoint; (5) fighting pollution and resource depletion and assuring ample resources for all species; (6) sustaining complexity, not complication; and (7) decentralization and local autonomy (Sessions 1987).

The most resistance to deep ecology principles, even among environmentally committed persons, is centered on three issues—ecological egalitarianism, human population reduction, and wilderness preservation (Sessions 1987). Writers such as Wendell Berry have tried to show the absurdity of ecological egalitarianism by posing questions like, "Is the life of a human child worth no more than that of a mosquito?" In response, Naess explained, "The right to live is one and the same, but vital interests of our nearest have priority of defense" (as quoted in Sessions 1987).

Many well-intentioned environmentalists are legitimately concerned about toxic wastes, acid rain, nuclear power plants, and other problems. But Gary Snyder has proposed what amounts to a litmus test to differentiate shallow and deep ecologists—and it is here that relevancy of the deep ecology movement to wildlife becomes clear. The crucial issue is one's attitude toward wildlife and wildlife habitat (Sessions 1987).

According to Snyder, ecological consciousness and the bioregional position calls for the "full rehabilitation of all wildlife" that was on the North American continent two hundred years ago. This has far-reaching implications, for if we really allow wildlife its place on the earth, it will be necessary to reduce the human population to accommodate that wildlife. Such a prospect would not be realistic in this century, or perhaps even in the next, but it is a long-range goal of deep ecology (Sessions 1987).

Ultimately, however, the deep ecology movement is concerned with fulfilling human potential. In Naess's view this involves an increasing maturity of the self—but a self that goes beyond the individual ego, and even other humans, to encompass nonhuman individuals, species, and ecosystems. This Naess called an "ecological self" (Sessions 1987).

Paul Shepard (1982) argued that humans have, built into their genetic makeup, a developmental ontogeny that includes an identification with the nonhuman. The problem is that modern humans living in urban/industrial societies get "stuck" in an adolescent phase of development for their entire lives. This perpetual adolescence promotes overly competitive, consumerist, and nature-destroying modes of action. By developing and living in societies that encourage humans to identify with the nonhuman world, people would be able to pass through their normal developmental stages. Then, many of our social ills and environmental problems would be resolved naturally (Sessions 1987).

Deep ecology, in some form, may be the philosophy of the future. It is "even more soundly rooted in the past than conventional anthropocentrism, and its message rings truer" (Meeker 1986). For the present, however, there are obstacles. Deep ecology is critical of virtually the entire environmental movement, from nineteenth-century conservationists who struggled to establish national parks to the Sierra Club and the current eco-activists. Thus, deep ecology has made few friends with other environmentalists. Even its terminology invites polarization. By adopting the "deep ecology" label, it has undoubtedly antagonized a lot of "shallow" ecologists (Meeker 1986).

## CONSERVATION BIOLOGY AND WILDLIFE BIOLOGY

The editors of *Conservation Biology: An Evolutionary-Ecological Perspective* denied that theirs was the first book in the field, and credited Raymond Dasmann's (1968) *Environmental Conservation* and David Ehrenfeld's (1970) *Biological Conservation* with priority (Soulé and Wilcox 1980a). It was, nevertheless, these editors who issued "an invitation to students and scientists . . . to participate in the vocation or avocation of conservation biology" (Soulé and Wilcox 1980b). In the preface to a second book with the same title, the tone and substance of Soulé's introductory comments indicated the extent to which he already regarded conservation biology as an established discipline: "Much has happened to conservation biology in the six-year interval between these two books. Many people now refer to themselves as conservation biologists, there is a new Society for Conservation Biology, and a new journal is being established. Partly a cause and partly as an effect of this movement, there is growing concern among biologists about biological diversity, genetic resources, and extinction" (1986).

Soulé's optimistic view of the field of conservation biology was supported in volume 1, number 1, of *Conservation Biology* when Peter Raven (1987) used the following title for his article reviewing the second *Conservation Biology* book: "Conservation Biology: A New Discipline Comes of Age." The journal's editor, David Ehrenfeld (1987), began an editorial in the same issue with the statement: "Conservation biology is now a discipline, a recognizable and coherent body of facts, theories, and technologies."

Such self-assured pronouncements were lent additional support by an auspicious group of biologists who contributed to one or other of the *Conservation Biology* books or to volume 1 of the journal: Archie Carr (posthumously), Jared Diamond, Paul Ehrlich, John Eisenberg, Daniel Janzen, Devra Kleiman, Robert May, Norman Myers, William Niering, Katherine Ralls, Daniel Simberloff, John Terbough, and E. O. Wilson.

Is it any wonder, then, that James Teer's (1988) review of the second *Conservation Biology* book, which began as "a report and welcome to a new professional organization with conservation of biodiversity as its founding and fundamental interest," later took a testy turn when he asked: "Why a new organization? Why did not these scientists join with an already established professional society whose interests and emphasis have been and are on conservation of the natural world?" Further along in the review Teer remarked, "Clearly, the new society has entered a niche presently filled by a number of professional societies." And then, "Yes, there is a 'hint of jealousy' . . . among resource managers in respect to the entry of a new group of scientist/educators into the arena of applied ecology. . . . What the [new] society proposes to be, the profession of wildlife ecology and management has been for all of its history."

Teer's comments provoked a response from Thomas Edwards, Jr. (1989), that was critical of the wildlife profession. The peer reviews of Edwards's article solicited by *Wildlife Society Bulletin* editor David Capen (1989) led to several short essays on the relationship between wildlife biology and conservation biology that Richard Yahner (1990) thought should be required reading for students and professionals in all natural resource fields. Those who delve into these brief articles will be treated to an interesting and thought-provoking discussion of the status of wildlife biology, as well as its relation to conservation biology. This summary seeks to present the major points and the flavor of the exchange.

Edwards was glad Teer asked why the Society for Conservation Biology (SCB) arose, given the presence of established societies with similar interests such as the Wildlife Society (TWS), "because it has forced me to ponder why I find many of the goals represented by SCB more exciting than those currently espoused by TWS." Continuing, Edwards viewed "the emergence of SCB as an unique opportunity to develop new and innovative approaches to managing wildlife" and suggested that wildlife biologists "have become a group of tinkerers with superb tactical skills," but with "little grasp of the theoretical foundations necessary to fully develop conservation strategy." Because of the reductionist approach often employed by wildlife biologists—"dissecting problems into their component parts and examining each in isolation"—he contended that "it frequently is difficult to place wildlife research into any kind of conceptual framework." Furthermore, he was troubled by "the limited emphasis given to synthesizing knowledge gained from the component parts into conceptual models that explain how underlying biological processes operate on and change natural systems" (1989).

Turning to Teer's comment that wildlife management continues its traditional emphasis on the consumptive aspect of wildlife, particularly in light of his statement that "what the [SCB] proposes to be, the profession of wildlife ecology and management has been for all of its history," Edwards suggested that conservation biologists might legitimately question the duality of "game" and "nongame" species. "The danger in continuing to emphasize [this] distinction is that, as the movement towards a broad-based conservation strategy grows, a narrowly defined emphasis on 'game' threatens to make an anachronism of much of wildlife management."

Two other points also received Edwards's attention: first, that wildlife management has emphasized a single-species approach to management, which should be expanded to encompass the kind of multispecies interactions that have largely been the province of community- and ecosystem-level studies; and second, that wildlife management has rarely emphasized the genetics of conservation (including such concepts as inbreeding depression and genetic drift), although there is a growing awareness that habitat preservation alone may not be sufficient to assure the survival of some species.

An anonymous reviewer (1989) began his contribution to the exchange by decrying the "parochialism, elitism, turf battles, and misleading characterizations [which] will only make the challenge [of conserving the world's wildlife resources] that much more difficult." In response to Edwards's assertion that there is limited attention to ecological theory within the wildlife profession, this reviewer contended "that ecological theory abounds" and "is the basis for most management of wildlife resources." The reviewer also believed that the "overemphasis on consumptive use . . . has changed considerably in the last decade" so that the wildlife profession "is not quite the deer and duck club [that Edwards] implied."

Considering "the pace of habitat degradation and destruction around the world," this reviewer also doubted "that wildlife has the luxury of sufficient time for theoretical ecologists alone to develop the expertise and data base of wildlife professionals" or for wildlife professionals "to come up to speed on all current ecological theory." Thus, only through a synergism of wildlife biologists and conservation biologists is there a chance for success. This means that wildlife biologists will have to put aside their defensive attitudes, and conservation biologists must stop discrediting or disregarding the contributions of wildlifers.

Eric Bolen (1989) viewed the broad goals of wildlifers and conservation biologists as not being mutually exclusive, but reflective of interests and professional backgrounds that are usually quite different. Wildlife management had its genesis in production-oriented schools of agriculture or forestry, which fostered the perspective of practitioner rather than theorist. Thus, the wildlife discipline developed from a different orientation than the "pure" biological sciences, such as genetics and systematics, with their links to evolutionary theory.

This, as Bolen observed, does not mean that wildlife biologists do not understand or appreciate the importance of ecological theory. In fact, pioneer wildlife researchers such as Paul Errington—who "formulated provocative ideas about carrying capacity, predator-prey relationships, and inversity"—made important contributions to the very foundations of ecological theory (1989). More recently, wildlife biologists have based management practices on theory from fields as diverse as animal behavior and island biogeography.

Rachel Carson's *Silent Spring*, the National Environmental Policy Act, and the Endangered Species Act brought about and signaled a changing societal emphasis, often accompanied by name changes in many state "game and fish" agencies, which became departments of conservation or wildlife. Now, state and federal wildlife agencies often direct "their resources toward salamanders, butterflies, and tortoises as well as to 'deer, ducks, and doves' " (Bolen 1989).

Noting that the history of the wildlife profession, which focused on game animals during its early decades, largely accounts for its traditional emphasis on "single-species" research and management, Bolen commented, "That scarcely lessens my pride in the research and management that led to recovery of wood ducks (*Aix sponsa*) or the return of Atlantic salmon (*Salmo salar*)." Furthermore, he doubted that much of this research was as narrow as critics imply; for example, "The landmark research into the pesticide contamination of raptors also considered the ecology of the species' prey base." Concluding, Bolen noted that wildlife management represents the empirical base and delivery system so necessary for transforming knowledge into practice, and in this way wildlife biology complements the basic sciences from which conservation biology springs.

Rhetorically asking "What's wrong with the questions we ask in wildlife research?" Thomas Gavin contended "that biological questions asked by wildlife biologists remain narrow in scope and potential applicability, and that our decisions to do site-specific, problem-oriented research in the short-term may have sold short our ability to solve the very problems we thought we were attacking directly" (1989). The point he sought to make was that the tradition of wildlife research has constrained both the way we ask questions and the kinds of questions asked, and that this approach is detrimental to the management of wildlife as well as to the wildlife discipline and profession. His thesis was that if we really understood the behavior of wildlife populations, then we could at least make biologically sound recommendations contributing to wise management.

Drawing on his own experience, Gavin noted that topics such as taxonomy and biogeography, which are not usually studied by wildlife biologists, may well be of paramount importance in resolving a research or conservation problem. Furthermore, he observed that investigators with a "pure" or "basic" science background, rather than resource-oriented biologists, now seem to be the ones making innovative suggestions for the management of wildlife populations.

Looking at the difference in the kinds of questions asked, Gavin argued that basic biologists tend to ask "why" questions and search for ultimate causes, whereas wildlife biologists generally ask "how" questions and look for proximate causes. If we ask the question "Why do snowshoe hares turn white in the winter?" the ultimate cause is the evolutionary advantage that this characteristic confers—most likely camouflage—operating through differences in survival and reproduction. The proximate cause is day length (photoperiod) mediated in this case by physiology—molting the brown fur and growing a white coat

(Brewer 1988). Unfortunately, wildlife researchers generally lack a background in evolutionary theory, or fail to see its value, and tend to avoid asking questions they feel are outside their discipline (Gavin 1989).

The classification of endangered species is just one sad example of why Gavin insisted wildlife biologists need to reach beyond the constraints of their usual expertise. In 1989 there were 1,566 animal species and 1,596 plant species awaiting evaluation for the Endangered Species List, yet U.S. Fish and Wildlife Service biologists could only process about fifty species a year. Wildlife biologists trained in systematics could help critique the classification of many of these organisms to help decide their evolutionary "uniqueness" in the event that preservation choices have to be made. The catch-22 is that wildlife students avoid learning the principles and techniques of systematics, management agencies think taxonomy is too esoteric to be useful, academic wildlife (and other applied ecology) departments see taxonomy as the domain of biology departments, and systematic biologists are too busy with the theoretical developments in their field to work on applied taxonomy (Gavin 1989).

Gavin concluded with a plea for a major overhaul in the way we define useful wildlife research. State and federal agencies that fund most wildlife research expect specific data they think are necessary for management purposes. Therefore, traditional funding sources strongly influence the kinds of research conducted. Time limits of graduate-student degree programs and the perceived needs of agency administrators also restrict research possibilities. By separating the data gathering procedures by which agencies obtain information for monitoring and problem-solving from the process of basic research, the needs of both management and research would be better met. "The conceptual development of the latter is necessary to make sense out of the former."

A short essay by Malcolm Hunter (1989) presented two principles of wildlife research. One he called the "aardvark principle" is exemplified by a researcher who embarks on a project with the thought, "It's been documented that lions, tigers, and bears exhibit territoriality and polygyny. I'll determine if aardvarks do, too." This amounts to defining questions from a species perspective. Ecologists who address conceptual questions may look askance at such research, and indeed there are too many species to conduct detailed studies on all aspects of the biology of each; hence, the shift to a more conceptual type of research seems inevitable. Still, Hunter contended, "even if one is concerned with genetic diversity or ecosystem diversity, it is usually necessary to deal with species . . . , thus wildlife biologists would not lose too much sleep over being adherents of the aardvark principle."

Of greater concern is the "Arcadia principle," in which a researcher thinks, "Lions are polygynous in Macedonia, Mesopotamia, and Medina; I'll determine if they are polygynous in Arcadia" (Hunter 1989). This amounts to limiting one's research vista to studying only proximate relationships. The problem with this approach is evident from an example using wildlife-habitat association studies: "There are about 1,500 species of terrestrial vertebrates in North America north of Mexico and four seasons of the year. If we assume that on average each species is found in ten states, then there are at least 1,500 × 4 × 10 = 60,000 studies of the form—'Habitat use by ruffed grouse in northern Virginia'—to be completed" (Gavin 1989). Replicating previous research is certainly valid and can be very useful; nevertheless, the problem of the Arcadia principle can be minimized when planning a study by evaluating the relevance of existing information based on ecological rather than political boundaries and by designing studies in such a way as to facilitate data comparisons. Although self-evident, these suggestions are often overlooked in practice (Hunter 1989).

The debate over conservation biology prompted Frederic Wagner (1989) to focus on some thoughts that had been troubling him for several years. In consequence, he expressed the concern that wildlife management has failed to be sensitive to change and to advance with the times—specifically, that we lack a clear sense of what we are about and that the quality of our applied science has not kept pace with developments in basic science.

The first issue is a question of values. Despite much discussion about the importance of considering social values, Wagner felt the wildlife profession has not fully embraced what he considers its central purpose; that is, management to satisfy social values. He also detected a lingering sense that our primary commitment is to "the resource." This, of course, raises the question of whether resources have intrinsic value.

Profound changes in social values accompanied the transition from a rural to our urban society, so that public expenditures for birdseed, binoculars, and field guides now greatly exceed the outlay for guns, shells, and hunting licenses. In Wagner's judgment the wildlife profession has not fully adjusted to these changes: it has not moved appreciably from its historic emphasis on consumptive uses and control of wildlife. While failing to minister to society's values, many management programs are strongly reflective of the traditional hunting, fishing, and trapping values often held by wildlife professionals. By failing to broaden its purview to effectively embrace protectionist and nonconsumptive values, as well as traditional consumptive interests, wildlife management has forfeited an opportunity for leadership in the conservation of all wildlife and the protection of biodiversity.

Wagner also charged that the quality of the applied science we call wildlife biology has not kept pace with basic scientific development. Dating the origin of the wildlife discipline to the 1933 publication of *Game Management,* in which Aldo Leopold constructed "a theoretical framework based on ecological and behavioral principles" for the wildlife management practices that had already been in use for several decades, Wagner pointed to the close association between applied wildlife programs and the ecology and behavior programs in university biology departments from the thirties through the fifties. Beginning in the late fifties and continuing through the eighties, these applied and pure disciplines diverged as behavioral ecology emerged from animal behavior, ecology emphasized competition-mediated community structure, and wildlife management generally retained its traditional concentration on single-species food habit and home range studies. A strong orientation toward theory, and greater sophistication in research methodology, accompanied the developments in "pure" ecology.

The consequences of this dichotomy include a frequent lack of scientific insight in the practice of wildlife management (compared with the explicit hypothesis statements and elegant experimental tests of "pure" ecology), the pursuit of largely separate agendas (with some wildlifers looking on conservation biologists "as too theoretical, too ivory-towerish, too unwilling to soil their hands in the day-to-day dirty work of managing wildlife on the land"), and a preference by many young, bright students for conservation biology programs rather than wildlife biology ones (Wagner 1989).

In conclusion Wagner noted that—with programs in federal and state agencies and private environmental organizations addressing such issues as preservation of endangered species, biodiversity, conservation of wetlands and riparian zones, control of vertebrate pests, and commercialization of wildlife on private lands, as well as traditional management for sport hunting—wildlife management has never been more diverse or complex than it is right now. Still, he felt that "we need to make a commitment to the full range of values which society assigns to wildlife resources, and we need to strengthen the teaching, research, and application of our science."

Jack Ward Thomas and Hal Salwasser (1989) wrote, in an essay in the journal *Conservation Biology,* that biological diversity has emerged as an important issue in natural resource management. They argued that the best chance to actually establish biological diversity as a land management objective is on public lands in the United States. Several factors favor this opportunity: these lands are publicly owned, existing regulations and legislation already direct attention to maintaining biological diversity, and there are appropriately trained biologists who could formulate and implement management plans. Since a large-scale set-aside of additional lands seems unlikely, the real test of maintaining biological diversity will occur on public lands already dedicated to multiple-use management.

They further argued that conservation biologists can perform a vital role by focusing attention on biodiversity as a management goal, by providing necessary information to guide management, by teaching and training agency personnel (and even sensitizing some of them to the importance of biodiversity), and by making sure that conservation biology practices are implemented on the land (Thomas and Salwasser 1989).

Aldo Leopold was in the vanguard of conservation thought and action throughout his professional life. "He was perhaps the first person to articulate the need to conserve biological diversity in its entirety" (Wilcove and Samson 1987). This commitment to the preservation of all species derived from two principles: first, an ethical belief that all species have an intrinsic right to exist; and second, a scientific appreciation for the complexity of ecosystems, which dictates that all species be preserved lest we discard a vital component that was perceived as being insignificant. The first principle is the essence of his famous essay "The Land Ethic"; the second is implicit in his admonition from another essay, "The Round River," that "to keep every cog and wheel is the first precaution of intelligent tinkering" (Leopold 1966).

It seems logical—almost inevitable—that, had Leopold lived a few more years, he would have tried to steer the Wildlife Society toward a position of leadership in the monumental effort to preserve biodiversity. Should wildlife biologists have resisted his salutary efforts to promote conservation biology, Leopold himself might well have moved on to establish the Society for Conservation Biology two or three decades before its actual 1985 beginnings.

## ANIMAL RIGHTS AND ANIMAL WELFARE

Wildlife biologists everywhere share a body of knowledge, specialized language, and certain values that create a professional bond and esprit de corps. Their outlook and beliefs often predispose them to certain convictions that make it difficult to identify with divergent viewpoints (Kennedy 1985). Understanding the motivations of animal-rights activists may be especially difficult, and the distinction between animal rights and animal welfare may not be clear (Schmidt 1990).

The terms *animal rights* and *animal welfare* have different meanings and refer to different philosophies, yet they are often used interchangeably. This leads to considerable confusion. The distinction between them is important because their doctrines are decidedly disparate, as is their stance toward wildlife management activities (Schmidt 1989).

*Animal rights* refers to the conviction that animals have rights equal (or similar) to those of humans. To animal-rights supporters, agricultural, biomedical, and other uses of animals cannot be condoned unless humans can ethically be treated in the same way (Schmidt 1989, 1990). The animal-rights philosophy rejects the concept of "speciesism," the idea that the interests of one species, usually *Homo sapiens*, can override the greater interests of another species (Singer 1975). Members of the animal-rights movement believe that even pests like house mice and Norway rats have the same right to a pain-free life as humans.

*Animal welfare* describes the view that we should strive to reduce the pain and suffering of animals. If you are repulsed by the thought of someone intentionally injuring an animal, then you are interested in animal welfare. In Schmidt's (1989, 1990) opinion, the majority of persons in the United States hold animal welfare concerns to some degree. An interest in animal welfare does not, however, imply giving rights to animals; animal rights is not a logical extension of the animal welfare philosophy.

How should wildlife biologists respond to the animal welfare coalition? Several wildlife professionals have urged wildlife biologists to take their solicitude seriously (see Schmidt 1989). Animal welfare concerns may be "a predictable ethical development of the moral fabric of a sophisticated culture which embraces a variety of religious, medical and political freedoms" (Schmidt 1989). Meanwhile, Schmidt (1990) has argued that wildlife professionals should not debate animal rights, which is divisive and tends to distract attention away from more important issues.

Some ways of utilizing animals will never meet with universal approval. Wildlife biologists should respond honestly to public concerns, should acknowledge that some techniques and procedures cause pain to animals, and should make real efforts to develop methodologies that reduce their suffering. Wildlife management can be compatible with animal welfare—but not with animal rights—"if the reduction of pain, suffering and unnecessary death are incorporated in the decision-making process" (Schmidt 1989).

The wildlife biologist and philosopher C. H. D. Clarke wrote: "Cruelty, or the willful infliction of pain, is not part of the purpose of hunting" (1958). Cruelty is likewise not part of the purpose of wildlife management. The humane treatment of wild animals should be part of the professional attitude of wildlife biologists (Schmidt and Brunner 1981). Everyone involved with animals, whether as an occupation or avocation, should have a genuine interest in animal welfare. There is no place in today's wildlife profession for those who do not.

## LOOKING TO THE FUTURE

A book devoted to human dimensions of wildlife would be remiss if it failed to mention the ultimate conservation problem of all, particularly when the problem involves both wildlife and people. That problem is the precipitous pace of human population growth that threatens to overwhelm wildlife and subvert the functioning of ecosystems, which are our very life support system.

Three million years passed from the dawn of human evolutionary history until the world population reached the 1 billion mark about 1850. Human numbers doubled to 2 billion by 1930. In the lifetime of many people living today, the population has more than doubled again—to 5.25 billion in 1990. Another billion people will be added during the decade of the nineties.

According to Nafis Sadik, executive director of the United Nations Population Fund, the population is increasing by 3 persons every second, 250,000 a day. In 1990 alone, 90 million to 100 million people were added to the global family. A 1984 United Nations projection showed world population leveling off at about 10 billion sometime in the next century, but it now seems likely the total will reach 14 billion ("Demographic Trends Seen Over-optimistic" 1990). Whether the earth can support such numbers is problematical. Even with 5 billion, half the world's humans live in perpetual poverty, malnourished, and continually on the verge of starvation.

Donald Mann, president of Negative Population Growth, contends that there is not one threat to the environment that would not be alleviated by a substantial reduction in human numbers. Conversely, there is not one environmental problem that will not be intensified—possibly to catastrophic proportions—by further population growth. Mann believes that reducing the world's population to between 1.5 billion and 2 billion, and a reduction in United States population numbers from over 250 million to between 100 million and 150 million, is necessary.

Just what the optimal population size should be is a topic for discussion. Unfortunately, the question is almost always absent from the agenda of critical national and international issues. Until we accept the notion that human numbers must be stabilized at a sustainable level, and until this goal is within sight, wildlife and wildlife habitats will continue to be sacrificed to the illusions of boundless human population growth and an ever-growing gross national product.

The situation is critical. Informed estimates suggest that we will lose between one-quarter and one-half of all species on earth (Myers 1984). Based on current assumptions of 10 million to 31 million species on our planet, we should anticipate losing between 3 million and 16 million species. Although the vast majority will be insects, it is quite possible that some 2,000 species of large, terrestrial vertebrates will be extinguished unless they can be captively bred. Most habitat for wildlife in the tropics will probably be lost (Soulé et al. 1986). How long is it likely to be before habitat for wildlife begins to increase rather than decrease? Informed speculation suggests the answer is a millennium, plus or minus five hundred years, barring additional human catastrophes such as nuclear war (Soulé et al. 1986).

In the face of such a grim forecast, we all need to act immediately and effectively to mitigate the inevitable disaster. On a personal level, it is imperative that we support the concept of a sustainable population size with our actions (one child per couple), our money (contributions to Zero Population Growth and Negative Population Growth will help publicize the effort), our votes (for politicians who recognize and are working to solve this fundamental problem), and our commitment to persuade family, friends, and colleagues of these needs. Whatever our involvement with wildlife—whether as active participant or passive TV viewer, consumptive hunter or nonconsumptive photographer, professional wildlife ecologist or hobby naturalist—we must all support policies that foster appropriate technologies, sustainable societies, and steady-state economies. There is no assurance of any future for wildlife or people until both are free from the mindless specter of boundless growth.

---

## SUGGESTED READING

Wilson, E. O. (ed.). 1988. *Biodiversity.* Washington, D.C.: National Academy Press. 521 pages. Important as the human dimensions of wildlife may be, they collectively comprise just one facet of the larger issue of human relations to, and impacts on, global biological diversity. Stephen Jay Gould called *Biodiversity* "the most comprehensive book, by the most distinguished group of scholars, ever published on one of the most important subjects of our (and all) times."

# References Cited

Adams, C. E., L. Newgard, and J. K. Thomas. 1986. "How High School and College Students Feel about Wildlife." *American Biology Teacher* 48:263–67.

Allen, D. L. 1970. "Historical Perspective." In *Land Use and Wildlife Resources,* edited by the Committee on Agricultural Land Use and Wildlife Resources, pp. 1–20. Washington, D.C.: National Academy of Sciences.

———. 1978. "The Enjoyment of Wildlife." In *Wildlife and America,* edited by H. P. Brokaw, pp. 28–41. Washington, D.C.: Council on Environmental Quality.

Allen, D. L., et al. 1973. "Report of the Committee on North American Wildlife Policy." *Transactions of the North American Wildlife and Natural Resources Conference* 38:152–78.

Amory, C. 1974. *Man Kind?: Our Incredible War on Wildlife.* New York: Harper and Row.

Anderson, D. R., and K. P. Burnham. 1976. *Population Ecology of the Mallard: 6. The Effect of Exploitation on Survival.* U.S. Fish and Wildlife Service Resource Publication no. 128.

Anderson, S., and J. K. Jones, Jr. 1967. *Recent Mammals of the World: A Synopsis of Families.* New York: Ronald.

Apple L. L. 1985. "Riparian Habitat Restoration and Beavers." In *Riparian Ecosystems and Their Management,* pp. 489–90. U.S. Forest Service General Technical Report no. RM-120.

Applegate, J. E. 1984. "Attitudes toward Deer Hunting in New Jersey: 1972–1982." *Wildlife Society Bulletin* 12:19–22.

Armstrong, E. A. 1958. *The Folklore of Birds.* London: Collins.

Arrow, K., and A. C. Fisher. 1974. "Environmental Preservation, Uncertainty, and Irreversibility." *Quarterly Journal of Economics* 55:313–19.

Arthur, L. M., and W. R. Wilson. 1979. "Assessing the Demand for Wildlife Resources: A First Step." *Wildlife Society Bulletin* 7:30–34.

Ashbrook, F. G. 1925. "Trapping Laws and the Fur Supply." *Journal of Mammalogy* 6:168–73.

Attebury, J. T., J. C. Kroll, and M. H. Legg. 1977. "Operational Characteristics of Commercial Exotic Big Game Hunting Ranches." *Wildlife Society Bulletin* 5:179–84.

Bailey, J. A. 1984. *Principles of Wildlife Management.* New York: John Wiley and Sons.

Banfield, A. W. F. 1961. "A Revision of the Reindeer and Caribou, Genus *Rangifer.*" National Museum of Canada Bulletin no. 177, Biological Series, no. 66.

Barry, R. G. 1983. "Late-Pleistocene Climatology." In *The Late Pleistocene,* edited by S. C. Porter, pp. 390–407. Volume 1 of *Late-Quaternary Environments of the United States,* edited by H. E. Wright, Jr. Minneapolis: University of Minnesota Press.

Bart, W. M. 1972. "A Hierarchy among Attitudes toward Animals." *Journal of Environmental Education* 3 (4): 4–6.

Barton, K. 1986. "Federal Wetland Protection Programs." In *Audubon Wildlife Report 1986,* edited by R. L. DiSilvestro, pp. 373–411. New York: National Audubon Society.

Batie, S. S., and D. B. Taylor. 1990. "Cropland and Soil Sustainability." In *Natural Resources for the Twenty-first Century,* edited by R. N. Sampson and D. Hair, pp. 56–77. Washington, D.C.: Island Press.

Bavin, C. R. 1978. "Wildlife Law Enforcement." In *Wildlife and America,* edited by H. P. Brokaw, pp. 350–64. Washington, D.C.: Council on Environmental Quality.

———. 1987. "Covert Wildlife Law Enforcement Operations." *Transactions of the North American Wildlife and Natural Resources Conference* 52:161–68.

Bean, M. J. 1978. "Federal Wildlife Law." In *Wildlife and America,* edited by H. P. Brokaw, pp. 279–89. Washington, D.C.: Council on Environmental Quality.

———. 1983. *The Evolution of National Wildlife Law.* Revised and expanded. New York: Praeger.

Beattie, K. H. 1981. "Warnings versus Citations in Wildlife Law Enforcement." *Wildlife Society Bulletin* 9:323–25.

Behrensmeyer, A. K. 1987. "Taphonomy and Hunting." In *The Evolution of Human Hunting,* edited by M. H. Nitecki and D. V. Nitecki, pp. 423–50. New York: Plenum Press.

Bentham, J. 1907. *An Introduction to the Principles of Morals and Legislation.* Reprint. Oxford: Clarendon Press, 1823.

Berryman, J. H. 1987. "Socioeconomic Values of the Wildlife Resource: Are We Really Serious?" In *Valuing Wildlife: Economic and Social Perspectives,* edited by D. J. Decker and G. R. Goff, pp. 5–11. Boulder: Westview Press.

Beuter, J. H. 1985. *Federal Timber Sales.* Washington, D.C.: Congressional Research Service.

Biggers, D. H. [Lan Franks, pseud.]. 1901. *History That Will Never Be Repeated.* Ennis, Tex.: Biggers' High-Grade Printing Office.

Bishop, R. C. 1987. "Economic Values Defined." In *Valuing Wildlife: Economic and Social Perspectives,* edited by D. J. Decker and G. R. Goff, pp. 24–33. Boulder: Westview Press.

Bockstael, N. E., and K. E. McConnell. 1981. "Theory and Estimation of the Household Production Function for Wildlife Recreation." *Journal of Environmental Economics and Management* 8:199–214.

Boddicker, M. L. 1981. "Profiles of American Trappers and Trapping." In *Proceedings of the Worldwide Furbearer Conference,* edited by J. A. Chapman and D. Pursley, 3:1918–49. Frostburg, Md.: Worldwide Furbearer Conference.

Bolen, E. G. 1989. "Conservation Biology, Wildlife Management, and Spaceship Earth." *Wildlife Society Bulletin* 17:351–54.

Borland, H. G. 1975. *The History of Wildlife in America.* Washington, D.C.: National Wildlife Federation.

Box, T. W. 1990. "Rangelands." In *Natural Resources for the Twenty-first Century,* edited by R. N. Sampson and D. Hair, pp. 101–20. Washington, D.C.: Island Press.

Boyle, S. A., and F. B. Samson. 1985. "Effects of Nonconsumptive Recreation on Wildlife: A Review." *Wildlife Society Bulletin* 13:110–16.

Bradford, W. 1952. *Of Plymouth Plantation, 1620–1647.* Edited by S. E. Morison. New York: Knopf.

Brady, S. J. 1988. "Potential Implications of Sodbuster on Wildlife." *Transactions of the North American Wildlife and Natural Resources Conference* 53:239–48.

Brande, J. 1980. "Worthless, Valuable, or What?: An Appraisal of Wetlands." *Journal of Soil and Water Conservation* 35:12–16.

Brewer, R. 1988. *The Science of Ecology.* Philadelphia: Saunders College Publishing.

Brian, M. 1988. "Year of the Elephant Campaign: Elephant Press Conference." *Wildlife News* 23 (2): 3.

Brocke, R. H. 1979. "The Name of the Nongame." *Wildlife Society Bulletin* 7:279–82.

Brokaw, H. P. (ed.). 1978. *Wildlife and America.* Washington, D.C.: Council on Environmental Quality.

Brown, P. J., and M. J. Manfredo. 1987. "Social Values Defined." In *Valuing Wildlife: Economic and Social Perspectives,* edited by D. J. Decker and G. R. Goff, pp. 12–23. Boulder: Westview Press.

Brown, T. C. 1984. "The Concept of Value in Resource Allocation." *Land Economics* 60:231–46.

Brown, T. L., and C. P. Dawson. 1978. "Interests, Needs, and Attitudes of New York's Metropolitan Public in Relation to Wildlife." Cornell University, Natural Resources Extension Series 13. Ithaca: Cornell University.

Bruggers, R. L. 1982. "The Exportation of Cage Birds from Senegal." *Traffic Bulletin* 4:12–22.

Bryan, H. 1980. "Sociological and Psychological Approaches for Assessing and Categorizing Wildlife Values." In *Wildlife Values,* edited by W. W. Shaw and E. H. Zube, pp. 70–76. University of Arizona Center for Assessment of Noncommodity Natural Resource Values, Institutional Series Report no. 1.

Bunn, H., and J. Kroll. 1986. "Systematic Butchery by Plio/Pleistocene Hominids at Olduvai Gorge, Tanzania." *Current Anthropology* 27:431–51.

Burch, E. S., Jr. 1972. "The Caribou/Wild Reindeer as a Human Resource." *American Antiquity* 37:339–68.

Burger, G. V., F. H. Wagner, and L. D. Harris. 1986. "Wildlife Prescriptions for Agricultural, Range, and Forest Landscapes." *Transactions of the North American Wildlife and Natural Resources Conference* 51:573–77.

Burnet, J. 1957. *Early Greek Philosophy.* 4th ed. New York: Meridian.

Burnham, K. P., G. C. White, and D. R. Anderson. 1984. "Estimating the Effect of Hunting on Annual Survival Rates of Adult Mallards." *Journal of Wildlife Management* 48:350–61.

Cain, S. A. 1978. "Predator and Pest Control." In *Wildlife and America,* edited by H. P. Brokaw, pp. 379–95. Washington, D.C.: Council on Environmental Quality.

Callicott, J. B. 1980. "Animal Liberation: A Triangular Affair." *Environmental Ethics* 2:311–38.

Campbell, B. 1983. *Human Ecology.* New York: Aldine.

Cann, R. L., M. Stoneking, and A. C. Wilson. 1987. "Mitochondrial DNA and Human Evolution." *Nature* 325:31–36.

Capen, D. E. 1989. "Political Unrest, Progressive Research, and Professional Education." *Wildlife Society Bulletin* 17:335–37.

Carey, J. 1986. "The Changing Face of America: Fifty Years of Land Use." *National Wildlife* (Apr.-May): 18–26.

Carter, H. L. 1983. "Robert Campbell." In *Trappers of the Far West,* edited by L. R. Hafen, pp. 297–308. Lincoln: University of Nebraska Press.

Causey, A. S. 1989. "On the Morality of Hunting." *Environmental Ethics* 11:327–43.

Chemers, M., and I. Altman. 1977. "Use and Perception of the Environment: Cultural and Developmental Processes." In *Children, Nature, and the Urban Environment: Proceedings of a Symposium-Fair,* pp. 43–54. U.S. Forest Service General Technical Report no. NE-30.

Christian, T. T. 1980. "Development and Economic Role of Aoudad Hunting in a Cattle Ranching Operation." In *Proceedings of the Symposium on Ecology and Management of Barbary Sheep,* edited by C. D. Simpson, pp. 104–5. Lubbock: Texas Tech University Press.

Claiborne, R. 1973. *The First Americans.* New York: Time-Life Books.

Clark, T. W. 1975. "Some Relationships between Prairie Dogs, Black-footed Ferrets, Paleo-Indians, and Ethnographically Known Tribes." *Plains Anthropologist* 20 (67): 71–74.

Clarke, C. H. D. 1958. "Autumn Thoughts of a Hunter." *Journal of Wildlife Management* 22:420–27.

Clarke, R., and F. Mitchell. 1968. "The Economic Value of Hunting and Outfitting in East Africa." *East African Agriculture and Forestry Journal* 33 (Special Issue): 89–97.

Clawson, M. 1959. "Methods of Measuring the Demand for and Value of Outdoor Recreation." Reprint no. 10. Washington, D.C.: Resources for the Future.

Clutton-Brock, J. 1989. *A Natural History of Domesticated Mammals.* Austin: University of Texas Press.

Cobb, J. B., Jr. 1980. Review of *Animal Rights: A Christian Assessment of Man's Treatment of Animals* by A. Linzey. *Environmental Ethics* 2:89–93.

Cocheba, D. J. 1987. "Opportunities for Improving Wildlife Management: An Economist's View." In *Valuing Wildlife: Economic and Social Perspectives,* edited by D. J. Decker and G. R. Goff, pp. 269–84. Boulder: Westview Press.

Cocheba, D. J., and W. A. Langford. 1978. "Wildlife Valuation: The Collective Good Aspect of Hunting." *Journal of Land Economics* 54:490–504.

Cohen, M. 1977. *The Food Crisis in Prehistory.* New Haven, Conn.: Yale University Press.

Connelly, N. A., D. J. Deckers, and T. L. Brown. 1985. "New Opportunities with a Familiar Audience: Where Esthetics and Harvest Overlap." *Wildlife Society Bulletin* 13:399–403.

Corbett, P. 1988. "Picasso's Masterpiece: What Is It Worth? Who Can Buy It?" *Connoisseur* 218 (918): 70–73.

Council on Environmental Quality. 1981. *Environmental Quality 1980: The Eleventh Annual Report of the Council on Environmental Quality.* Washington, D.C.: GPO.

Cowardin, L. M., V. Carter, F. C. Golet, and E. T. LaRoe. 1979. *Classification of Wetlands and Deepwater Habitats of the United States.* Washington, D.C.: Office of Biological Services.

Cronon, W. 1983. *Changes in the Land: Indians, Colonists, and the Ecology of New England.* New York: Hill and Wang.

Crowe, D. M. 1983. *Comprehensive Planning for Wildlife Resources.* Cheyenne: Wyoming Game and Fish Department.

Crutchfield, J. A. 1962. "Valuation of Fishery Resources." *Land Economics* 38 (5): 145–54.

Cutright, P. R. 1956. *Theodore Roosevelt, the Naturalist.* New York: Harper.

Dagg, A. I. 1970. "Wildlife in an Urban Area." *Naturaliste Canadien* 97:201–12.

———. 1974. "Reactions of People to Urban Wildlife." In *Wildlife in an Urbanizing Environment,* edited by J. H. Noyes and D. R. Progulske, pp. 163–65. Holdsworth Natural Resources Center Planning and Resource Development Series no. 28. Amherst: University of Massachusetts Cooperative Extension Service.

Dasmann, R. F. 1968. *Environmental Conservation.* New York: John Wiley and Sons.

———. 1981. *Wildlife Biology.* New York: John Wiley and Sons.

Davis, R. K., and D. Lim. 1987. "On Measuring the Economic Value of Wildlife." In *Valuing Wildlife: Economic and Social Perspectives,* edited by D. J. Decker and G. R. Goff, pp. 65–75. Boulder: Westview Press.

Decker, D. J., and T. A. Gavin. 1987. "Public Attitudes toward a Suburban Deer Herd." *Wildlife Society Bulletin* 15:173–80.

Decker, D. J., and G. R. Goff (eds.). 1987. *Valuing Wildlife: Economic and Social Perspectives.* Boulder: Westview Press.

Deknatel, C. 1979. "Wildlife Habitat Development on Private Lands: A Planning Approach to Rural Land Use." *Journal of Soil and Water Conservation* 34:260–63.

"Demographic Trends Seen Over-optimistic." 1990. *Popline* 12 (Jan.-Feb.).

Devall, B., and G. Sessions. 1985. *Deep Ecology: Living as If Nature Mattered.* Layton, Utah: Gibbs Smith.

DeVoto, B. 1954. "Conservation: Down and on the Way Out." *Harper's,* Aug., 66–74.

Doughty, R. W. 1983. *Wildlife and Man in Texas: Environmental Change and Conservation.* College Station: Texas A&M University Press.

Douglas-Hamilton, D. H. 1979. *The African Elephant Action Plan.* IUCN/WWF/NYZS Elephant Survey and Conservation Programme.

Downing, R. L. 1987. "Success Story: White-tailed Deer." In *Restoring America's Wildlife, 1937–1987,* edited by H. Kallman, C. P. Agee, W. R. Goforth, and J. P. Linduska, pp. 45–57. Washington, D.C.: U.S. Fish and Wildlife Service.

Dwyer, J. F. 1980. "Economic Benefits of Wildlife-related Recreation Experience." In *Wildlife Values,* edited by W. W. Shaw and E. H. Zube, pp. 62–69. University of Arizona Center for Assessment of Noncommodity Natural Resource Values, Institutional Series Report no. 1.

Dwyer, T. J., and J. D. Nichols. 1982. "Regional Population Inferences for the American Woodcock." In *Woodcock Ecology and Management,* T. J. Dwyer and G. L. Storm, technical coordinators. U.S. Fish and Wildlife Service Wildlife Research Report no. 14.

Edmunds, S., and J. Lety. 1973. *Environmental Administration.* New York: McGraw-Hill.

Edwards, E. E. 1940. "American Agriculture—the First Three Hundred Years." In *Farmers in a Changing World, The Yearbook of Agriculture 1940,* pp. 171–276. Washington, D.C.: U.S. Department of Agriculture.

Edwards, T. C., Jr. 1989. "The Wildlife Society and the Society for Conservation Biology: Strange but Unwilling Bedfellows." *Wildlife Society Bulletin* 17:340–43.

Ehrenfeld, D. W. 1970. *Biological Conservation.* New York: Holt, Rinehart, and Winston.

———. 1987. Editorial. *Conservation Biology* 1:6–7.

Ehrlich, P. R. 1986. *The Machinery of Nature.* New York: Simon and Schuster.

Eisenberg, J. F. 1981. *The Mammalian Radiations: An Analysis of Trends in Evolution, Adaptation, and Behavior.* Chicago: University of Chicago Press.

Eltringham, S. K. 1984. *Wildlife Resources and Economic Development.* New York: John Wiley and Sons.

Errington, P. L. 1956. "Factors Limiting Higher Vertebrate Populations." *Science* 124:304–7.

———. 1963. *Muskrat Populations.* Ames: Iowa State University Press.

Estes, J. A., R. Jamieson, and E. Rhodes. 1982. "Activity and Prey Selection of the Sea Otter (*E. lutris*): Influence of Population Status on Community Structure." *American Naturalist* 120:242–58.

Estes, J. A., N. S. Smith, and J. F. Palmisano. 1978. "Sea Otter Predation and Community Organization in Western Aleutian Islands, Alaska." *Journal of Ecology* 59:822–33.

Evans, R. D., J. Tieger, and J. P. Graham. 1988. "Conservation Easements: Farmers Home Administration Inventory Lands and Debt Restructuring." *Transactions of the North American Wildlife and Natural Resources Conference* 53:263–65.

Fagan, B. M. 1989. *People of the Earth: An Introduction to World Prehistory.* 6th ed. Glenview, Ill.: Scott, Foresman.

Favre, D. S. 1983. *Wildlife: Cases, Law, and Policy.* Tarrytown, N.Y.: Associated Faculty Press.

Fazio, J. R., and L. A. Belli. 1977. "Characteristics of Nonconsumptive Wildlife Users in Idaho." *Transactions of the North American Wildlife and Natural Resources Conference* 42:117–28.

Feltus, D. G., and E. E. Langenau, Jr. 1984. "Optimization of Firearm Deer Hunting and Timber Values in Northern Lower Michigan." *Wildlife Society Bulletin* 12:6–12.

Flader, S. L. 1978. *Thinking like a Mountain: Aldo Leopold and the Evolution of an Ecological Attitude toward Deer, Wolves, and Forests.* Lincoln: University of Nebraska Press.

Ford, A. (comp. and ed.). 1951. *Audubon's Animals: The Quadrupeds of North America.* New York: Studio Publications/Thomas Y. Crowell.

Fortner, R. W., and V. J. Mayer. 1983. "Ohio Students' Knowledge and Attitudes about the Oceans and Great Lakes." *Ohio Journal of Science* 85:218–24.

Fox, W. 1990. "The Meanings of 'Deep Ecology.' " *Trumpeter* 7:48–50.

Frobenius, L., and D. C. Fox. 1937. *Prehistoric Rock Pictures in Europe and Africa.* New York: Museum of Modern Art.

"Furs and the War." 1942. *Anti-Steel-Trap League News* 9 (1): 11.

"The Future of Wildlife Resources Cannot Afford Strange or Unwilling Bedfellows." 1989. *Wildlife Society Bulletin* 17:343–44.

Galton, F. 1865. "The First Steps towards the Domestication of Animals." *Transactions of the Ethnological Society of London* n.s. 3:122–38.

Gavin, T. A. 1989. "What's Wrong with the Questions We Ask in Wildlife Research?" *Wildlife Society Bulletin* 17:345–50.

Geist, V. 1985. "Game Ranching: Threat to Wildlife Conservation in North America." *Wildlife Society Bulletin* 13:594–98.

———. 1988. "How Markets in Wildlife Meat and Parts, and the Sale of

Hunting Privileges, Jeopardize Wildlife Conservation." *Conservation Biology* 2:15–26.

Gentile, J. R. 1987. "The Evolution of Antitrapping Sentiment in the United States: A Review and Commentary." *Wildlife Society Bulletin* 15:490–503.

Gilbert, D. L. 1975. *Natural Resources and Public Relations.* 2d ed. Washington, D.C.: Wildlife Society.

———. 1978. "Sociological Considerations in Management." In *Big Game of North America: Ecology and Management,* edited by J. L. Schmidt and D. L. Gilbert, pp. 409–16. Harrisburg, Pa.: Stackpole Books.

Gilbert, F. F. 1982. "Public Attitudes toward Urban Wildlife: A Pilot Study in Guelph, Ontario." *Wildlife Society Bulletin* 10:245–53.

Giles, R. H. 1971. "The Approach." In *Wildlife Management Techniques,* edited by R. H. Giles, pp. 1–4. 3d ed. rev. Washington, D.C.: Wildlife Society.

———. 1978. *Wildlife Management.* San Francisco: W. H. Freeman.

Giles, W. L., D. L. Leedy, and E. L. Pinnell. 1970. "New Patterns on Land and Water." In *Land Use and Wildlife Resources,* edited by the Committee on Agricultural Land Use and Wildlife Resources, pp. 55–91. Washington, D.C.: National Academy of Sciences.

Gillis, M., and R. Repetto. 1988. "Conclusion: Findings and Policy Implications." In *Public Policies and the Misuse of Forest Resources,* edited by R. Repetto and M. Gillis, pp. 385–410. Cambridge: Cambridge University Press.

Giovengo, R. D. 1988. "An Undergraduate Curriculum in Conservation Law Enforcement." *Wildlife Society Bulletin* 16:218–21.

Goldman-Carter, J. L. 1988. "Effects of Swampbuster Implementation on Soil, Water, and Wildlife Resources." *Transactions of the North American Wildlife and Natural Resources Conference* 53:249–62.

Goldstein, J. H. 1988. "The Impact of Federal Programs and Subsidies on Wetlands." *Transactions of the North American Wildlife and Natural Resources Conference* 53:436–43.

Gordon, S. 1930. "Giving the Game Policy the Laboratory Test." *Transactions of the American Game Conference* 17:7–17.

Gosling, L. M. 1981. "Demarkation in a Gerenuk Territory: An Economic Approach." *Zeitschrift für Tierpsychologie* 56:305–22.

Gosling, L. M., and M. Petrie. 1981. "The Economics of Social Organization." In *Physiological Ecology: An Evolutionary Approach to Resource Use,* edited by C. R. Townsend and P. Callow, pp. 315–45. Oxford: Blackwell Scientific Publications.

Gottschalk, J. S. 1978. "The State-Federal Partnership in Wildlife Conservation." In *Wildlife and America,* edited by H. P. Brokaw, pp. 290–301. Washington, D.C.: Council on Environmental Quality.

Grant, C. 1980. "The Desert Bighorn and Aboriginal Man." In *The Desert Bighorn: Its Life History, Ecology, and Management,* edited by G. Monson and L. Sumner, pp. 7–39. Tucson: University of Arizona Press.

Grant, W. E. 1974. "The Functional Role of Small Mammals in Grassland Ecosystems." Ph.D. diss. Colorado State University.

Gray, G. G., and J. S. Larson. 1982. "Estimating Relative Demand for Wildlife: Conservation Activity Indicators." *Environmental Management* 6:373–76.

Gray, G. G., J. S. Larson, and D. A. Braunhardt. 1979. "Urban Conservation Leadership and the Wildlife Resource." *Urban Ecology* 4:1–9.

Green, M., L. Hogee, T. Milliken, and G. M. Oza. 1983. "Scient to the Orient." *Traffic Bulletin* 5:47.

Greenwalt, L. A. 1978. "The National Wildlife Refuge System." In *Wildlife and America,* edited by H. P. Brokaw, pp. 399–412. Washington, D.C.: Council on Environmental Quality.

Griffin, C. R. 1989. "Protection of Wildlife Habitat by State Wetland Regulations: The Massachusetts Initiative." *Transactions of the North American Wildlife and Natural Resources Conference* 54:22–31.

Grigg, G. 1989. "Kangaroo Harvesting and the Conservation of Arid and Semi-arid Rangelands." *Conservation Biology* 3:194–97.

Grimwood, I. 1968. "Endangered Mammals in Peru." *Oryx* 9:411–21.

Gruber, H. E., and P. H. Barrett. 1974. *Darwin on Man: A Psychological Study of Scientific Creativity.* New York: E. P. Dutton.

Gutermuth, C. R. 1971. "Role of Policy-making Boards and Commissions." Paper presented at the Seventh Annual Short Course in Game and Fish Management. Colorado State University.

Guthrie, R. D. 1967. "The Ethical Relationship between Humans and Other Organisms." *Perspectives in Biology and Medicine* 11:52–62.

———. 1982. "Mammals of the Mammoth Steppe as Paleoenvironmental Indicators." In *Paleoecology of Beringia,* edited by D. M. Hopkins, J. V. Matthews, Jr., C. E. Schweger, and S. B. Young, pp. 307–26. New York: Academic Press.

Guynn, D. E., and J. L. Schmidt. 1984. "Managing Deer Hunters on Private Lands in Colorado." *Wildlife Society Bulletin* 12:12–19.

Hadingham, E. 1979. *Secrets of the Ice Age: A Reappraisal of Prehistoric Man.* New York: Walker.

Hagenstein, P. 1990. "Forests." In *Natural Resources for the Twenty-first Century,* edited by R. N. Sampson and D. Hair. Washington, D.C.: Island Press.

Hair, J. D., and G. A. Pomerantz. 1987. "The Educational Value of Wildlife." In *Valuing Wildlife: Economic and Social Perspectives,* edited by D. J. Decker and G. R. Goff, pp. 197–207. Boulder: Westview Press.

Hallenbeck, C. 1940. *Álvar Núnez, Cabeza de Vaca: The Journey and Route of the First European to Cross the Continent of North America, 1534–1536.* Port Washington, N.Y.: Kennikat Press.

Halls, L. K. 1978. "White-tailed Deer." In *Big Game of North America: Ecology and Management,* edited by J. L. Schmidt and D. L. Gilbert, pp. 43–65. Harrisburg, Pa.: Stackpole Books.

Hardin, G. 1968. "The Tragedy of the Commons." *Science* 162:1243–48.

Harper, F. 1958. *The Travels of William Bartram.* Naturalist's ed. New Haven, Conn.: Yale University Press.

Hartman, F. E. 1973. "Hunting Is Big Business." *Pennsylvania Game News* 44 (9): 26–31.

Hendee, J. C., and C. Schoenfeld (eds.). 1973. *Human Dimensions in Wildlife Programs.* Washington, D.C.: Wildlife Management Institute.

Henning, D. H. 1974. *Environmental Policy and Administration.* New York: American Elsevier.

Henry, W. 1976. "A Preliminary Report on Visitor Use in Ambroseli National Park." University of Nairobi Institute of Developmental Studies Working Paper no. 263.

Hervey, D. F., R. R. Hill, and D. L. Leedy. 1970. "Influence of Land Management on Wildlife." In *Land Use and Wildlife Resources,* edited by the Committee on Agricultural Land Use and Wildlife Resources, pp. 92–148. Washington, D.C.: National Academy of Sciences.

Hester, J. J. 1967. "The Agency of Man in Animal Extinctions." In *Pleistocene Extinctions: The Search for a Cause,* edited by P. S. Martin and H. E. Wright, Jr., pp. 169–92. New Haven, Conn.: Yale University Press.

Hickey, J. L., and D. W. Anderson. 1968. "Chlorinated Hydrocarbons and Eggshell Changes in Raptorial and Fish-eating Birds." *Science* 162:271–72.

Hill, E. P. 1987. "Beaver Restoration." In *Restoring America's Wildlife, 1937–1987,* edited by H. Kallman, C. P. Agee, W. R. Goforth, and J. P. Linduska, pp. 281–84. Washington, D.C.: U.S. Fish and Wildlife Service

Hirst, S. M. 1975. "Ungulate-Habitat Relationships in a South African Woodland/Savanna Ecosystem." *Wildlife Monograph* 44.

Hopkins, D. M. 1982. "Aspects of the Paleogeography of Beringia during the late Pleistocene." In *Paleoecology of Beringia,* edited by D. M. Hopkins, J. V. Matthews, Jr., C. E. Schweger, and S. B. Young, pp. 3–28. New York: Academic Press.

Hughes, J. R. 1978. "Archeology of Palo Duro Canyon." *Panhandle-Plains Historical Review* 51:35–57.

Hunter, M. L., Jr. 1989. "Aardvarks and Arcadia: Two Principles of Wildlife Research." *Wildlife Society Bulletin* 17:350–51.

"Hunters in Italy." 1981. *Oryx* 16:127.

Husar, J. 1986. "Hunters Are Original Protectors of Wildlife." *Chicago Tribune,* Dec. 3, 1986, sect. 4, p. 4.

———. 1987. " 'Rambo-style' Deer Hunters Coming under Heavy Fire." *Chicago Tribune,* Dec. 2, 1987, sect. 4, p. 4.

Hvenegaard, G. T., J. R. Butler, and D. K. Krystofiak. 1989. "Economic Values of Bird Watching at Point Pelee National Park, Canada." *Wildlife Society Bulletin* 17:526–31.

Ip, P.-K. 1983. "Taoism and the Foundations of Environmental Ethics." *Environmental Ethics* 5:335–43.

Isaacs, B., and D. Howell. 1988. "Opportunities for Enhancing Wildlife Benefits through the Conservation Reserve Program." *Transactions of the North American Wildlife and Natural Resources Conference* 53:222–31.

Jackson, D. (ed.). 1966. *The Journals of Zebulon Montgomery Pike, with Letters and Related Documents.* 2 vols. Norman: University of Oklahoma Press.

Jacquemot, A., and F. L. Filion. 1987. "The Economic Significance of Birds in Canada." In *The Value of Birds,* edited by A. W. Diamond and F. L. Filion, pp. 15–21. International Council for Bird Preservation Technical Publication no. 6.

Janzen, D. H. 1983. "The Pleistocene Hunters Had Help." *American Naturalist* 121:598–99.

Jordan, T. G., and M. Kaups. 1989. *The American Backwoods Frontier: An Ethnic and Ecological Interpretation.* Baltimore: Johns Hopkins University Press.

Karr, J. R. 1981. "An Integrated Approach to Management of Land Resources." In *Wildlife Management on Private Lands,* edited by R. T. Dumke, G. V. Burger, and J. R. March, pp. 164–92. Madison: Wisconsin Chapter of the Wildlife Society.

Kastner, J. 1978. *A Species of Eternity.* New York: E. P. Dutton.

Keith, L. B. 1963. *Wildlife's Ten-Year Cycle.* Madison: University of Wisconsin Press.

Kellert, S. R. 1976. "Perceptions of Animals in American Society." *Transactions of the North American Wildlife and Natural Resources Conference* 41:533–46.

———. 1980a. "Americans' Attitudes and Knowledge of Animals." *Transactions of the North American Wildlife and Natural Resources Conference* 45:111–24.

———. 1980b. "Contemporary Values of Wildlife in American Society." In *Wildlife Values,* edited by W. W. Shaw and E. H. Zube, pp. 31–60. University of Arizona Center for Assessment of Noncommodity Natural Resource Values, Institutional Series Report no. 1.

———. 1981. "Trappers and Trapping in American Society." In *Proceedings of the Worldwide Furbearer Conference,* edited by J. A. Chapman and D. Pursley, 3:1971–2003. Frostburg, Md.: Worldwide Furbearer Conference.

———. 1987. "The Contributions of Wildlife to Human Quality of Life." In *Valuing Wildlife: Economic and Social Perspectives,* edited by D. J. Decker and G. R. Goff, pp. 222–29. Boulder: Westview Press.

Kellert, S. R., and M. O. Westervelt. 1981. *Historical Trends in Animal Use and Perception.* Washington, D.C.: U.S. Fish and Wildlife Service.

———. 1983. "Children's Attitudes, Knowledge, and Behaviors toward Animals." Washington, D.C.: U.S. Fish and Wildlife Service.

Kennedy, J. J. 1985. "Viewing Wildlife Managers as a Unique Professional Culture." *Wildlife Society Bulletin* 13:571–79.

Kenney, J. P. 1975. *Police Administration.* Springfield, Ill.: Charles C. Thomas.

Kimball, T. L. 1975. "Foreword." In *Natural Resources and Public Relations,* by D. L. Gilbert, pp. vii–viii. 2d ed. Washington, D.C.: Wildlife Society.

Kimball, T. L., and R. E. Johnson. 1978. "The Richness of American Wildlife." In *Wildlife and America,* edited by H. P. Brokaw, pp. 3–17. Washington, D.C.: Council on Environmental Quality.

King, R. T. 1966. "Wildlife and Man." *New York Conservationist* 20:8–11.

Klein, D. R. 1973. "The Ethics of Hunting and the Antihunting Movement."

*Transactions of the North American Wildlife and Natural Resources Conference* 38:256–67.

Knox, M. L. 1990. "In the Heat of the Hunt." *Sierra* 75 (6).

Krantz, G. S. 1970. "Human Activities and Megafaunal Extinctions." *American Scientist* 58:164–70.

Krebs, C. J. 1988. *The Message of Ecology.* New York: Harper and Row.

Krutch, J. W. 1957. "A Damnable Pleasure." *Saturday Review* 17.

Kurtén, B. 1968. *Pleistocene Mammals of Europe.* Chicago: Aldine.

Kurtén, B., and E. Anderson. 1980. *Pleistocene Mammals of North America.* New York: Columbia University Press.

Labisky, R. F., D. Stansbury, and S. C. Smith. 1986. "Fish and Wildlife: The Forgotten Resource in National Policy." *Transactions of the North American Wildlife and Natural Resource Conference* 51:538–42.

LaHart, D. E., and C. R. Tillis. 1974. "Using Wildlife to Teach Environmental Values." *Journal of Environmental Education* 6:42–48.

Langford, W. A., and D. J. Cocheba. 1978. "The Wildlife Valuation Problem: A Critical Review of Economic Approaches." Canadian Ministry of Fisheries and the Environment, Occasional Paper no. 37.

Langner, L. L. 1989. "Land-Use Changes and Hunter Participation: The Case of the Conservation Reserve Program." *Transactions of the North American Wildlife and Natural Resources Conference* 54:382–90.

Larson, J. S. 1982. "Understanding the Ecological Value of Wetlands." In *Research on Fish and Wildlife Habitat,* edited by W. T. Mason, Jr., pp. 108–18. Washington, D.C.: U.S. Environmental Protection Agency.

Lautenschlager, R. A., and R. T. Bowyer. 1985. "Wildlife Management by Referendum: When Professionals Fail to Communicate." *Wildlife Society Bulletin* 13:564–70.

Legge, A. J., and P. A. Rowley-Conwy. 1987. "Gazelle Killing in Stone Age Syria." *Scientific American* 255:88–95.

Leonard, J. W. 1973. "Remarks of the Session Chairman." *Transactions of the North American Wildlife and Natural Resources Conference* 38:151–52.

Leopold, A. 1930. "The American Game Policy in a Nutshell." *Transactions of the American Game Conference* 17:281–83.

———. 1933. *Game Management.* New York: Charles Scribner's Sons.

———. 1949. *A Sand County Almanac and Sketches Here and There.* London: Oxford University Press.

———. 1966. *A Sand County Almanac with Other Essays on Conservation from Round River.* New York: Oxford University Press.

Leopold, A., et al. 1930. "Report to the American Game Conference on an American Game Policy." *Transactions of the American Game Conference* 17:284–308.

Leopold, A. S. 1978. "Wildlife and Forest Practice." In *Wildlife and America,* edited by H. P. Brokaw, pp. 108–20. Washington, D.C.: Council on Environmental Quality.

Leuschner, W. A., V. P. Ritchie, and D. F. Stauffer. 1989. "Opinions on Wildlife:

Responses of Resource Managers and Wildlife Users in the Southeastern United States." *Wildlife Society Bulletin* 17:24–29.

Levy, G. R. 1948. *The Gate of Horn: A Study of the Religious Conceptions of the Stone Age and Their Influence upon European Thought.* London: Faber and Faber.

Lewin, R. 1983. "What Killed the Giant Mammals?" *Science* 221:1036–37.

Lewis, D., G. B. Kaweche, and A. Mwenya. 1990. "Wildlife Conservation outside Protected Areas—Lessons from an Experiment in Zambia." *Conservation Biology* 4:171–80.

Linzey, A. 1976. *Animal Rights: A Christian Assessment of Man's Treatment of Animals.* London: SCM Press.

Lipske, M. 1986. "Our Long Love Affair with Nature: Fifty Years of Recreation." *National Wildlife* (Apr.-May): 36–45.

Livingston, D. 1858. *Missionary Travels and Researches in South Africa.* New York: Harper.

Loftin, R. W. 1984. "The Morality of Hunting." *Environmental Ethics* 6:241–50.

Ludwin, W. G., and P. A. Chamberlain. 1989. "Habitat Management Decisions with Goal Programming." *Wildlife Society Bulletin* 17:20–23.

Lumsden, C. J., and E. O. Wilson. 1981. *Genes, Mind, and Culture: The Coevolutionary Process.* Cambridge: Harvard University Press.

———. 1983. *Promethean Fire: Reflections on the Origin of Mind.* Cambridge: Harvard University Press.

Lund, T. A. 1980. *American Wildlife Law.* Berkeley: University of California Press.

Lyons, J. R., and T. M. Franklin. 1987. "Practical Aspects of Training in Natural Resource Policy: Filling an Educational Void." *Transactions of the North American Wildlife and Natural Resources Conference* 52:729–37.

Macaulay, A. J. 1989. "New Approaches to Waterfowl Habitat Management: The Canadian Experience." *Transactions of the North American Wildlife and Natural Resources Conference* 54:71–74.

McCorkle, C. O., Jr. 1981. "Trends in American Agriculture Relevant to Wildlife Management on Private Lands." In *Wildlife Management on Private Lands,* edited by R. T. Dumke, G. V. Burger, and J. R. March, pp. 11–16. Madison: Wisconsin Chapter of the Wildlife Society.

McDivitt, J. H. 1987. "Price and Value Alternatives for Wildlife." In *Valuing Wildlife: Economic and Social Perspectives,* edited by D. J. Decker and G. R. Goff, pp. 101–8. Boulder: Westview Press.

Madsen, C. R. 1981. "Wildlife Habitat Development and Restoration Progress." In *Wildlife Management on Private Lands,* edited by R. T. Dumke, G. V. Burger, and J. R. March, pp. 209–17. Madison: Wisconsin Chapter of the Wildlife Society.

———. 1989. "New Approaches to Wetland Management through the North American Waterfowl Management Plan: The U.S. Experience." *Transactions of the North American Wildlife and Natural Resources Conference* 54:67–70.

Madson, J. 1985. *Up on the River.* New York: Nick Lyons Books/Schocken Books.

Mager, R. F. 1962. *Preparing Instructional Objectives.* Palo Alto, Calif.: Fearon.

Manfredo, M. J. 1989. "Human Dimensions of Wildlife Management." *Wildlife Society Bulletin* 17:447–49.

Marshall, L. G. 1988. "Land Mammals and the Great American Interchange." *American Scientist* 76:380–88.

Martin, E. B. 1980. "The Craft, the Trade, and the Elephants." *Oryx* 15:363–66.

Martin, E. B., and C. Martin. 1982. *Run Rhino Run.* London: Chatto and Windus.

Martin, P. S. 1967. "Prehistoric Overkill." In *Pleistocene Extinctions: The Search for a Cause,* edited by P. S. Martin and H. E. Wright, Jr., pp. 75–120. New Haven, Conn.: Yale University Press.

Martin, P. S., and H. E. Wright, Jr. (eds.). 1967. *Pleistocene Extinctions: The Search for a Cause.* Proceedings of the Seventh Congress of the International Association for Quaternary Research, vol. 6. Sponsored by the National Academy of Sciences/National Research Council. New Haven, Conn.: Yale University Press.

Martin, W. E., and R. L. Gum. 1978. "Economic Value of Hunting, Fishing, and General Outdoor Recreation." *Wildlife Society Bulletin* 6:3–7.

Matthews, O. P. 1986. "Who Owns Wildlife?" *Wildlife Society Bulletin* 14:459–65.

Matthiessen, P. 1987. *Wildlife in America.* New York: Viking.

Meeker, J. W. 1986. "Some Earthly Speculations: How Deep Is Deep?" *Wilderness* 49 (172): 51–53.

Meine, C. 1988. *Aldo Leopold: His Life and Work.* Madison: University of Wisconsin Press.

Miller, E. J., and P. T. Bromley. 1989. "Wildlife Management on Conservation Reserve Program Land: The Farmers' View." *Transactions of the North American Wildlife and Natural Resources Conference* 54:377–81.

Miller, J. D. 1975. "The Development of Pre-adult Attitudes toward Environmental Conservation and Pollution." *School Science and Mathematics* 75:729–37.

Minnich, D. W. 1978. "The Role of a Wildlife Planner." *Proceedings of the International Association of Fish and Wildlife Agencies* 67:68–78.

Mitchell, B., B. W. Staines, and D. Welch. 1977. *Ecology of Red Deer—A Research Review Relevant to their Management in Scotland.* Cambridge: Graphic Art Ltd.

Mitchell, J. G. 1982. "The Trapping Question: Soft Skins and Sprung Steel." *Audubon* 84:64–89.

Moore, R. C. 1977. "The Environmental Design of Children-Nature Relations: Some Strands of Applicative Theory." In *Children, Nature, and the Urban Environment: Proceedings of a Symposium-Fair,* pp. 207–14. U.S. Forest Service General Technical Report no. NE-30.

More, T. A. 1977. "An Analysis of Wildlife in Children's Stories." In *Children,*

*Nature, and the Urban Environment: Proceedings of a Symposium-Fair,* pp. 89–94. U.S. Forest Service General Technical Report no. NE-30.
———. 1977a. "The Demand for Nonconsumptive Wildlife Uses: A Review of the Literature." U.S. Forest Service General Technical Report no. NE-52.
———. 1979b. "Wildlife Preferences and Children's Books." *Wildlife Society Bulletin* 7:274–78.
Morell, V. 1990. "Running for Their Lives." *International Wildlife* 20 (3): 4–13.
Morison, S. E. 1971. *The European Discovery of America: The Northern Voyages, A.D. 500–1600.* New York: Oxford University Press.
Morlan, R. E., and J. Cinq-Mars. 1982. "Ancient Beringians: Human Occupation in the Late Pleistocene of Alaska and the Yukon Territory." In *Paleoecology of Beringia,* edited by D. M. Hopkins, J. V. Matthews, Jr., C. E. Schweger, and S. B. Young, pp. 353–81. New York: Academic Press.
Morse, W. B. 1987. "Conservation Law Enforcement: A New Profession Is Forming." *Transactions of the North American Wildlife and Natural Resources Conference* 52:169–75.
Mossiman, J. E., and P. S. Martin. 1975. "Simulating Overkill by Paleoindians." *American Scientist* 63:304–13.
Müller-Beck, H. 1982. "Late Pleistocene Man in Northern Alaska and the Mammoth-Steppe Biome." In *Paleoecology of Beringia,* edited by D. M. Hopkins, J. V. Matthews, Jr., C. E. Schweger, and S. B. Young, pp. 329–52. New York: Academic Press.
Myers, N. 1984. "Genetic Resources in Jeopardy." *Ambio* 13:171–74.
Naess, A. 1973. "The Shallow and the Deep, Long-range Ecology Movements: A Summary." *Inquiry* 16:95–100.
Nelson, R. D., and H. Salwasser. 1982. "The Forest Service Wildlife and Fish Habitat Relationships Program." *Transactions of the North American Wildlife and Natural Resources Conference* 47:174–83.
Nicolaisen, J. 1963. "Ecology and Culture of the Pastoral Tuareg, with Particular Reference to the Tuareg of Ahaggar and Ayr." *National Museum, Copenhagen, Etnografisk Raekke* 9.
Nilsson, G. 1980. *Facts about Furs.* Washington, D.C.: Animal Welfare Institute.
Niven, C. D. 1963. *History of the Humane Movement.* New York: Transatlantic Arts.
Odum, H. T. 1971. *Environment, Power, and Society.* New York: Wiley-Interscience.
Ortega y Gasset, J. 1972. *Meditations on Hunting.* New York: Charles Scribner's Sons.
Owen, O. S. 1975. *Natural Resource Conservation: An Ecological Approach.* 2d ed. New York: Macmillan.
Owen-Smith, N. 1987. "Pleistocene Extinctions: The Pivotal Role of Megaherbivores." *Paleobiology* 13:351–62.
Pamp, F. E., Jr. 1955. "Liberal Arts as Training for Business." *Harvard Business Review* 33:42–50.

Parker, I. S. C., and E. B. Martin. 1982. "How Many Elephants Are Killed for the Ivory Trade?" *Oryx* 16:235–39.

Patterson, J. H. 1979. "Can Ducks Be Managed by Regulation?: Experiences in Canada." *Transactions of the North American Wildlife and Natural Resources Conference* 44: 130–39.

Payne, N. F. 1980. "Furbearer Management and Trapping." *Wildlife Society Bulletin* 8:345–48.

Peek, J. M. 1989. "A Look at Wildlife Education in the United States." *Wildlife Society Bulletin* 17:361–65.

Peterle, T. J., and J. E. Scott. 1977. "Characteristics of Some Ohio Hunters and Non-hunters." *Journal of Wildlife Management* 41:386–99.

Peterson, I. 1990. "Poetry Lessons: Bridging the Chasm between the Sciences and the Humanities." *Science News* 138:396–97.

Peyton, R. B., and E. E. Langenau, Jr. 1985. "A Comparison of Attitudes Held by BLM Biologists and the General Public towards Animals." *Wildlife Society Bulletin* 13:117–20.

Phenicie, C. K., and J. R. Lyons. 1973. *Tactical Planning in Fish and Wildlife Management.* U.S. Fish and Wildlife Service Resource Publication no. 123.

Phillips, P. C. 1961. *The Fur Trade.* 2 vols. Norman: University of Oklahoma Press.

Plato. 1985. *The Republic.* Trans. R. W. Sterling and W. C. Scott. New York: W. W. Norton.

Pomerantz, G. A. 1985. "The Influence of 'Ranger Rick' Magazine on Children's Perceptions of Natural Resource Issues." Ph.D. diss., North Carolina State University.

Potts, R. 1984. "Hominid Hunters? Problems of Identifying the Earliest Hunter-Gatherers." In *Hominid Evolution and Community Ecology,* edited by R. Foley, pp. 129–66. London: Academic Press.

Povilitis, A. J. 1980. "On Assigning Rights to Animals and Nature." *Environmental Ethics* 2:67–71.

Powell, R. A. 1982. "Ecological 'Nonarguments' and Human Value Judgements." *Wildlife Society Bulletin* 10:141.

Prescott-Allen, C., and R. Prescott-Allen. 1986. *The First Resource: Wild Species in the North American Economy.* New Haven, Conn.: Yale University Press.

Purdy, K. G., and D. J. Decker. 1989. "Applying Wildlife Values Information in Management: The Wildlife Attitudes and Values Scale." *Wildlife Society Bulletin* 17:494–500.

Raven, P. H. 1988. "Our Diminishing Tropical Forests." In *Biodiversity,* edited by E. O. Wilson and F. M. Peter, pp. 119–22. Washington, D.C.: National Academy Press.

Read, H. 1955. *Icon and Idea: The Function of Art in the Development of Human Consciousness.* London: Faber and Faber.

Reid, W. V., and K. R. Miller. 1989. *Keeping Options Alive: The Scientific Basis for Conserving Biodiversity.* Washington, D.C.: World Resources Institute.

Reiger, G. 1978. "Hunting and Trapping in the New World." In *Wildlife and*

*America,* edited by H. P. Brokaw, pp. 42–52. Washington, D.C.: Council on Environmental Quality.

Reiger, J. F. 1986. *American Sportsmen and the Origins of Conservation.* Rev. ed. Norman: University of Oklahoma Press.

Rejeski, D. W. 1982. "Children Look at Nature: Environmental Perception and Education." *Journal of Environmental Education* 13 (4): 27–40.

Repetto, R. 1988. "Subsidized Timber Sales from National Forest Lands in the United States." In *Public Policies and the Misuse of Forest Resources,* edited by R. Repetto and M. Gillis, pp. 353–83. New York: Cambridge University Press.

Ripple, R. E., R. F. Biehler, and G. A. Jaquish. 1982. *Human Development.* Boston: Houghton Mifflin.

Robinson, A. Y. 1988. "Implementation of Conservation Compliance: Implications for Soil, Water, and Wildlife." *Transactions of the North American Wildlife and Natural Resources Conference* 53:210–21.

Robinson, J. M. 1968. *An Introduction to Early Greek Philosophy.* Boston: Houghton Mifflin.

Robinson, W. L., and E. G. Bolen. 1984. *Wildlife Ecology and Management.* New York: Macmillan.

Roe, H. R., and Q. C. Ayres. 1954. *Engineering for Agricultural Drainage.* New York: McGraw-Hill.

Rolson, H., III. 1983. "Values Gone Wild." *Inquiry* 16:181–207.

———. 1986. "Beauty and the Beast: Aesthetic Experience of Wildlife." *Trumpeter* 3 (3): 29–34.

Roseberry, J. L. 1979. "Bobwhite Population Responses to Exploitation: Real and Simulated." *Journal of Wildlife Management* 43:285–305.

Sampson, R. N. 1988. "Institutional Challenges in Implementing Conservation Compliance." *Transactions of the North American Wildlife and Natural Resources Conference* 53:205–9.

Schindler, P. T. 1988. "President's Letter." *Wildlife News* 23 (2): 2.

Schmidt, R. H. 1989. "Animal Welfare and Wildlife Management." *Transactions of the North American Wildlife and Natural Resources Conference* 54:468–75.

———. 1990. "Why Do We Debate Animal Rights?" *Wildlife Society Bulletin* 18:459–61.

Schmidt, R. H., and J. G. Bruner. 1981. "A Professional Attitude toward Humaneness." *Wildlife Society Bulletin* 9:289–91.

Schoenfeld, C. A. 1978. "Environmental Education and Wildlife Conservation." In *Wildlife and America,* edited by H. P. Brokaw, pp. 471–84. Washington, D.C.: Council on Environmental Quality

Schultz, G. E. 1978. "The Paleontology of Palo Duro Canyon." *Panhandle-Plains Historical Review* 51:59–86.

Schweitzer, A. 1922. *On the Edge of the Primeval Forest.* London: Black.

———. 1923. *Civilization and Ethics.* London: Black.

Schweitzer, D. H., D. A. Scott, A. W. Blue, and J. P. Secter. 1973. "Recreational

Preferences for Birds in Saskatchewan." In *Human Dimensions in Wildlife Programs,* edited by J. C. Hendee and C. Schoenfeld, pp. 42–49. Washington, D.C.: Wildlife Management Institute.

Seagle, S. W., R. A. Lancia, D. A. Adams, M. R. Lennartz, and H. A. Devine. 1987. "Integrating Timber and Red-Cockaded Woodpecker Habitat Management." *Transactions of the North American Wildlife and Natural Resources Conference* 52:41–52.

Sessions, G. 1987. "Deep Ecology and the New Age." *Earth First!: The Radical Environmental Journal* 8 (8).

Shackleton, D. M., and C. C. Shank. 1984. "A Review of the Social Behavior of Feral and Wild Sheep and Goats." *Journal of Animal Science* 58:500–509.

Shanks, B. 1984. *This Land Is Your Land: The Struggle to Save America's Public Lands.* San Francisco: Sierra Club Books.

Shaw, J. H. 1985. *Introduction to Wildlife Management.* New York: McGraw-Hill.

Shaw, W. W. 1975. *Attitudes toward Hunting: A Study of Some Social and Psychological Determinants.* Michigan Department of Natural Resources Wildlife Division Report no. 2740.

Shaw, W. W., and W. R. Mangun. 1984. *Noncomsumptive Use of Wildlife in the United States.* U.S. Fish and Wildlife Service Resource Publication no. 154.

Shaw, W. W., and E. H. Zube (eds.). 1980. *Wildlife Values.* University of Arizona Center for Assessment of Noncommodity Natural Resource Values, Institutional Series Report no. 1.

Shay, R. 1980. "The Sagebrush Rebellion." *Sierra* 65 (1): 29–32.

Shepard, P. 1982. *Nature and Madness.* San Francisco: Sierra Club Books.

Simons, E. L. 1989. "Human Origins." *Science* 245:1343–50.

Singer, P. 1975. *Animal Liberation: A New Ethics for Our Treatment of Animals.* New York: New York Review Books.

———. 1977. *Animal Liberation.* New York: Avon.

Smith, A. G., J. H. Stoudt, and J. B. Gollop. 1964. "Prairie Potholes and Marshes." In *Waterfowl Tomorrow,* edited by J. P. Linduska and A. L. Nelson, pp. 39–50. Washington, D.C.: Bureau of Sport Fisheries and Wildlife.

Smith, R. N. 1974. "Problems with Urban Wildlife." In *Wildlife in an Urbanizing Environment,* edited by J. H. Noyes and D. R. Progulske, pp. 113–15. Holdsworth Natural Resources Center Planning and Resource Development Series no. 28. Amherst: University of Massachusetts Cooperative Extension Service.

Solman, V. E. F. 1974. "Aircraft and Wildlife." In *Wildlife in an Urbanizing Environment,* edited by J. H. Noyes and D. R. Progulske, pp. 137–41. Holdsworth Natural Resources Center Planning and Resource Development Series no. 28. Amherst: University of Massachusetts Cooperative Extension Service.

Sorg, C. F., and J. Loomis. 1985. "An Introduction to Wildlife Valuation Techniques." *Wildlife Society Bulletin* 13:38–46.

Soulé, M. E. 1986. "Preface." In *Conservation Biology: The Science of Scarcity and Diversity,* edited by M. E. Soulé, pp. ix–x. Sunderland, Mass.: Sinauer Associates.

Soulé, M. E., and B. A. Wilcox. 1980a. "Conservation Biology: Its Scope and Its Challenge." In *Conservation Biology: An Evolutionary-Ecological Perspective,* edited by M. E. Soulé and B. A. Wilcox, pp. 1–8. Sunderland, Mass.: Sinauer Associates.

———. 1980b. "Preface." In *Conservation Biology: An Evolutionary-Ecological Perspective,* edited by M. E. Soulé and B. A. Wilcox, pp. xi–xiv. Sunderland, Mass.: Sinauer Associates.

Soulé, M., M. Gilpin, W. Conway, and T. Foose. 1986. "The Millenium Ark: How Long a Voyage, How Many Staterooms, How Many Passengers?" *Zoo Biology* 5:101–13.

Speth, J. D. 1989. "Human Evolution: New Questions." Review of *The Evolution of Human Hunting,* edited by M. H. Nitecki and D. V. Nitecki. *Science* 243:241–42.

Steinhart, P. 1986a. "Can We Solve the Great Goose Mystery?" *National Wildlife* 24 (3): 5–16.

———. 1986b. "For Wildlife, the Struggle Continues: Fifty Years of Wildlife." *National Wildlife* 24 (3): 5–16.

Steinhoff, H. W. 1980. "Analysis of Major Conceptual Systems for Understanding and Measuring Wildlife Values." In *Wildlife Values,* edited by W. W. Shaw and E. H. Zube, pp. 11–21. University of Arizona Center for Assessment of Noncommodity Natural Resource Values, Institutional Series Report no. 1.

Steinhoff, H. W., R. G. Walsh, T. J. Peterle, and J. M. Petulla. 1987. "Evolution of the Valuation of Wildlife." In *Valuing Wildlife: Economic and Social Perspectives,* edited by D. J. Decker and G. R. Goff, pp. 34–48. Boulder: Westview Press.

Stevens, R. O. 1944. *Talk about Wildlife.* Raleigh, N.C.: Bynum.

Stoddard, C. H. 1951. "Wildlife Economics—a Neglected Tool of Management." *Land Economics* 27:248–49.

Stoddart, L. A., A. D. Smith, and T. W. Box. 1975. *Range Management.* 3d ed. New York: McGraw-Hill.

Stringer, C. B., and P. Andrews. 1988. "Genetic and Fossil Evidence for the Origin of Modern Humans." *Science* 239:1263–68.

Stuber, P. J. (comp.) 1988. *Proceedings of the National Symposium on the Protection of Wetlands from Agricultural Impacts.* U.S. Fish and Wildlife Service Biological Report no. 88 (16).

Sumner, L. W. 1979. Review of *Animal Liberation,* by P. Singer, and *Animal Rights and Human Obligations,* edited by T. Regan and P. Singer. *Environmental Ethics* 1:365–70.

Swift, E. F. 1967. *A Conservation Saga.* Washington, D.C.: National Wildlife Federation.

Talbot, L. M. 1987. "The Ecological Value of Wildlife to the Well-being of

Human Society." In *Valuing Wildlife: Economic and Social Perspectives,* edited by D. J. Decker and G. R. Goff, pp. 179–86. Boulder: Westview Press.

Tanner, T. 1980. "Significant Life Experiences: A New Research Area in Environmental Education." *Journal of Environmental Education* 11 (4): 20–25.

Taylor, W. P. 1913. "Fur-bearing Mammals: An Unappreciated Natural Resource." *Science* 37:485–87.

Teague, R. D. 1979. "The Roles of Social Sciences in Wildlife Management." In *Wildlife Conservation: Principles and Practices,* edited by R. D. Teague and E. Decker, pp. 55–60. Washington, D.C.: Wildlife Society.

Teels, B. 1990. "Wetlands." In *Natural Resources for the Twenty-first Century,* edited by R. N. Sampson and D. Hair, pp. 121–42. Washington, D.C.: Island Press.

Teer, J. G. 1988. Review of *Conservation Biology: The Science of Scarcity and Diversity. Journal of Wildlife Management* 52:570–72.

Thomas, J. W., and H. Salwasser. 1989. "Bringing Conservation Biology into a Position of Influence in Natural Resource Management." *Conservation Biology* 3:123–27.

Thomas, K. 1983. *Man and the Natural World: A History of the Modern Sensibility.* New York: Pantheon.

Thwaites, R. G. (ed.). 1904. *Original Journals of the Lewis and Clark Expedition, 1804–1806.* 7 vols. New York: Dodd, Mead.

Tiner, R. W., Jr. 1984. *Wetlands of the United States: Current Status and Recent Trends.* Newton Corners, Mass.: U.S. Fish and Wildlife Service.

Tobias, S., and L. S. Abel. 1990. "Scientists and Engineers Study Chaucer and Wordsworth: Peer Perspectives on the Teaching of Poetry." *English Education* 22:165–78.

Todd, A. W. 1981. "Ecological Arguments for Fur-Trapping in Boreal Wilderness Regions." *Wildlife Society Bulletin* 9:116–24.

Towell, W. E. 1979. "The Role of Policy Making Boards and Commissions." In *Wildlife Conservation: Principles and Practices,* edited by R. D. Teague and E. Decker, pp. 49–54. Washington, D.C.: Wildlife Society.

Triandis, H. C. 1971. *Attitude and Attitude Change.* New York: John Wiley.

Tucker, P., and D. H. Pletscher. 1989. "Attitudes of Hunters and Residents toward Wolves in Northwestern Montana." *Wildlife Society Bulletin* 17:509–14.

U.S. Bureau of the Census. 1986. *Statistical Abstract of the United States: 1987.* 107th ed. Washington, D.C.: Department of Commerce.

U.S. Fish and Wildlife Service. 1988. *1985 National Survey of Fishing, Hunting, and Wildlife Associated Recreation.* Washington, D.C.: Department of the Interior.

Urich, D. L., J. P. Graham, and P. E. Kelley. 1986. "Statewide Planning Using the Wildlife and Fish Habitat Relationships System." *Wildlife Society Bulletin* 14:22–30.

Vereshchagin, N. K. 1967. "Primitive Hunters and Pleistocene Extinction in the Soviet Union." In *Pleistocene Extinctions: The Search for a Cause,* edited by P. S. Martin and H. E. Wright, Jr., pp. 365–98. New Haven, Conn.: Yale University Press.

Wagner, F. H. 1978. "Livestock Grazing and the Livestock Industry." In *Wildlife and America,* edited by H. P. Brokaw, pp. 121–45. Washington, D.C.: Council on Environmental Quality.

———. 1989. "American Wildlife Management at the Crossroads." *Wildlife Society Bulletin* 17:354–60.

Wallace, A. R. 1876. *The Geographical Distribution of Animals.* Vol. 1. London: Macmillan.

Ward, D. V. 1978. *Biological Environmental Impact Studies: Theory and Methods.* New York: Academic Press.

Welker, R. H. 1955. *Birds and Men: American Birds in Science, Art, Literature, and Conservation 1800–1900.* Cambridge, Mass.: Belknap.

Wendorf, F., and J. J. Hester. 1962. "Early Man's Utilization of the Great Plains Environment." *American Antiquity* 28:159–71.

Wengart, N. 1962. "The Ideological Basis of Conservation and Natural Resources Policies and Programs." *Annals of Science* 364 (Nov.).

West, F. H. 1983. "The Antiquity of Man in America." In *The Late Pleistocene,* edited by S. C. Porter. Vol. 1 of *Late-Quaternary Environments of the United States,* edited by H. E. Wright, Jr. Minneapolis: University of Minnesota Press.

Whiteside, R. W., D. C. Guynn, Jr., and H. A. Jacobson. 1981. "Characteristics and Expenditures of Deer Hunters Using Two Areas in Mississippi." *Wildlife Society Bulletin* 9:226–29.

Wilcove, D. S., and F. B. Samson. 1987. "Innovative Wildlife Management: Listening to Leopold." *Transactions of the North American Wildlife and Natural Resources Conference* 52:327–32.

Wilcox, B. A. 1980. "Insular Ecology and Conservation." In *Conservation Biology: An Evolutionary-Ecological Perspective,* edited by M. E. Soulé and B. A. Wilcox, pp. 95–117. Sunderland, Mass.: Sinauer Associates.

Wildlife Management Institute Staff. 1978. "The Future." *Big Game of North America: Ecology and Management,* edited by J. L. Schmidt and D. L. Gilbert, pp. 417–24. Harrisburg, Pa.: Stackpole Books.

Wilson, E. O. 1983. "Statement." In *The Garden of Eden: A Conservation Film,* produced and directed by L. R. Hott and R. M. Sherman. The Nature Conservancy and Florentine Films.

Woodwell, G. M. 1967. "Toxic Substances and Ecological Cycles." *Scientific American* 216 (3): 24–31.

Wywialowski, A. 1977. *The Anti-hunting Movement—The People Involved, Their Attitude Development, and Implications for Wildlife Management.* Master's thesis. Iowa State University.

Yahner, R. H. 1990. "Wildlife Management and Conservation Biology Revisited." *Wildlife Society Bulletin* 18:348–50.

Young, J. S., D. M. Donnelly, C. F. Sorg, J. B. Loomis, and L. J. Nelson. 1987. *Net Economic Value of Upland Game Hunting in Idaho.* USDA Forest Service Resource Bulletin no. RM-15, Rocky Mountain Forest and Range Experiment Station.

Zeuner, F. E. 1963. *A History of Domesticated Animals.* London: Hutchinson.

Zimring, F. E., and G. Hawkins. 1973. *Deterrence.* Chicago: University of Chicago Press.

# Index